Those Oldies but Goodies

Art Rodriguez

Dream House

ISBN: 0-967-1555-4-1
Library of Congress
Catalog Card Number: 2004096689

Edited by
Margarita Maestas-Flores

Cover Illustration and Production by
Alvarez Design & Illustration
AlvarezDesign75@yahoo.com

CONTENTS

1   RELEASED

It was Sunday morning. Dennis and Phil came into my house and greeted my mother, my two brothers, and my sister. I left with my friends. As we drove away, I said, "Hey, man, let's get some beer and go cruising downtown. Maybe we can find some girls."

Dennis had come to my house to pick me up in his cool 1964 Chevy Impala. It had deep chrome rims and was light brown with red pinstripes. When he would greet someone or was next to some girls, he would gun his engine for his cool pipes to be heard.

I had just been released from the California Youth Authority after serving three years. My good friends Dennis and Phil had telephoned to ask if I wanted to go out with them. I told them I had been looking forward to having a good time for three years. I was ready!

Times were hard while I was imprisoned. I always dreamed of going out again and being with my friends. People I knew on the outside thought I was a big shot for being imprisoned; however, it was no fun. There was nothing big about being a prisoner. There was always someone telling you when to get up and when to go to bed. You had to ask to go to the bathroom, a stall with no doors. Someone had to watch you all the time unless you were locked in a cell.

The first few days after I was released from Preston, in Ione, California, I planned to stay home with my mother, my brothers Eddie and Victor, and my sister Mildred, or Tita as we called her. I had a lot of lost time to cover. Victor, my little brother, was fourteen years old; Tita was sixteen; and Eddie, whom I went to jail with, was twenty years old. He had been released a month earlier than I, and he already had a job at a chrome plating shop.

My mother moved to Emory Street during this time; Emory Street is on the north side of San Jose. She was having problems with crank callers and threats. Because of this she became scared and moved. Now that my brother and I were home, we told her she had nothing to worry about because we would protect her.

Things looked different when I arrived home. The house seemed small. When I left to jail, I lived in our house on Virginia Place. The house on Emory Street seemed small because in Preston I stayed in a very large dayroom with several guys and slept in a large dorm with bunk beds.

My mother had a boyfriend for whom Eddie, Tita, and I didn't care. This man was all right when he wasn't drinking; but once he started drinking, he was different. He didn't like us very much either.

Here I was, back with my friends. I really looked forward to this. Everyday that I was locked up I thought about being out in the streets with my partners. Before I was arrested, we had to do most of our partying by walking. However, now we could drive because we were old enough.

Dennis entered the freeway. The car windows were open. It was a nice, warm summer day. We headed to the eastside and exited Highway 101 on Alum Rock Avenue. As we went over the overpass, there was a Tico's Tacos restaurant next to the freeway. Phil told Dennis to stop at the gas station one block up, where Dennis and Phil always bought their beer. Neither one of them was twenty-one years old yet, but the owners of the gas station didn't care. A person has to be twenty-one in order to buy beer in California.

We pulled into the parking strip next to the little store that was part of the gas station. I took out the $5.00 my mother had given me. Dennis told me not to worry about the money because he and Phil were welcoming me back.

I was glad to be out of jail and swore to myself that I would never go back again. I wanted to stay out of trouble and felt that if I ever went back it would be for something minor.

Phil and Dennis were putting their money together to buy the beer. Dennis was 5'10", medium built, and had wavy brown hair and a baby face. Phil was 5'4", stocky, with wavy black hair. He loved to fight. Dennis said as he opened the car door, "OK, I'll be right back."

He stepped out of the car and walked into the store.

"Hey, Phil, have you seen any of my old girlfriends around?"

Phil chuckled and asked, "Which ones? You had a lot of them, man!"

When I went to jail, I was going out a lot. I had one steady girl-friend. She lived on McGinness Avenue off of Story Road on the eastside of San Jose; her name was Linda. I would go to her house often and got along very well with her family. However, when I went to jail, she found out I was writing to two other girls and decided to drop me.

"Any of them," I answered Phil.

"Yeah, I see them all the time."

"Oh yeah, where?" I asked.

"All over. You know, at the Jose, parties, and the Flats." The Jose was the Jose Theater on Second Street.

"Oh yeah, what's the Flats?"

"Tortilla Flats is at Alum Rock Park, homey."

"I never heard of the Tortilla Flats. Where is it in the park?"

Alum Rock Park is a nice, big park in the east foothills in San Jose. It is part of the Diablo Mountain Range. It is a canyon and is filled with oak trees and has a running creek going through it. In the main part of the park, there was a zoo and a concession building with a carousal and a playground. There was a large indoor swimming pool where we would swim a lot when we were young. The main area also had green grass that was maintained for visitors by the City of San Jose. There were many barbecue pits. It was a very nice place for families.

"Yeah, man, you know when you go into the park, where the booth to pay is?"

"Yeah."

"You go around the other way, toward Eagle Rock. Right there. All that flat part is Tortilla Flats. Everyone goes on Sundays, and they park all around there."

I asked, "Who goes, just the homeboys?"

"Heck no, man. If it was just guys, why would we want to go? Girls and guys go! It's really cool, man. You'll like it."

While I was locked up, I remembered my sister telling me something about someone getting shot at Alum Rock Park. She had said there were fights all the time, and she didn't like to go because of that. I wondered if she was talking about the Flats in the park.

I saw Dennis step out of the front door of the store with a case of beer. I thought, "That's a lot of beer for the three of us." However, I didn't mind.

Dennis opened the back door and put the box of beer next to me.

"If we need more, we'll get it later," Dennis said.

Dennis started his car. He had installed cool sounding pipes on his Impala. He stepped on the gas pedal twice, so we could hear his pipes. People at the gas station turned to stare at us; his pipes were attracting attention. We drove out of the gas station.

Phil asked, "Hey, Art, pass me a beer, man. I'm dying of thirst!"

During this time it was no big deal to drink in a car. If a cop stopped someone with beer, he usually made him dump it out; or the officer might even take the driver in for the night, depending on how drunk the person was. I didn't want to go in for the night because I was on parole and knew I would definitely get sent back to YA (California Youth Authority).

I took out a beer for Phil and handed it to him. "Here you go, man."

I pulled out another beer and passed it to Dennis. He reached for it without turning his head, not wanting to take his eyes off the road. I then took one out for myself. I opened my beer, taking a drink out of the can.

"Where we going, Dennis?"

"I don't know, man. Maybe we'll cruise up Alum Rock Avenue and then to the Flats for a little while. If nothing is happening at the Flats, we could ask around if there are any parties. We could go downtown for a while, check things out, and then go to the parties. What do you think, Art?"

"That sounds good to me."

I was looking forward to seeing some of the people I used to know before I left. Maybe I would see some of them downtown or at the Jose Theater, which was in the same area. A lot of young people hung out on Sundays in this part of the city.

"Hey, Phil, remember when we were younger and we broke into the little store on Alum Rock? I think it was the Alum Rock Market."

Phil answered, "Yeah, man, I remember! How could I forget? Poor people. I think we burned them good." Phil took a swallow of his beer as he shook his head.

There were things we had done in our younger days of which we were not proud.

"Yeah, 'poor people' is right. I think we did a lot of damage there and didn't get anything. Heck man, I got caught!"

"Yeah, I remember when the cop car you were in and the cop car I was in were side-by-side. The cop asked you if I was one of the guys you were with. I remember hearing you say, 'No, that's not one of them. I don't know that guy.' They let me go a little while later."

"Yeah, I remember that. What was your story then? I can't remember if you told me about it."

Dennis asked, "Where was I that night?"

I laughed and answered, "I can't remember, man. Maybe your father didn't let you come with us. He probably thought we were up to no good, man."

"Na, my father liked you guys."

Dennis' father worked with my father at the American Can Company for twenty-five years. They knew each other well. However, they didn't hang out together. Tex, Dennis' father, had his own group of friends and all of his brothers. When they were young, they were the way we were now. They liked to party and fight.

Phil came back to what I asked him. "The cops picked me up on King Road and asked if I had been at Alum Rock Market. I don't know if they thought I was stupid enough to tell them, 'Sure I was there!'"

We all laughed.

"The cops put me in one of the cars and parked in front of the Alum Rock Market. They kept asking me questions about the break-in. I told them I didn't know what they were talking about. I told them I was at Henry's house." Henry was a friend who lived on King Road and Saint James Street.

"Oh, yeah, good story, ese," I cut in. "Ese" is slang for guy.

"Yeah, so then I heard on the cop's radio that they caught another guy with their dog."

"Yeah, man, that was me!"

"Yeah, I know. Then they brought you next to our car, and that's when I heard you say you didn't know me. I was hoping they didn't put our addresses together. Heck, man, then they would know we were neighbors!"

We all laughed. By this time we were going up past Capital Avenue, getting closer to Alum Rock Park. Dennis said, "Yeah, then they would come and pick me up, too, because they would know I lived one house down from you, Phil."

The rest of the way to the park, we talked about different things— who got married, who died, and who went to jail.

We were traveling slowly up the hill by the Country Club's golf course. We went over the hill and down into the park. The road to the entrance of the park was small with many curves. To the right of the road was a wall of rock shooting up straight. On the left was a very steep cliff with many bushes and oak trees. The other road going out of the park was the same.

"Hey, man, I remember when I was young. My father and his friends had an accident here," I reminisced.

"Oh, yeah?" Phil asked, "What happened?"

2 TRAPPED

My father enjoyed going out with his friends and partying. He had bought a brand new 1957 Cadillac. It was two-door, beige, with a light brownish top. His friends Ray, (or Green Eyes), Henry, and George were with him. They had been drinking all night at Ralph's bar, their hangout on Story Road. From there they went to Henry's house until morning. One of my father's friends from the American Can Company was having a barbecue at Alum Rock Park. He invited my father and his friends.

On the way to the park, my father and Green Eyes were drinking a fifth of whiskey, drinking it as they drove. The two guys in the back seat were beer drinkers. All were really bombed by this time. My father was telling them a story about someone he was angry with at work. As he spoke while driving on the small road entering the park, he drove a little fast.

As he took a drink from his whiskey bottle, from nowhere a car came around the bend, also traveling fast. My father pulled the steering wheel hard to the left and lost control. He remembered feeling his front wheels leave the ground. He saw the bushes and then an oak tree directly in front of him as he was going over the cliff. In an instant everything went black.

The next thing he remembered, he was lying on the street. He opened his eyes and saw the blue sky. The scent was of oak trees. He raised his head and looked around the area. Green Eyes was standing a few feet away, gazing down the embankment. Green Eyes was getting over his shock of what had just happened. Blood dripped down his forehead and onto his shirt. There was a police car a few yards away blocking the road. Five cars were behind the cop car, and people had stepped out of their vehicles to watch what was happening. The cop was down at the wreck trying to see what he could do for the other two men trapped in the Cadillac.

"What happened?" my father asked Green Eyes.

Green Eyes looked fine except for the little blood he had on him. He looked down at my father and answered, "Joe, at least we're all alive."

My father tried to sit up, but it felt as if someone was knocking the breath out of him. He moaned.

"Joe, I wouldn't try to move for a while. You're banged up pretty good. You hit your head kind of hard. Lie down and wait for the ambulance. They'll take care of you."

"How are Henry and George?"

"Not too hot, buddy. But alive."

My father slowly pushed himself up so that he could sit and hold himself up with one arm. The other arm was holding his chest. He wanted to go down and help his two friends. Green Eyes made it sound as if they were in really bad condition.

"Joe," Green Eyes said, "I took care of the beer and whiskey. I threw them away from the car."

My father hadn't even thought of that. However, he was relieved he didn't have to worry about it.

From a distance they could hear sirens approaching. The cars that were lined up waiting to enter the park started to back up slowly. There was another officer who was directing them in order to make room for the emergency vehicles.

My father could see his car from where he sat. The cop was standing on the driver's side of the vehicle talking to someone in the Cadillac.

Green Eyes started to make his way back down the embankment to where the car was. He yelled out something to the cop that wasn't understandable.

Once Green Eyes was down by the car, he went to the passenger side and climbed into the window. In a few seconds the officer said something in a loud voice. The only thing my father was able to understand was the word, "OK."

The cop reached into the car and pulled. Henry's black, wavy hair started to show; then the rest of his body appeared. "OK, I'm free!" Henry yelled. He fell to the ground. He quickly stood and leaned against the car. There was blood on his forehead. He was holding his arm, as it was badly hurt.

Henry looked into the car and said something to George. On the passenger side Green Eyes' feet showed as he pushed himself free. Once Green Eyes was out and on his feet, he came around to where Henry was standing. Green Eyes helped Henry, putting his arm around his shoulder. They started uphill to make their way up the cliff to the paved road.

The ambulance, a tow truck, and two more motorcycle cops arrived. The ambulance stopped, and the attendants stepped out quickly and ran to the back of their vehicle. They pulled out the stretcher. Both of the attendants ran with the stretcher to where my father was sitting. He looked up at them and pointed down to his friends. They helped Green Eyes and Henry up the rest of the way and placed Henry next to Dad. They then made their way down the hill, back to the Cadillac where the cop was still standing on the driver's side. My father put his hand on Henry's head and asked, "¿Comó estas, mi amigo?"

"I don't know, Joe. My arm really hurts. Feels like it's broken but I'm not sure. Man, this hurts."

My father tapped him lightly on the forehead, feeling sorry for him.

The cop, tow truck driver, and the two ambulance attendants all tried to pull the door open; but it was jammed shut. They needed tools to remove George.

Green Eyes was standing on the street.

"Hey, Green Eyes, ¿comó esta, George (how is George)?"

"It looks like he has broken legs, Joe; but I'm not sure. He's sitting back there with the seat smashed on his legs. He's in a lot of pain. Even if they could open the door, I don't know how they're going to take him out of there."

With those words my father really felt bad. Even though they were all drinking and knew what could happen, my father told himself that it was his fault because he was driving and it was his car. The cop came back up the hill with the ambulance attendants. They put Henry on the stretcher and were taking him to the ambulance. The cop went to his police car and called someone on his radio. Next, he stepped to where they were on the pavement.

"How is everyone here? Do you think you are going to be OK for a little while?"

Green Eyes asked the cop, "How you going to get him out of there?"

"I just called the fire department. They're on the way up. They'll have the tools to take the door off. I think I'll send one of you with your friend to the hospital right now. You," the cop pointed to Green Eyes. "You can go with your friend."

"No, don't take me first. Take my friend Joe. He is hurting worse than me."

My father didn't want to go first either. He wanted to make sure his friend George was out and safe. Even if he couldn't do anything, he could watch.

"Green Eyes, you go. I'll be OK. I have to make sure George is OK. I have to."

Green Eyes didn't feel as if he was hurt, but he was very sore and wanted to be checked out anyway.

"Are you sure, Joe? I'm all right. I can stay. If they need help, I can help."

"No, you go. I have to wait."

"All right, Joe. I'll go. I'll see you there." Green Eyes then turned and walked to the ambulance where Henry was.

"Looks like you got a couple of broken ribs. I think you also got smacked on your head. It knocked you out for a while. How do you feel now?" the cop asked.

My father didn't notice the pain until that moment. Now that the officer mentioned his head, he felt the headache. He moved his hand up and over his head to see if there were any wounds. He did find a sore spot; however, the bleeding had stopped.

"Not too good. But I know I'll be all right."

"What about my car?" my father asked, not really worried about the damage. He wanted to know where they were going to take it so that he could make arrangements for it.

"The car is damaged, but nothing that can't be fixed."

"No, I mean, where are you taking it?"

"We'll let you know later. I'm not sure. Do you want us to take it anywhere specific?"

"No, not yet."

The ambulance left; and another one arrived, as did the fire truck. Three fire fighters were heading down the embankment with large tools in their hands. When they arrived at the car, one of them stuck a large tool into the door jam. Two pulled on the tool. The door popped open. The fire person put his large tool under the front seat. Another one put another long tool behind the seat. All pulled and pushed at the same time. The seat moved. They knew what they were doing. One of the fire fighters was halfway into the car. The ambulance attendants made their way down with a stretcher.

When George was out of the car, he and my father were taken to the hospital. George had a broken leg. Henry had a broken arm and a concussion. My father had four broken ribs and injuries to his head. Fortunately, no one was killed.

"And the cop didn't bust your dad?" Dennis asked.

"No, for what? As far as the cops were concerned, he wasn't drinking. There was nothing in the car. Green Eyes got rid of it, remember?"

Phil added, "They fixed his car. I know, because I remember he had that car for a few years."

"Yeah, I remember right after that, every week, sometimes we would go with him to George's and Henry's house. My father would take them $25 every week to help them out, which was a lot of money in those days. He would make $100 a week, and that was good money."

"Hey, man, that was cool for your dad to do that," Phil expressed.

"Yeah, my mother said he did it for two reasons. The first was to help them out because they were his friends. The second reason was because he didn't want them to sue him."

"Really? You think they would have sued him?"

"I don't think they would have, but I know they really wouldn't because my father was giving them money. You never know nowadays."

Dennis remarked, "Hey, man, if I go over this hill, does that mean you might sue me?"

We all laughed.

3 TORTILLA FLATS

We came to the bottom of the canyon of Alum Rock Park. There was a small booth where we had to pay 50 cents to be able to enter. We paid and made a left to the Tortilla Flats, driving a quarter of a mile farther.

As we drove into the flat area, I saw that it was a quarter of a city block parking area. It was hard dirt and gravel. Around the outside of the parking area, it was wooded with oak trees, with a few picnic tables and barbecue pits. Completely around the area were parked cars backed into the parking spaces. There were cool, low-rider cars and some older vehicles. There were even some psychedelic-painted cars and vans with hippies in them. There were young people, males and females, in all the cars or standing around them. They were listening to music, talking to one another, and drinking beer. The entire center portion was clear of cars. There were vehicles, but they were not parked. They were stopped while people talked to each other, and then they moved. The restrooms were located where we first drove into the parking area. When the young people used the restrooms, they stopped and talked to other people they knew.

Dennis asked, "Hey, where do you guys want to park?"

"I don't know," Phil answered. "Let's drive slow in front of the cars first to see who's here, and then we'll park."

"Sounds good to me, Phil."

We drove into the area slowly. As we drove in front of the cars, everyone in the car or standing would turn to see who we were. In the first two cars the people were inside. We really couldn't tell who they were.

In the next car, there were three girls standing next to it; one was sitting inside with the door open. In the next one a guy stepped out of his car as we passed; his shirt was unbuttoned. Dennis slowed to a stop. The guy came to the window on the passenger side.

"Hey, Dennis, how's it going, man?"

"Hey, man, what's up? Where are the parties today?"

The guy laughed and said, as he looked around, "This is the party for today, man. Want a joint?"

"No, that's OK, Danny. I don't want to get busted with my partner. He just got out. He was locked up for a while. Thanks."

"Órale, ese," the guy greeted me.

"Hey, man. I'm Art Rodriguez."

"Yeah, I remember you. You were one of the guys who killed them guys by Happy Hollow Park, right? I remember."

Happy Hollow was on Keys Street. We had been in a fight, and 2 guys were killed three years previously. There were 11 guys on our side that night, three years ago, and about three times more of the guys whom we were fighting. However, no one ever knew who killed whom. No one told.

"Yeah, man, I was locked up for that." I was never scared to say it. If anyone ever had a problem with it, I was always ready to go toe-to-toe with them.

"Yeah, ese, I was there at that party that night but left earlier. Hey, ese, I'm glad I left; or I might be getting out of jail, too," the guy said as a joke.

I didn't say anything, just nodded my head and took a drink of my beer. I didn't think it was funny, just glad I was out of jail now and didn't want to look back. During the three years I was locked up, I never thought about the damage and hurt we caused the families of the guys who were killed.

Dennis offered the guy a beer. He said they had a lot of beer in their car.

"I'll talk to you in a while when you park, man. I'll walk to your short." A short was one of the terms we used when we were referring to a car.

"All right, Danny, take care, man."

We started to move again. As we drove by the next few cars, we didn't know anyone. A few cars down there were two guys. One had his foot on the bumper, and the other was listening really seriously to what the first one was saying. They both stopped talking and turned to look at us.

Dennis said to Phil, "Look, Phil. Look who's here."

Phil stared hard at them. The guy with his foot on his bumper lowered his foot and turned all the way around, staring at us. Dennis stopped the car, put it in neutral, and started to open his car door.

I'm going to get him right now, man!"

"Cool down, Dennis," Phil said, "There'll be plenty of other times to finish the fight."

I knew they weren't friends. I put my beer on the floor, ready to get out of the car, wanting to back up Dennis. Dennis closed his door.

"Yeah, you're right, Phil. Next time."

I reached down for my beer. The two guys looked worried because they thought they had a fight on their hands. They stared at us as we left.

I thought, "I'm ready right now!" Right then I felt the urge to fight. I loved to fight, but I thought, "I better cool it right now. I'm out to have fun. I don't want to mess things up right away for myself."

As we passed, I asked, "Who was that? Did you have a fight with him?"

Phil answered, "Yeah, we did. At a party a few weeks ago, him and his friends got smart with us. We were just about to throw the first blow, but things got out of hand. The people who lived there asked us to leave right away. We told him that we would take care of him another time."

"I wanted to make that time right now," Dennis said. Phil laughed.

Dennis laughed, too, and continued, "We could have; but I think since this is Art's first time out with us, we should be careful. I don't want to take him back home and have his mother be mad with us for getting him all roughed up."

"No, don't worry about my mother. She won't say anything."

"I don't know," Dennis said. "I don't want to take any chances right now."

We drove past a few more cars. A little farther ahead were four young, pretty girls. When they saw Dennis' Impala, they waved and started to walk in our direction. Dennis stopped. Two girls went to Phil's side, and two went to Dennis' side.

"Dennis! Hey! How are you?"

"I'm good! How about you girls. How have all of you been? What's going on? Any parties today?"

"Not yet," the girl on Dennis' side answered. "It's too early still. Maybe later there will be. Someone here will tell us where they are. Are you staying, Dennis; or are you just cruising by?"

"I don't know. It depends on what I can get from you!" Dennis replied as he laughed.

"What you can get from us? You mean what we can get from you!" the girls laughed. So did we.

She continued, "Do you have any beer?"

Dennis smiled and asked me for a beer. "Yeah, as a matter of fact, I do." I passed him the beer, and he handed it to her.

"Thanks a lot, Dennis! You are so nice!"

"Want a beer?" Phil asked the girls on his side.

"Hey, yeah!" one of them answered.

Phil looked back at me and said, "Hey, Art, give me a beer for all the girls."

I took out three beers and passed them to Phil. "Here you go," he said.

One of the girls looked at me and asked, "Hey, who is that?"

Phil introduced me. "Art, this is Teresa; Ruby; and, on that side, Joann and Tracy. I would ask them to get in with us, but they are way too young. They sure don't look like it, but they really are."

"No we aren't!" Teresa exclaimed.

"Yeah, you are. How old are you, fourteen?" Phil asked.

Teresa looked embarrassed, "Maybe."

"Maybe?" Dennis answered and continued. "Now if their sisters were here, then we would take them for a ride."

"Yeah, she would go with you anytime."

I didn't say anything because I had been out of jail for only a week. I was shy around the girls.

Dennis said, "OK, girls, time for us to move on. Have fun."

All four girls, at the same time, moved away from the car and yelled out, "Bye!" One of them said, "Thanks!"

We pulled away from them.

There was a space between cars on the back side of the parking area. Dennis said, "We'll park here in the shade. We could drive all the way around and come back, but this parking space might be taken."

"That's cool," I replied.

Dennis backed his car, gunned his pipes, and turned off the engine. We sat in our car drinking our beer. We saw some guys on the other side start yelling at others in another car. I said, "Hey, man, there is going to be a show for us in a little bit."

A cop car came cruising slowly into the Flats. We noticed that about every ten minutes or so they would pass to make sure everyone was behaving. When the cop entered the Flats, everyone hid their beers or whatever they were drinking. The cop didn't stop to check out anyone. If they would have, in almost every car they would have found something for which to bust them. The drinking law in California was twenty-one years. The cops would take our beer or make us dump it.

From the other side I saw a hippie walking toward us. Dennis said, "There comes Johnny."

So many things had changed over the time I was imprisoned. Before I went to jail, there were no hippies. Now I saw them all over town.

Phil answered, "Yeah, there he comes. I wonder what he has to offer us today."

"What does he have?" I asked.

Dennis answered, "Hey Art, you remember Johnny Ramirez?"

"Yeah, I know Johnny."

"That's him. He turned hippie."

I couldn't believe it!

"That's Johnny?" I answered, shocked. Johnny used to be a loco. He was a tough guy, a fighter. The last time I saw him, he was going to get some guy for giving him a dirty look. He used to wear khakis pants and Pendleton shirts. Now he was a hippie, dressed in a long gown, with long hair, a headband, and sandals. This wasn't the same Johnny I knew.

"Yeah, man," Phil commented. "A lot of our old friends have changed. They're hippies now. They live here and go and spend a few days on the road or at Haight Ashbury in San Francisco."

"Oh, yeah? What's over there?"

"Man, Art, we have to take you there! It's really cool."

Johnny approached our car, came to Dennis' window, and said, "Peace. How are you guys doing, groovy?"

"Hey, Johnny, how is the flower child today?"

"I'm happy, full of love and peace. Want some?"

Phil asked, "What do you have?"

"I have everything. LSD, Grass, STP—whatever you want. I have it on sale right now. I have White Lightening, and you know how good that is. You'll be hip to the world with this, man."

"Hey, Art, you ever try White Lightening?"

"No, not yet. But I think I'll pass on it right now."

"Art Rodriguez, is that you?"

"Yeah, it's me Johnny. How you been? Looks like you changed, man."

"Yeah, this is the life. We're all together and all one, full of love. We want the world to be full of peace. Join us, Art. Free love and you'll have peace."

I laughed not knowing what to say. This wasn't the same Johnny I knew in school. It seemed as if someone transferred into his body, and I was talking to someone else.

"I'm here, man. And I do have peace," I said.

"When did you get out, Art?"

"Last week, man. Finally home!"

"You know what, Johnny," Dennis said, "I think we'll pass right now. We're cool."

"All right. If you change your mind, let me know. I'll be over there with my brothers. Hey, when you leave, and if I don't catch a ride yet, can you take me down to my pad?"

"Sure," Dennis answered.

"OK, let me know when you leave. Peace," Johnny said as he walked away and back to where his friends were parked.

At that time we saw the same guys on the other side of the Flats starting to really get angry with guys from a few cars away. One guy from the first car was standing in front of the vehicle as he yelled, cussed, and shook his fist at the other person. From the other car one of the persons stepped in front of his vehicle. His friends all followed and stood as if waiting for a fight to start.

There were two girls in the second car. From where we sat, it appeared as if they were upset and were telling their boyfriends to stay back and not to say anything in return. There were four guys standing in front of the second vehicle. One of them started walking fast toward the guy who was yelling.

I commented, "Looks like he's not going to take it anymore."

"Yeah, I would've gone after him when he first yelled, right away, man," Dennis said.

"Me too," Phil confirmed.

"Yeah, so would I. Well, that's what drinking will do to you," I commented and continued. "Beer makes you really brave, braver than you already are!" Phil and Dennis laughed and agreed.

The three other guys from the second car, with beer bottles in their hands, were right behind their friend, ready to fight. The group of five persons from the first car also started walking toward the four guys to meet them.

"Hey, man, here they go!" I said, waiting for a good show.

The first guy from the second car approached the lead guy who was doing all the yelling. From 15 feet he threw his beer bottle hard and fast. The bottle hit the person he was aiming for on the forehead, and the victim's head tilted back with the impact. He stopped and reached up, grabbing his head as if he were in a lot of pain.

"One down," I said. Dennis and Phil didn't say anything. They didn't want to miss a second of the show we were having.

All the other guys from both sides threw their beers, some cans, and some bottles. Everyone started fighting. There was dust everywhere from the commotion all around them. We saw one guy jabbing in and out, in and out as he threw punches. The person he was jabbing stood and took the beating without hitting back. Two of the others from the first car were fighting with one guy who was dancing around in a large area, exchanging blows with the both of them. Two others were wrestling on the ground. By this time the girls were out of the vehicle and crying for them to stop. The first guy who was hit with the beer bottle recouped and started throwing blows at anyone in front of him. From where we sat, it appeared he even hit one of his own friends. It was crazy!

The fight lasted a minute-and-a-half, which is a long time when you are fighting. A police car drove into the Flats. The cop turned on his siren and flashing lights, even though he was only a few yards away.

When the people who were fighting heard the siren, all but the two owners of the cars and the girls took off running. The owners of the cars and the girls stayed to face the music. One of these guys was the person who first received the bottle to his forehead.

The cop stayed in his car for a few seconds as he radioed for help. A girl handed a cloth to the guy with the bleeding forehead to press against his wound. The cop stepped out of his police car and approached the girls and guys.

"Well, it's over. You guys want to leave? In a little while there's going to be a lot of cops here, and the fun will be over. They'll probably want to interview everyone here. Should we go?" Dennis asked.

"Yeah, let's go. We'll cruise around and see what we find," Phil answered.

"Yeah, that's cool," I answered. "If we stay here, they might take away our beer; and we don't want that to happen."

Dennis started his engine and gunned his pipes; so Johnny, our hippie friend, would know we were leaving. The cop turned around and looked at us. "Uh, oh, I think I got the wrong person's attention."

We pulled out of the parking space and drove to where Johnny was. He came out and approached the passenger side of our car. "Peace. You leaving already?"

"Yeah, we're going to go, man. We don't want to be here when all the cops come," Dennis replied.

"I think I'll stay. I'll catch a ride from someone else later. Are you sure you don't want any acid? I have good stuff!"

"No, man. Anyway, there are going to be too many cops here in a few minutes. OK, Johnny, we'll see you later, man."

"Peace," Johnny said as he walked away.

Dennis turned his head to look at me and said, "Hey, Art, is there anything to cover the beer back there?"

"Yeah, there's a coat or something back here on the floor." I picked it up. It was a coat.

"Good, here is my beer."

Phil handed me his beer also. Dennis insisted, "Cover all the beer under it, just in case that cop wants to stop us. We don't want him to see the beer."

"OK," I replied as I covered our stash.

Once I was done, Dennis stepped on the gas and started moving slowly in the lowered, light brown 64 Impala. As we made our way to the exit of the Flats, the police officer turned, looked at us, and looked back at the people he was interviewing. The cop told all of them to stay right where they were. He took a few steps toward us and put his hand up, indicating for us to stop. Dennis stopped the car. We had a large audience because everyone at the Flats had their eyes on us. Some of them were probably also thinking of leaving.

"Where you boys going?" he asked, as his eyes scanned all of us and the interior of the car, including the covered beer on the back floor. I hoped the cop wouldn't give us a bad time. I didn't want to end up fighting with a cop and going back to jail.

"We're leaving, Officer, going home," Dennis replied.

"Did you see what happened here?"

"No, Officer, we didn't."

"What do you mean? You were parked across from here and had to see what was going on."

"Officer, we didn't see anything. What else can I say?"

"OK, you boys be careful; and don't get into any trouble." The cop knew we were no part of the fight and were not guilty of anything, even though he knew we were lying about seeing the fight.

We drove slowly out of the Flats. As we moved down the road, a cop car approached, flashing lights and siren sounding. As he went by our car, his brake lights illuminated.

Dennis' Impala attracted a lot of attention because of its appearance. It was lowered with deep chrome rims and really looked cool. The cop was looking at us in his rear view mirror as he almost came to a full stop. He was talking on the radio. Then the brake lights went off, and he continued down the road.

As we went by the pay booth, we turned left, driving into the main part of the park. There was another cop racing down the road toward the Flats.

"Hey, man, I think something else must have happened down there. There's too many cops for that little fight," I said.

"No," Phil answered. "They make a big thing out of nothing. That's just the way they are."

The main part of Alum Rock Park had a cool, running creek between the grassy section and the large parking lot. There were little bridges made of stone crossing over to the parking lot. We saw people with their coolers, boxes, and picnic baskets crossing over to spend the afternoon. We drove slowly. It brought back to mind many times we as a family spent our days at Alum Rock Park.

THE
STONE
BRIDGE

rturo, Edmundo!" Dad called out. "Carry these boxes to the car. Then get your things. We're going to Alum Rock Park. Hurry!" When my father said hurry, he meant hurry. I ran to get ready, getting my play clothes. "Arturo! ¿Adónde vas? (where you going?)"

"To get ready, Dad," I answered as I came to a stop. I looked at Dad to see what he was going to say.

"No!" he said demandingly. "First take this to the car!"

My father didn't seem as if he were in a good mood. Usually, when we went to a park or went somewhere to have fun, he would be nice.

I ran back and grabbed the big box and carried it to the trunk of the car. It was too high for me to reach, so I put it down on the ground by the trunk. I ran to get ready.

Dad yelled at Eddie and me, "Put on your good clothes because we're not staying there all day. We have to go somewhere later!"

"Oh, man!" I thought. "So why are we going there? We won't be able to have fun."

The real story was that we were invited to someone's house in the afternoon, but my father felt like going to the park. He liked to lie on a blanket and read for hours.

We got ready and left. We parked by the stone bridge toward the end of the grassy area. Over the stone bridge in the grassy area, there was a large, round, white fountain. In the park there were many stone bridges. There were four pillars around it and in the center, all the way around the fountain. There were some that had different, stinky water coming out of them. The water was called mineral water. Some people would fill bottles of it, feeling it was good for their health.

We carried the boxes to where we were going to be. As we were crossing the bridge, I looked down to the creek and thought, "Man, I'm going to have fun!" Then I remembered I was wearing my good shoes and clothes.

Once we were over the other side of the old rock bridge, my father instructed, "Arturo, Edmundo, take the blankets out of the box and spread them there," he said as he pointed. Eddie and I did as he wished. We had to move the box a few times because Dad wasn't happy with our task. He took out his pillow from the other box and threw it on his blanket. My mother sat down and said, "This is nice, Joe, not a lot of people here today."

My father answered, "No, not yet. It's still early. It will fill up in a little while." My father sat down and then placed his head on my mother's lap. "Millie, where is my book?"

Mom reached into the box and found it. She handed it to my father.

Victor was an infant, and Tita was just a little girl. He was asleep; and Tita made herself busy with Gee Gee, her doll.

Eddie and I were bored. First, we sat on the blanket looking around, watching the people who were there. Some were going for a hike to the back part of the park, which went a few miles behind the creek; and others sat on the grass or were coming for the stinky water with jugs. My arms were behind me, holding myself upright. I didn't complain because if I did my father would become really upset with me, and I knew it. Once in a while I did complain; and either I was punished or was spanked. If my mother was at the park without my father, I could complain all I wanted. There was nothing to worry about; it was very unlikely that I would get beat by my mother.

Eddie stood up and said with enthusiasm, "I'm going to the bridge to look down! Want to come, Arthur? Let's go!"

I hoped my father didn't tell us we couldn't go. I stood and said, "OK!"

My father lifted his head and put his book down for a moment. "Muchachos, you can play; but don't get dirty! And don't get in the water! If you do, haw, haw, haw, haw!" my father sang his sarcastic laugh, as if he would give us a good spanking if we did.

"OK, Dad. Is it OK if I go down to the water, to look at the little fish?"

"Sí, but don't get wet! You have your good shoes on! Just look. Don't play with them. If you get wet, you will have to answer to me!"

My father was very strict about our clothes. If he paid good money for them, we better not ruin them. He didn't want them to wear out fast. If we wore our clothing out too quickly, we knew we would receive a beating. I recall a time, on the way home from school, when he saw me walking through puddles of water with my new, pointed shoes that I didn't like. Man, I received a beating for that!

Eddie and I made our way through all the bushes, down the rocky slope to the creek. The creek was filled with large rocks and small ones. It was just a stream of water in the summer months with little minnows. One could easily cross the creek by stepping on and over the rocks.

"Eddie, look at that fish!" I exclaimed as I pointed. The water was clear, and the day was warm. Being on the rocks made it a little warmer than it really was. It smelled like oak trees and green grass.

"Yeah, cool," Eddie said as he stood on a large rock himself. The fish moved away from us. I stepped to the large rock where Eddie was standing. My shoes were slippery, and I almost fell.

"Be careful, Arthur! You don't want to fall. You know what Dad will do if you fall in the water. I don't want to be around for that."

"Neither do I," I thought.

I jumped over a few more rocks to try to get to where the little fish were. Eddie stood on the same rock, trying to be very careful. As I jumped over from a large rock to a smaller one, I slipped! "Oh, man!" I said, really upset.

"Arthur! I told you . . . ."

I fell in the water and was soaked. It was cool. I stood up, feeling really scared. The first thing I thought about was my father up on the grass. Looking to make sure he wasn't looking down, I hurried and stepped to the rock, getting out of the water. I stood on the rock, drenched. The water was draining from my pants and shoes. I looked at myself and said, "I'm going to be killed!"

"Man, Arthur! Dad is going to be mad; and you're right, he will probably kill you!"

My shoes were filled with water. "Yeah, I know he's going to kill me!"

I removed my shoes and dumped the water from them, not knowing what I should do. Eddie looked me over but didn't know what to tell me. He and I knew that I might be murdered that very day. Then Eddie said, "Arthur, take your socks off, too; and put them with your shoes on this rock. They can dry in the sun. And if you lie on a big rock, you might dry off." I did what Eddie said.

"You should take off your pants and put them on a rock. That way they'll dry faster."

"Heck, no! I'm not going to take off my pants! I would rather get hit than let someone see me with nothing on."

"No one wants to see you."

At that moment we heard Dad call us. I was scared. Eddie said, "I'll go up and see what he wants. I hope we ain't leaving right now."

"We just got here," I said. I agreed with Eddie and hoped we weren't leaving.

Eddie made his way up the side of the creek through the brush. When he arrived where our father was, Dad had just yelled again, "¡Arturo y Edmundo!"

"I'm right here, Dad," Eddie said as he went through the brush.

"Where is your brother?"

"He is farther down by the bridge. He can't hear you."

"OK, go and get him. I want you to go to the snack bar and buy five hot dogs for us. Take Arturo with you, so he can help you carry them." We had brought two large bottles of Coke and some cups but no food.

"OK, Dad. I will. I'll get him."

Eddie took the money from Dad and headed back down the hill to the creek to get me.

I was waiting nervously to see what Eddie was going to say. "Arthur, Dad wants you and me to go buy some hot dogs."

"Me? I can't go. Oh, no. What am I going to do?"

"Don't worry. I'll go by myself. I can carry them."

Eddie was a good brother.

"Eddie, tell Dad I didn't want any so that you can carry them easier."

"Are you sure? I could still carry five of them."

"Yeah. I hope he don't get mad at me for not going."

"I'll tell him you did go with me but that you went back to the creek by the bridge, and it was easy for me to carry them."

I agreed. Eddie went and came back in a little while, carrying two hot dogs. "How did it go?" I asked.

"Dad said he will talk to you later, Arthur. He said we're leaving in a few minutes. Did your things dry? Here is a hot dog for you."

"A little. I don't think he will notice. Only if he touches me. Then he will. You can have my hot dog. I don't feel like eating." I was just too nervous.

In ten minutes I heard Dad yell, "Arturo, Edmundo! Come here!"

I put on my socks and shoes as fast as I could. My pants were still wet, but my shirt was almost dry. My shoes looked dull from the water. When Eddie and I reached the top where my father was standing, Eddie went through the bushes first. I followed. Dad was standing, and Mom was folding the blanket. He stared at me because he knew I was wet, but he didn't say anything. Mom glanced at me, also knowing I was wet. Dad gave me a hard look and told me to start taking the boxes we brought. He wouldn't take his eyes off me. I thought he was wondering what he should do˜either tell me off, spank me, or not say anything at all, just play dumb.

"Eddie," Mom said, "take these two boxes; and go with your brother."

Eddie caught up with me. "Arthur, I think he noticed but didn't say anything."

"I know. I hope he doesn't tell me anything later." We were going over the bridge to the car. "I hope he isn't waiting to tell me something when we get home."

When we arrived at the car, we put the boxes by the trunk. I stayed there. Eddie went back to see if they needed any more help.

On the way home we stopped at the house of one of Dad's friends. and Eddie and I waited in the car. Sometimes we had to wait for Dad for a long time. It was hot. In a while we started fighting and wrestling. In an hour the front door to the house opened; Dad, Mom, (holding Victor), and Tita appeared. Dad was standing by the front door talking to his friend. As Dad spoke, he did what he often did˜brushed his hair back with his hand when it fell to his face. In a few minutes they came to the car and stepped inside.

On the way home Eddie called me a name. I yelled out an uglier name and said it really loud, almost yelling. Dad told us to sit still or else. I knew there wasn't much he could do because he was driving. Eddie jabbed me with his elbow in my ribs. It hurt. I yelled at him and called him stupid. Eddie didn't like being called stupid because my father always called him that when he became angry at him. Eddie hit me in the leg lightly, so Dad couldn't see. I yelled at him again. Dad really became angry at me.

"Arturo! ¡Quieto! (Behave!) I'm already going to get you when we get home for ruining your shoes. I told you not to get in the water! And now you are fighting? Ay, ay, ay, ay," he said as he reached with his arm to the back to our legs. He felt my leg but passed it. Upon feeling another leg, he yelled, "¡Estupido!" He pinched as hard as he could, turning the flesh hard as he pinched. However, it wasn't I who yelled in pain. It was Eddie! My father pulled the car over after hearing Eddie yell in agony and knew he had pinched the wrong kid.

He felt bad for Eddie and told me he was going to take care of me later. By the time we arrived home, he didn't say anything. I think he felt bad that he punished the wrong kid. Eddie's entire thigh stayed black and blue for weeks. Dad never spanked me for that one.

5 THE GET AWAY

e drove through the main part of the park and then traveled up the road on the hill that exited Alum Rock Park. It was now 2:30 p.m.

Once we left the park, we were driving down Alum Rock Avenue. I lifted my beer to take a drink when I caught sight of a cop car going past us on the other side of the road. I had the beer up to my lips when I made eye contact with the cop. Pulling the can down, I exclaimed, "Oh, man!"

"What? What happened?" Dennis asked, realizing that the cop had just passed.

"That cop, he saw me drinking my beer!" I looked back, and Dennis had his eyes on the rear view mirror. Phil turned around, too. We all saw the cop's brake lights illuminate. Dennis stepped on the gas, pushing the accelerator to the floor. He made an immediate left after the next bend in the road, turning down a side street. Phil and I hung on because Dennis was driving very fast.

Just a few houses down, there was another street. Dennis pulled hard on the steering wheel. We turned, skidding around the corner.

I looked behind and didn't see the cop. "He's not there. Maybe he forgot about us," I said hopefully.

"No way, Art. He's not going to forget about us. They don't like it when someone tries to get away from them," Phil explained.

Dennis was still driving fast, making a lot of turns. We kept driving down the side streets. We were by Mt. Hamilton Road on the east foothills, not too far from Alum Rock Park. "That's right. They sure don't like it. Heck, we have been through this a lot of times. Sometimes we get away, and sometimes we get caught," Dennis said, laughing a little, feeling the excitement.

We made another right. As we did, we saw a cop car passing the street two blocks ahead. Dennis stepped on the gas harder as the cop stopped right in the middle of the intersection.

"Man! They got us!" I yelled, not wanting to get busted right away.

"No, they don't have us yet! They don't have us until they've got us!" Dennis said loudly as he continued to make turns. We saw another cop down the street. Dennis continued, "Now I'll try my last trick!" He turned down another street and drove into a long driveway. He went all the way back behind the house, down the long driveway. When we were in the back, he turned off his engine.

We sat there for a few seconds, hearing the engines of police cars racing down the streets. We saw a Latino family looking out the back window at us. Phil stepped out of the car and said, "I'll be right back." He went to the back door and knocked. Someone looked out the back window and opened the door.

"Hola, ¿qué pasa (Hello, what's happening?")

Dennis and I could hear them talking but couldn't see the person. It was a ladies' voice. "Is Charlie here?"

"No Charlie here. You maybe have wrong house," the woman answered in broken English.

I said to Dennis, "I bet they are wondering why we really came back here."

"Yeah, maybe. But, hey, it's better then getting caught by the cops."

"Yeah, it is."

"Charlie doesn't live here? Really? I was sure this was the house. What street is this?"

"This is Porter."

"Oh, man. This looks like his street, but I think he lives a block down. I'm sorry we parked in your back yard, but we always park in Charlie's back yard. OK, sorry. We'll go to his house. Sorry."

"Oh, it's OK, don't worry about it," the lady answered.

Phil came back to the car and stepped inside. Dennis said, "Now let's see how long we can stay here." We could hear the cop cars racing up and down the streets.

"Are we going to leave?" I asked.

Dennis looked at me and responded, "Not if we can help it. We'll wait a few minutes."

We sat in the car for five minutes. Dennis then looked at Phil and told him, "Go tell them my car won't start. Tell her that when my car gets warmed up it takes a few minutes to get going again. What kind of people live here?"

"Looks like a Mexican family. She didn't speak English too well; she had an accent. I think it'll be all right if we stay a bit."

"You never know. She might not like it that three guys are in her back yard. She's probably scared, man. Go tell her about my car. Maybe she will believe you."

"OK, you got it," Phil acknowledged as he stepped out of the car again.

I saw Phil knock a second time. "Hello," he said. The same lady came to the door.

"Yes?"

"Our car won't start. When it's warmed up, it has to cool down to start again. I hope you don't mind." Phil looked like an innocent kid.

The lady looked as if she felt sorry for him. "Esta bien. Quedate todo el tiempo que quieras. (It's all right. Stay as long as you want.)"

"I wonder what she is saying? Do you understand Spanish, Art?"

"Yeah. She said it's OK, not to worry about it."

"Cool," he answered. Even though Dennis was Latino, like many Latinos he was second or third generation Mexican-American. His grandparents spoke English in their homes.

I agreed and also said, "Cool."

"Yeah, it always seems to work. Now the cops think we did a magic trick! Pretty good, huh?"

"Yeah, good one. You learned a lot since I've been gone, man!"

Phil stepped into the car. "Pass me a beer, Art. Might as well enjoy it back here."

"Yeah, pass me one too," Dennis stated.

"Yeah, might as well," I agreed as I passed them two beers.

Within fifteen minutes we didn't hear the cop cars racing around us anymore. Dennis said, "I think we better go because these people might call the cops on us for sitting back here drinking beer."

"I don't think they will," Phil answered. "The lady was kind of nice. I don't think she minds. Heck, maybe she knows we're trying to get away from the cops and is helping us."

Laughing, I replied, "I don't think so, man. I think if she knew the cops were after us, she would be scared and call them." I took a drink of beer.

"Yeah, I think we should go," Dennis said as he started the engine.

All three of us were done with the beers we had just opened. Phil took all the full and empty cans and put them into the trunk. He backed slowly out of the driveway.

We started moving down the street. When we turned the corner two blocks away, we saw a cop car parked next to the curb. Dennis made a left and headed back to Alum Rock Avenue, driving slowly, not wanting to attract attention. The cop who was parked didn't notice us. Once we were on Alum Rock, we went the speed limit and escaped safely.

We drove to Second Street by the Jose Theater downtown. There were people standing around in front of the theater. Dennis gunned his engine. The Jose Theater, during that time, was our mall, a place where we all gathered to see our friends. However, on this day we weren't planning on stopping. We just wanted to check out the scene.

Dennis drove his car into the parking lot across the street, where we parked and sat in the car. Phil got out, opened the trunk and took out three beers. We wanted to play it safe, so we left the rest of the beer in the trunk. Someone from the front of the theater ran across the street to where we were.

"Hey, man! ¿Qué pasa? What's happening, hommies?"

"Hey, Flaco, how are you, man?"

Flaco looked to the back seat where I was seated and asked, "Hey, Art! Man, when did you get out?"

"A week ago, ese. How are you? What's up?"

"Cool, man. I heard you were getting out soon. How was it in there?"

"It was alright, Flaco. Hey, I heard your cousin got sent up right after we did. I met a guy who knows you and your cousin."

"Yeah, man. He and my other cousin both went to YA for fighting and beating up a cop. Then they wrecked into the cop's car. He really got busted, man. They beat the heck out of him before taking him in. What was the bato's (guy's) name who knows me?"

"I don't know his real name, just his nick name, Little John. I think he's from Los (Los Angeles)."

"Yeah, that's what I heard about your cousin. Too bad he didn't go to Preston with me. I needed some homeboys there. There weren't too many of us. I was out numbered, man."

"I can't remember or don't know who that guy is. But, yeah, I know what you mean. Hey, man, maybe we can get together sometime."

"Sure, Flaco. Just let me know. I'm staying with my mother on Emory Street."

Dennis cut in, "Hey, Flaco, have you heard of any parties going on today?"

"Not too many things going on because it's Sunday. But I did hear of a party during the day, right now on Delmas Street, the westside." Delmas was by Spencer, where I grew up as a young kid. This was the house we lived in when I was sent to the store in the dark and thought I saw monsters.

"Who's having it?" Dennis asked.

"Some girl I know. I think she's having a barbecue. She told me to come, but I thought I would come here instead."

"Oh, yeah," I asked. "What's her name?"

"Yolanda. She lives on Delmas. Do you know her? I can't remember her last name." After spending the last three years locked up, I wasn't too good on names.

"No, I don't think so. But if I seen her I would know."

"Dennis asked, "Hey, you having a good time here; or do you want to go to the barbecue and take us with you?" When Dennis asked, I thought this was a really good idea.

"Sure, I'll take you guys. There's nothing happening here anyway."

Flaco stepped into the car next to me in the back seat.

"Want a beer?" I asked.

Flaco replied that he did. I asked Phil if he would get another one out of the trunk. Phil got back in and handed it to Flaco and said, "Be careful, there's a lot of cops around." I really didn't have to tell him that because we all knew to be careful.

We drove to Delmas Street.

"Hey, man, slow down." I said. We were driving by Spencer and Virginia, a block away from Delmas. "See that little house there, the white one? That's where I lived when I was a little kid."

"Cool, Art. Hey, I didn't know you were from the westside," Phil commented.

I laughed and answered, "Yeah, man, till I was seven years old. Then we moved to Virginia Place on the eastside."

This part of town was on the westside, with Virginia Avenue on this side of town. It was the old part of San Jose with many of the homes built in the old Victorian style. Most of the houses had little front yards with very large back yards. There were a lot of shrubs and flowers. In the past it was mainly an Italian neighborhood, but now many Mexican-American families lived here.

As we drove up to the stop sign at Delmas, Dennis asked Flaco which way to turn.

"Make a right, man. It's only a few houses down, I think."

We saw all the cars parked in the driveway and on the street. There wasn't a parking space on the whole block. The houses had long driveways going all the way to the back. We were moving slowly down the street to see who was having a party. Some people were in the front yard and looked at us. Four guys in a 1969 low-rider Ford passed us. "That's it. This is where Yolanda lives. Now see if you can find parking."

Phil said, "We'll find parking, but it might be around the corner. I hope it's OK with Yolanda that you're bringing us, man."

Flaco answered, "If it's not, we'll just leave. When we get there, I'll let you know if she wants us to leave or stay; but I'm sure it'll be all right."

6 CHEMISTRY

ennis drove his car around the corner and found parking. "Yeah, just let us know. Then we'll leave, Flaco."

A block-and-a-half down we found a parking space open. We parked and stepped out of the car. The evening was still sunny and warm. It was five o'clock. We all started to walk toward the party and barbecue. Almost at the corner from Yolanda's house, we could smell the meat they were barbecuing. A carload of girls drove by as we were walking.

"Hey, look at that," I commented as we all turned to look. They were driving a 1957 Chevy two-door, lowered and clean, blue and white. It appeared the girls were saying something as they all turned and looked at us. They were pretty girls as far as I could see, about our age. They were laughing. I continued, "I wonder if they're going to be there, too. Maybe they're looking for parking."

"I don't know," Flaco answered. We were turning the corner and were a few houses down from Yolanda's home.

As we approached Yolanda's house, there were young people who were staring at us. They were about our ages, both guys and girls. As we stepped by, Flaco asked one of them, "Hey, ese, this is where Yolanda lives, right?"

The house was an older home, and it was kept up very nicely. The grass was green and mowed. There were flowers all around the lawn and rose bushes with many different colored roses next to the asphalt driveway and in front of the house.

"Yeah, she does," the taller guy answered. "She's back there," he said as he motioned his head towards the back. "Are you friends of hers?" He was wearing dark shades, as was his partner. The guy had his arm around one of the three girls. Keeping straight faces, the girls were motionless. I felt they didn't like us being at this gathering. It appeared as if they thought we were there to start trouble.

"Yeah, she invited us."

"She did? You must be good friends of hers. Go ahead back there. Make yourselves at home," he said as if he were part of the family. Once we said we were invited, he lightened up his hard expression.

We walked down the long driveway and went all the way to the back yard. The fence that separated the house from the next door neighbors' looked new. We could hear a lot of people talking and some laughing. The smell of meat cooking was apparent. It smelled very good, making my stomach growl. At the end of the driveway, there was a high wooden gate that was partly open.

We entered the back yard. It was nice with green trees all over and one very large tree in the center of the yard. I recognized it to be a Chinese Elm because it was the same as the large tree in our back yard on Emory Street. Tables and chairs were all over the place. Most of the front part of the back yard was green grass. There were people of all ages, even little kids running around the yard. Some of the people turned to look at us. We didn't see any guys like the four of us in the crowd. It appeared as if it were a family get-together.

Three older men stopped talking and turned our way. They looked at us as if they were wondering who we were. I waved to them as if I knew them. They returned the wave and went back to their conversations.

We followed Flaco as he took the lead. I was hoping it was all right that we were at the gathering. Most parties were open to whoever wanted to attend, however, not this one.

I thought back to the girls who drove by when we parked and wondered if the word was getting around that this was one of our wild parties.

There were mostly adults standing around where the food was located. We walked toward two men who were cooking meat on a large grill. The barbecue pit was made of red brick with a large tabletop as part of it and was covered with light brown tile. The two men appeared as if they were really working hard, turning meat over as fast as they could. The fire was burning hot. There were drops of sweat on their foreheads. All around the area were chairs with people sitting on them, talking and laughing. They were sitting around the tables and under the trees.

I saw a beautiful girl moving around some dishes. She looked at us as we approached. Light complected; with ruby cheeks; tall and thin, her hair was long and reddish brown, wavy. She looked very nice. She had pretty brown eyes, wore red lipstick, and was very attractive. Her smile is what caught my attention. When she smiled, it sent a feeling all the way to the pit of my stomach. I could feel my heart pump faster, thinking to myself that I just had to meet this girl. She was my type, the type who touched my inner feelings.

Phil noticed how I was looking at her and moved his elbow to hit my side. "Hey, don't stare so hard. You'll get us all kicked out of here." We both chuckled.

I knew he was kidding, but he was right. I should not be staring so hard. Knowing I was going to meet her very soon, I realized at that moment that I wanted her to be my girlfriend.

She looked at Flaco and then at us. Her eyes stopped on me as she smiled. I loved that smile. It was nice.

"Hey! Hi, how are you guys?" she asked as we were nearing her. She put down the dishes she was handling, picked up a cloth to wipe her hands, and turned toward us.

Her eyes passed all of us again and stopped with me, as if she recognized me. At that moment I remembered her. She was a girl I knew before I was sent to the California Youth Authority. I thought, "Or maybe it's her sister because she didn't look this beautiful when I left." She was wearing a colorful Mexican apron.

Because she wouldn't take her eyes off me, I said, "Hi, Yolanda. Remember me, Art Rodriguez?"

She kept her smile and answered, "Yeah, I think I do. I'm not sure. Oh, Art Rodriguez? Yeah, how can I forget! You look older now. Where have you been?"

"You look beautiful, Yolanda. I've been out of town for a while. But I'm back now, for good."

"Oh, thank you, Art." She blushed a little and then continued, "Yeah, my memory is coming back. I remember now. You were sent away. When did you get out?"

Before I answered, I remembered that Phil, Dennis, and Flaco had not yet greeted Yolanda. "Just a few days ago. It's nice to be home with my family and friends. You know Dennis and Phil, right?"

She looked at them as if she didn't see them standing next to me. "Yes, I know them." She looked at Dennis and Phil and said, "Hi, you guys. How are you? Nice of you to come."

Yolanda had a pleasant way about her. She smiled and spoke excit-
edly, as if we made her day because we came to her house. She didn't
lose her smile; it seemed as if it was part of her everyday expression. I
couldn't take my eyes off her. "And you know Flaco, right?" I chuckled
to myself because he was the one who was invited. We just tagged along
with him.

"Flaco? You mean Jeff."

I looked at Flaco and repeated, "Jeff?"

"Yeah, man, that's my real name. But, hey, Flaco sounds better."

"In fact, Jeff said you invited him; and he thought you wouldn't
mind if he brought us. I hope it's OK?"

"Oh, yes. I am really glad you could come! I always wondered what
ever happened to you, Art. I think of you every so often."

"You do? I mean, you have, really?" I answered, smiling and surprised. I felt good knowing that someone like her was thinking about me
while I was away.

"Yes, I did, I mean, do." She laughed because she was getting confused. Yolanda turned, pointed to one of the men who was barbecuing,
and said, "That's my father, Art. Would you like to meet him? Come this
way."

She took my hand and led me in the direction of her father. I looked
back at Dennis and Phil. They looked at me as if they were saying, "Hey,
man, what do you have that we don't?" But at the same time, they could
also be saying, "Go for it. You got it made. I wish I was in your place
right now!"

I chuckled to myself, feeling it was the chemistry. Convinced that
she was really attracted to me and I to her, I wondered how she was
going to introduce me to her father. As I stepped to where her father was
cooking, she still had a smile.

My memory was flashing back to when I met her for the first time.

7 THE BUSY SIGNAL

When I was fourteen, my friends and I called the local radio station, KLIV, to dedicate songs to our girlfriends or just girls; however, it was always busy. When you received the busy signal, if you listened closely, you could hear other young people talking in between the busy signal tones. "Hello (beep) who (beep) are (beep) you (beep)?"

One of the other people on the line would answer, "I'm (beep) Linda. (beep) What (beep) school (beep) do (beep) you (beep) go (beep) to (beep)?

"(beep) Overfelt. (beep) What's (beep) your (beep) phone (beep) number (beep)?"

One would have to have good timing to be able to talk through the busy signal. In time almost every dedication made was for everyone on the busy signal. The radio station had no idea what the busy signal was.

In one instance I asked for a girl's phone number. When I called her, she sounded really nice. I told her to meet me in front of the variety store on the southwest corner of White Road and Alum Rock Avenue. Phil and I took a bus to the corner. The only person we saw was a very large girl who had her hair ratted up everywhere. She looked like a pregnant spider. When we stepped off the bus, Phil and I saw her. He spoke through the side of his mouth, covering his mouth with his hand as if he were going to cough. The girl stared at us as if she knew one of us was the guy she was supposed to meet. I looked at Phil and told him, "Let's keep walking and catch the bus around the corner." I didn't want to meet her after all!

Two weeks later Yolanda was on the busy signal line. I called her on her telephone. We talked three different times. The following Sunday I met her at the Jose Theater. I tried to put my arm around her as the movie was playing; however, she wouldn't let me. That was the last time I saw Yolanda until the barbecue.

As we stepped to where her father was cooking, there were people standing around talking and laughing, drinking beer. I didn't know why she was treating me so special. I thought maybe she remembered me well and had always liked me.

"Dad, I want you to meet a good friend of mine, Art. Art, this is my father Juan."

"Welcome, boy. I hope you have a good time here. My muchacha (girl) told me she was inviting some friends. I told her any friend of hers is a friend of mine, as long as you treat my mija well."

"Thank you, sir. I know I will."

"Mija, tell your mother to bring me the large pot to start putting some of this meat into."

"OK, Daddy." She turned and walked away. I wondered if he had sent her away so he could talk to me privately.

"You didn't come alone, I see."

"No, those are my friends—Jeff, Dennis, and Phil."

"How long have you known my Yolanda?" he asked, not looking at me. He kept turning over the meat. I could tell the meat on the grill was almost done.

"Well, I think I have known her ever since I was fourteen or fifteen. But I haven't seen her for a long time."

"Do you work or go to school?" he asked as he was stacking the beef on the corner of the grill. The meat was done, and the pot had not yet arrived.

"No, I'm looking for a job right now. I just got out of school." I answered, not lying. The prison where I served my sentence was called Preston School of Industries.

"I see. So what did you learn there?"

I thought this man was asking a lot of questions, as if I were asking for his daughter's hand in marriage when I had really just met her again a few minutes ago. Even though I knew Yolanda when I was younger, I really didn't know her well. We didn't talk to each other very much back then.

"High school. I had to get some credits that I needed to graduate."

Just as I said this, Yolanda brought the pot. "Here, Daddy."

"Thank you, Mija."

"You're welcome, Daddy. We're going to go back over there with Art's friends. And if you need another pot, just flag me over. I'll get whatever you need."

"OK, Mija. And boy," he said as he looked at me, "nice to meet you. Be nice to my baby."

"Nice to meet you too, sir; and I will."

Yolanda said, "Let's go over there, Art," as she looked to where Jeff, Phil, and Dennis were sitting. They had found chairs against a wall. Yolanda kept glancing at me and smiling. It was a nice feeling for me.

Phil asked, "So, Art, what happened? Did he like you?" Dennis and Jeff were also waiting for my answer. They were asking in a joking manner because Yolanda was treating me so special.

"Yeah," I answered, smiling and thinking it was funny. "He wanted to know who you guys are. He said that if you were my friends and you behaved then you could stay!" I said jokingly.

Both Yolanda and I sat down on two chairs. Yolanda sat next to me. I felt she really liked me since she decided to sit next to me. Maybe I had made a big impression on her when we were younger, and she never forgot about it.

"Art, how was it when you were in jail? How long has it been that you've been out?"

Before I answered, I looked around the yard and saw people laughing and enjoying themselves. Chairs were all over the place. Some chairs had people on them, and some didn't. It looked as if everyone was having a really good time. Farther back in the yard, the small children were running around, holding hands and laughing. "Well, it was a long time. All together it was about 32 months, 5 days, 6 hours, and 17 minutes. Do you want the seconds too? Because I know them," I asked, jokingly.

Yolanda laughed. "No, that's OK."

"As I said earlier, I have only been out for one week. And it feels good to be here. I never want to go back again. I'm really going to try hard not to go back. When I was locked up, I thought of being home every minute. I couldn't wait for the day I walked out of there, and it finally came."

"That's good. I'm glad to hear that. I don't know how you could have gotten into that trouble because you were so nice. When I read it in the newspaper the day after it happened, I couldn't believe it was the same Art Rodriguez I knew. You were so nice, and I thought it just couldn't be you."

Jeff cut in, "Yolanda, do you think you can get us anything to drink?

I mean like beer or something?"

Before Yolanda answered, she went into deep thought for a second and then said, "Yeah, I can. I'll get you some paper cups, and that way no one will know you're drinking. I'll be right back." Yolanda stood up from her chair and stepped into the house.

"Cool, Jeff," Dennis said. "I needed a beer. I was getting dry. I was just going to take a walk to my car and have one."

"Yeah, me too, man." Phil agreed.

"Hey, Art," Jeff said, "she really likes you, man. What did you do to her. Put a spell on her?"

I laughed and then answered, "Nothing, man. The last time I saw her was when I was a kid. I met her on the busy signal. Remember the busy signal on KLIV?"

"Yeah," Phil answered.

Dennis laughed and commented, "Yeah, I remember the busy signal. Hey, that was fun." He laughed again. "I remember I filled up my little black book there!"

"The busy signal, what's that?" Jeff asked.

"We used to meet girls there. It was on the KLIV radio station. But after the station management found out why their lines were jammed and everyone was calling just to get the busy signal, they shut it down."

"I never heard of that," Jeff commented.

"Hey, so what are we going to do, man? Stay here or go somewhere else?" Dennis asked.

"I don't know. Whatever you want," Phil answered and then continued. "We should let Art make the decision because we're the ones who brought him out to have a good time."

"Yeah, what do you want to do, Art?" Dennis asked. He added, "He's going to want to stay here. Someone is interested in him, man! He isn't going to leave now!" The three of them laughed.

Just then Yolanda stepped out of the house, holding four large paper cups. She stated, "Here you go. No one knows I'm giving you this. So if anyone finds out, leave me out of it. My dad will really be upset with me."

"Cool," I said, reaching for my beer. "I'll never tell." Jeff, Dennis, and Phil reached for theirs.

We were all happy now. More young adults entered the back yard. Yolanda stood and headed toward them. They were probably the friends whom she really invited.

Dennis and Phil both said at the same time, "Nice babes!"

Jeff didn't say anything but was all eyes. I commented, "Yeah, man, they are nice looking. But, what can I say? I already found someone for today."

They all looked at me and chuckled. Dennis looked hard at the guys who arrived with them and said to Phil, "Hey, isn't that Freddie's little brother? What's his name?"

Jeff was studying the guys and then responded, "Yeah, that's him. That's Mikie. He's cool."

Phil added, "Not with us. He and his brother want to rumble with us, man."

Jeff appeared perplexed and answered, "Why?"

Phil responded, "Because Dennis took his brother's girlfriend out."

"Too bad," Jeff answered. "I hope nothing happens here. I don't want to mess up Yolanda's party."

"Na, we won't do anything here. If I have a problem with him, I'll take care of it later with his brother. Let's see what he says."

Yolanda pointed toward us. It seemed as if she were telling them to sit where we were. Then they all started walking towards us. Mikie noticed who we were and had a worried expression.

Yolanda introduced us. "Mikie, Luis, Tomas, Sally, Marie, and Vickie, this is Art, Phil, Dennis, and Jeff."

Mikie didn't seem as if he wanted any problems. He greeted, "Órale."

At the same time all the girls said hello to us.

We all looked at the girls and answered, "Hi."

"Well, that was easy," Yolanda expressed as she turned to bring more chairs to where we were standing. Mikie looked uncomfortable. Mikie and his brother, as well as Jeff, were from the westside, where we were at the moment.

Dennis and Phil wanted to get to know the girls. They didn't know if they were the girlfriends of these guys; however, they were going to find the answer. Mikie seemed young. I asked him, "So, Mikie, what school do you go to?"

"I'm going to continuation high school right now. I don't want to, but my mother tells me I have to make up some credits." He spoke with a gentle voice.

"Are you Art Rodriguez who went to jail for those murders two or three years ago?"

"Yeah, that's me. Why, you have a problem with me?" I asked, as if I didn't like the way he asked the question. When I was locked up, my mother received a lot of threats because of what my brother and I had done. She even had to move out of her house on Virginia Place and move to the house on Emory Street. I was determined that if anyone gave me any problems or said anything bad about us I was going to take care of it right away.

"No, I just hear my brother and his friends talk about it a lot."

"Yeah? What do they say?"

Mikie had an expression as if he had put his foot into his mouth. "Not too much. Just that they know the families of the guys you fought with."

"Hey, Mikie, do me a favor, man. Tell your brother and his friends that I'm out now." I was never charged with murder. I was charged with assault.

"Sure, I will," Mikie answered, not taking it in a challenging way. We both took drinks of our beers.

I looked at Yolanda; she smiled at me. I returned the smile. For some reason it seemed she really liked me more as the minutes passed. I was a little stunned because of this. She seemed to be overreacting to my presence.

We stayed in the same spot and made small talk with Mikie's friends. They seemed to be all right. We laughed and told jokes.

Yolanda brought us and the guys who arrived more beer. In a while she returned for yet another refill.

We served ourselves plates of food. It was really good. I needed it because I hadn't eaten since the morning before Dennis and Phil picked me up from my house. During this time Yolanda's father turned up the music; he and others started dancing on the concrete patio area where they had been cooking.

Every once in a while, someone would step to where we were sitting and introduce themselves to us. They asked us questions, such as what school we went to and where we worked. When they asked me, I answered that I had just finished school and was now looking for work.

"Oh," one lady answered. "Have you gone to the unemployment office on the eastside? A friend of mine just went there and got a really good job that pays well."

I didn't remember an unemployment office anywhere on the east side. I knew of one on the westside on Julian Street by Andy's Pet Shop.

"No, where is it?"

"Right on Alum Rock Avenue. It's a few buildings over on the westside of King Road. The front wall has black tile half way up. If you are going east, it's on the right side." On the corner of Alum Rock and King Road was a Safeway store that later turned into the new unemployment office. This now is the Mexican Heritage Plaza.

I told her I would try it because I really needed a job right away.

In a while Dennis wanted to leave. Yolanda didn't want me to go. She said she would have someone take me home later.

I looked at Dennis and Phil because I was out with them. "What do you think?" I asked them.

Dennis looked at Phil and asked the same thing, "What do you think, Phil?"

Phil looked as if he didn't want to leave me.

Dennis answered his own question, "All right. We'll stay a little longer."

"Cool," I thought.

Later in the evening we became a little high from the beers Yolanda brought us. People were starting to leave. Mikie and his friends had already left. Dennis asked me if I was ready. I told him I was, but I wanted to talk to Yolanda first.

I asked her if she wanted to go for a walk. She stood up and came with me. We walked down the long driveway and down the sidewalk towards Virginia Street. I held her hand when we went around the corner to Virginia Street. "Can I call you in the morning?"

"That will be nice. What time?"

"I don't know. What time do you get up?"

"The time you want to call me. I'll put the phone by my bed; so when you call, I'll be waiting."

"I'm not sure when I'll wake up. It depends on what time I go to bed tonight. Maybe around nine?"

"That's fine. If you want to call earlier, that will be all right, too."

"Good," I answered. I wanted to tell Yolanda something sweet, but I didn't know what to say.

We walked past two more houses. When we were almost to the corner on Delmas, I stopped, faced her, reached for her other hand, and looked into her eyes. I said, "Yolanda, I really liked being here with you today. I had a lot of fun, and you have a really nice family. I'm really glad I found you. I think things are going to go well for us." She appeared happy. She liked the thoughts I shared with her.

"Thank you, Art. I'm glad you came, too. I really meant what I said about thinking of you every so often while you were away."

My hand let go of hers and came up to brush her hair back over her shoulder. I expressed, "I don't know if anyone has ever told you this, but you have the most beautiful eyes I have ever seen." My eyes stared into hers.

She smiled and asked, "Really, you think so?"

I answered softy, "Yeah, I wouldn't lie to you."

"You are so nice, Art. I knew there was something there when I first saw you."

"Really?" I asked. I came close to her and kissed her soft lips.

WHITE
LIGHTNING

The following day I went to the unemployment office I was told about on Alum Rock Avenue. They had many jobs posted on boards against the far wall when one walked into the building; however, most of them were for sales people with experience. I wasn't confident enough to be a sales person.

The following week I called Yolanda twice a day, and we talked for a good while. We started to get to know each other.

I went out looking for a job, filling out applications all over the city. Because I didn't know how to spell, I used business cards, writing my information in small print on the blank side. When I filled out applications, I copied what I had written on the business card.

That Friday Dennis called and asked if I was going to be around my house. He wanted to pick me up in the evening and go do something. I told him I would be around and that I would like to take Yolanda with us. He answered, "No problem."

After finishing my telephone call with him, I called Yolanda and asked if she wanted to go with us. "Where are we going?"

"Just hanging out, maybe to a party, maybe to a drive-in."

San Jose, during this time, had many drive-in theaters. There was the Fox on North First Street, Tropicana on Alum Rock Avenue, The Spartan on South First, the El Rancho on Almaden and Alma, San Jose Drive-in on North 13th Street, and a few others.

"Sure, what time?"

I answered, "About six."

"OK, I'll be ready. What should I wear?"

"I don't know. Anything you want."

"No, I mean what kind of clothes should I wear? Are we going to any nice places? Should I wear dress-up clothes or hang-around clothes?"

"Hang-around clothes. I don't think we're going anywhere fancy. I don't have any money to go to a nice place."

"Yeah, I know. OK, I'll be ready."

When Dennis arrived at my house, I was waiting. I came out of the house and stepped into his car. "Hey, man, how's it going?"

As we drove away, Dennis answered, "Good. What's new? Find a job yet?"

"No, man. A few places said they were going to call me, but they never did. I really need a job. Money is tight!"

"Yeah, I bet."

We turned the corner onto Walnut and back onto University, making our way to Coleman.

"Yeah, I think it's the assault that's messing me up."

"Assault? What do you mean it's messing you up?"

"Yeah, they ask on the applications if I have ever been arrested; so I put down assault."

Dennis laughed. "Hey, man, you don't tell them you've been in jail for assault. No wonder no one has hired you yet. Heck, if I owned a company, I wouldn't hire you either! Man, you'll probably beat everyone up who works there and me, too!"

"Yeah, but if I don't, they'll find out anyway."

"No, man, not for the kind of job you're looking for. No way, Art. And if they do find out, what are they going to do? Fire you? Hey, you won't be losing anything. You'll just be back where you started."

"Yeah, you're right. That's kind of dumb of me. I think I'll write down I've never been arrested before."

"Or just leave it blank. Put a line through it. Yeah, man. That's funny. You've been putting down assault."

We were on Coleman now and entering Highway 17, heading to the eastside.

"Where are we going right now?"

"I think we'll pick up Phil first. See if he has anything in mind. Then we'll pick up the girls in a while and go cruising for a while."

"So, what's the story with Mikie's brother?"

"Mikie, at Yolanda's house?"

"Yeah."

"Nothing really. His girlfriend wanted to come with us one day. I was with Phil, Ray, and her. Her friend went with us. We went to some parties and down to Bert's house." Ray was Phil's cousin. He hung out with us a lot.

"Did you two do anything to make him so upset?"

"No, not really. We just made out. That's all. She told me she didn't like him anymore and wasn't going out with him because she broke up with him. I think they had a fight, and she was using me to get back at him."

"If I'm around, Dennis, don't worry, man. I'll take care of him for you."

"Na, that's OK. I can handle him. He's no big deal," Dennis said confidently.

We were now on Highway 101, approaching the eastside.

"Hey, whatever happened to Cecilia, remember her?"

"You mean Cecilia, the tall girl? She had sisters, Becky, Judy, and Eva?"

"Yeah, that's her."

"I don't really know. Once in a great while I see them at a party or something. In fact, I think I saw one of her sisters at the Flats not that long ago. Why? Were you writing to her when you were locked up?"

"No, I wish. I was just wondering. I always liked her and thought about her when I was locked up. What about Stella, you know, she had a sister named Bobby, Rudy's old girlfriend?"

"I see Stella around town. You liked her, right?"

"Yeah, I did. She was my girlfriend. I think I was her first boyfriend."

"Oh, yeah, cool. I didn't know that."

"Yeah, I was young then. I don't really think she liked me all that much. But it was cool meeting her at the Jose all the time."

We were now getting off the freeway on Alum Rock Avenue, heading toward King Road.

"I didn't know you went out with her."

"Well, I really didn't go out with her. We went to the Jose a few times, made out; but we were young then. We used to talk on the phone all the time."

We made a right on King Road toward Virginia Place. Dennis said, "I talked to Phil before coming. He said he would be waiting for us."

In a few minutes we made a right on Virginia Place. I saw Phil sitting on his front lawn waiting for us. When he saw us, he stood. Dennis pulled into his driveway and backed out onto the street. Phil stepped in, and Dennis started to leave. "Hey, Art, Dennis, how's it going?" Dennis lived two houses down. In between their houses was where the Lopez girls lived.

"Dennis said, "Hey."

Then I repeated, "Not too much, man. How are you?"

"I'm good, man. I have a surprise for you later."

"Oh, yeah, what is it?"

"I'm not telling. You'll see later. I think you'll like it."

"Hey, man, I already have a girl," I answered jokingly.

"No, it's not a girl. Hey, talking about a girl, I hear you are already in love and hen pecked!"

"In love? Man, that's a big word. I like her, but I don't know about being in love and being hen pecked. I don't think that could ever happen to me."

"That's what I heard. I heard you can't come out on weekdays because she won't let you," he said. I could tell from the way he was speaking that he was smiling as he said this, but I couldn't see his face because he was in the back seat.

"No, who told you that?"

"I'm not telling," he answered, giggling.

I looked back at him, and he was really smiling. He put his arm over the seat as he was getting comfortable. Dennis spoke up and said, "I didn't say that. I said he might not want to come out because he had this thing with Yolanda."

Phil laughed again and raised his voice, "No you didn't, man! You said she wouldn't let him!"

Dennis looked at me and explained, "No, don't believe him, Art. You know that's not true. I wouldn't say that. You know me!"

Phil remarked, "There you go, making me into the bad guy again!"

Dennis changed the subject, "Hey, where do you guys want to go?"

"What time is it? I told Yolanda we were going to pick her up around five."

Phil commented, "Let's go get some beer; then we'll go pick up Norma. You're taking Norma, right, Dennis?"

"Yeah."

"Then we'll go and get Yolanda."

I asked, "What about you? Are you going to have a lady next to you tonight?"

"No. I wanted to take Rebecca, but she didn't want to come. She said she had plans. I think her father won't let her come."

We did as Phil said, bought beer and picked up the girls. The beer was no problem even though all of us were under twenty-one years of age. There were places that sold us beer. Before I was sent to jail, I also had a few places to buy beer, even though I was really young, such as Bubbles on San Antonio and House of Pizza on Almaden. A guy who worked there would sell me all the beer I wanted. That was a long time ago, and I didn't know if they would know me anymore.

Once we picked up the girls, we all decided to go to the Tropicana Drive-in on Alum Rock. A drive-in theater is an outside theater where you park your car next to a pole that has a speaker hooked to a wire. You hang the speaker on the car window and enjoy the show.

On the way to the drive-in, Phil asked, "OK, man, ready for your surprise?"

Yolanda then asked, "What surprise?"

I cut in and said, "He has been telling me that he has a surprise for me, but I told him I already have you!" Yolanda smiled.

"OK, Phil, what do you have for him?" Dennis asked.

Phil reached into his shirt pocket and pulled out a pill. "This."

"What is that?"

"Just take it. You'll like it," Phil insisted, as if he really had something good for me.

"What is it, man, drugs?" In those days, because of the hippie movement, drugs were really going strong. There were all types being introduced. When I was locked up, I heard about a lot of them from guys who were just arriving at YA. "No, man, I don't want it. I just got out, and you want me to take a pill?"

"What do you mean?" Phil asked. "You've been out for two weeks. That's long enough. I have been saving this for you."

"What is it?"

Phil answered in a spooky, low-shrill voice with his palm open and the pill showing, "White Lightening!"

"What in the heck is White Lightening?"

Yolanda spoke up, "It's LSD. It will take you on a weird trip."

I asked Yolanda, "Have you taken it before?"

"Yeah, once. I think everyone has."

"Really, what kind of trip?" I had no idea what LSD was like. The only thing I ever took or smoked was pot.

Dennis and Norma weren't saying anything. Dennis seemed as if he really didn't want me to take it, but he wasn't going to say anything.

As his hand shook wickedly with the pill in his palm, Phil demanded, "Come on, take me! I'll give you a little ride! Try me. You'll like me!"

"I don't know, man. What if it really sends me on a really weird trip, and I end up making a fool of myself in front of these girls?"

"You never tried it?" Yolanda asked.

"No, they didn't have this around before I went to jail. I don't know. I don't want to get hooked."

Phil replied, "You won't get hooked on this, man. This is safe."

"How about you guys? Are you going to take it, too? You, Yolanda?"

Phil answered, "I only have one, and I got it just for you because you haven't been around."

"I don't know. I heard about it, and I don't know," I answered, worried. Yolanda hit me with her elbow on the side. "Don't be scared. It's not going to hurt you. Everyone takes it."

"Man, OK, but I don't know. I feel like this isn't right."

After Yolanda said everyone takes it, I didn't want to sound like a chicken. I took the pill of LSD out of Phil's hand, threw it in my mouth, and swallowed it. "OK, there. I hope I'm OK with it and don't blow it."

Dennis laughed, "Hey, you're going on a trip now. Don't worry. It'll only last about eight hours. If you take STP, it'll last three days."

"Three days!" I exclaimed. I didn't want to be loaded for three days.

Phil explained, "But don't worry. This isn't STP. You'll be all right in the morning."

"What do you mean I'll be all right in the morning? Do you mean I won't be all right before then?"

Norma wasn't saying anything. I heard she didn't get loaded or do any kind of drugs. They said she didn't even drink. I asked her, "Norma, have you ever taken this stuff?"

"No, I'd rather not. I know someone who lost it taking it."

"Lost it?" Now I became a little worried. "What do you mean they lost it? Man, I hope I don't loose it."

Norma answered, "Yeah, some people go on bad trips, you know, like a nightmare. I know a person, and I heard of others who became schizophrenic. You know, they hear voices and talk to themselves all of their lives. But not everyone. I don't want to take any chances with my brain. That's for sure."

I looked at Phil and remarked, "Hey, Phil, if that happens to me, I'm coming to live with you, man! You'll have to live with a crazy person and take care of me!"

Phil, Dennis, and Yolanda laughed. Norma didn't think it was funny.

We stopped at the store to buy more beer and some snacks. We didn't want to run out of beer. On the way to the Tropicana Drive-in, I didn't know what to expect from the drug I had just taken. I didn't know if I was going to feel high as if I were drinking or what.

Before arriving at the drive-in, Dennis pulled to the side of the road. "OK, who wants to get in the trunk?" Some drive-ins charged per car, but this one was the cheapest for us because they charged per person. As many of us as possible would get into the trunk and hide. Once inside the drive-in grounds, the driver would open the trunk. Everyone would get out and get into the car. Phil, Norma, and Yolanda agreed to get into the trunk. Everyone thought this was fun.

We drove into the pay booth area. Dennis looked at the guy in the booth. The guy said, "$1.50." Dennis took $2.00 from his pocket and paid. The guy at the booth looked at me strangely. I looked into his eyes, and I could see into his pupils. I saw something move inside his eyes. The guy seemed as if he were talking to me as he stared at me. I followed his pupils inside his brain. I heard a cry. "Help! I'm trapped in here," a little voice said.

"Yes? Is something wrong?" the young man asked in the pay booth.

"Art, man, hey, you all right?" Dennis asked.

"What?" I answered as I looked at Dennis coming out of my trance. "Yeah. Yeah, I am."

I looked back at the guy in the booth, and my eyes caught his pupils again. I felt their pull. I started falling into them a second time. I had to find out who was crying for help. Our car started moving, and I lost eye contact.

"Hey, man, you scared the heck out of that guy. How are you feeling, huh?" Dennis asked as he was drove slowly, staring at me.

"What? I'm what?"

Dennis laughed. "Yeah, it hit you. Take it slow, Art. Try to enjoy it. Let me know if anything happens."

As we were driving, it looked as we were moving in really slow motion. Even Dennis' voice sounded weird, as if one had a record on the wrong speed, a slow speed. I didn't know what was wrong with me. "Was I dreaming?" I asked myself.

We went to the farthest row from the snack bar. The snack bar was a building in the middle of the parking area. Parking for the drive-in was half full. Dennis, stepping out of the car, went to the back. I didn't notice him leaving. As far as I knew, I saw Dennis at my side. The next time I looked, he was gone.

"Man, I thought, where did he go? Did I make him disappear?" I heard something and felt the car move. I didn't know what was happening. Lights from other cars behind us started flashing, and horns started honking. This happened when people saw young adults sneaking into the drive-in and stepping out of a trunk.

"What the heck is going on?" I asked myself. I thought a UFO was landing. All of a sudden the doors opened, and everyone was getting into the car. Once everyone was in, Dennis drove the car to another location of the parking area.

"Hey, Art's tripping, man."

Phil looked at me and asked, smiling, "Hey, how does it feel?"

I looked down at my hands and thought, "What is he talking about? I'm not feeling anything."

"Huh, Art," Yolanda asked. "How does it feel? Do you like it?"

I heard someone mention LSD; then I realized I was feeling this way because of the LSD. "Yeah, I think I do," I said slowly, doubting if that were true. Everyone started laughing. I asked, "What are you laughing about? Did something happen?"

Yolanda patted my arm and said, "No, nothing funny happened. Just the way you said it was funny. Everything is OK," she assured.

There were five of us in the car. I was in the back seat with Phil and Yolanda. I felt as if they were getting closer, and the car was shrinking. Dennis and Norma were in the front seat. It seemed as if the seat was moving back. "Man, I got to get out of here. I'm going to be squashed," I thought.

Yolanda turned to look at me. The movie had already begun when we arrived. I looked at Yolanda. She was facing me, and she said something. She seemed too close. I could see every little thing on her face. Her nose really seemed large. I could see the pores on her nose. They seemed as if they were big, and something was moving in them. She appeared very scary. Her eyes seemed really wide and blinked in slow motion. I felt I had to get out of there and fast.

"Hey, let me out! I have to go to the bathroom."

Norma opened her door and pulled the seat forward, so I could leave. I couldn't remember how I ended up in the back seat. I remembered being in the front with Dennis. I thought I was going crazy. As I stepped out, I asked where the bathrooms were. I couldn't remember. It had been a long time since I had been to this drive-in.

Norma answered, "Right there where the snack bar is. Just walk in. You'll see a sign that says, "Restrooms.' "

"K," I answered and walked away.

The snack bar wasn't that far, but it seemed as if I were taking a lot of steps to get there. After passing three rows of cars, I looked back. I saw what looked like thousands of cars, row after row after row. I thought, "Man, I hope I can find my way back."

I went into the snack bar and saw the sign. There were a lot of people. Some were in line; some were talking; and others were leaving. I stepped into the bathroom, into a stall, and did my business. As I was standing there, I saw on the side of the toilet a piece of newspaper that someone left. It was a cruise ship advertisement. I looked at it and saw the people on the deck of the ship. They started to move. My eyes focused even closer. Then someone yelled, "The ship is sinking! The ship is sinking!" I saw two children who were crying on the deck. No parents were nearby. Poor kids! Someone needs to help them! "Kids!" I yelled in my mind. "Do you need my help? Can you hear me?" The little girl looked up to the sky at me. I asked if she saw me in the sky.

She yelled, "Yes! Help us! Where is my mommy?"

"I don't know, but I'll try to find her."

My eyes were leading me down into the ship, down one flight of stairs. People were running in a panic. I went into a large room with sofas and chairs and asked loudly, "Does anyone know where the little girl's mother is?" No one answered.

I went down a long hallway; something was telling me to go there. I felt the ship move, and then a big explosion occurred. It was sinking!

"Oh, no! Should I stay or should I go? I forgot my way out! Which way did I come in? Where is out?"

People were running all around, yelling, "Get your life jackets! Your life jackets!"

"Life jackets?" I thought.

My eyes led me through other doors. People were running past me as if they didn't know I was there. "Stop! Stop! Listen to me! I don't think this is real!" I said doubtfully. I didn't know if I were having a dream, or this was really happening. I felt the floor move. The ship was sinking. I was going to die with all these people.

"Help, someone! Help!" My eyes led me to the people who were running! Now I was one of them. I was going to die!

Boom, boom, boom! A heavy knock sounded. "Hey, buddy, you done in there? You OK in there?"

I returned from the weird trip to where I was, standing over the toilet. "Man! What the heck? Yeah, I'm done. I'm coming out right now." That was a really weird trip. "Man, how long have I been in here?" I asked myself. I fixed myself up and opened the door. Someone was standing there. "Hey," I said.

"You OK?" the man asked.

"Yeah, I'm fine, thanks. How are you?"

The man just stared at me as if he knew I was loaded. I stepped to the wash basin and looked into the mirror, saying, "Man! I look like an old wino!" I thought I looked cool; but I was all messed up, sweating, my hair was pointing in every direction. I appeared as if I had crawled out from a gutter. I turned the water on and washed my hands; I splashed water on my face. "I don't know if I can handle this stuff I am on," I thought. This feeling had never happened to me in my entire life; it was very different and scary.

I walked out of the bathroom and through the snack bar area, stepping outside. The fresh air hit me, and it felt good. I started walking to where we were parked. I walked through a few rows of cars, seeing Dennis' car. I approached the passenger side, opened the door, and sat in front. Something wasn't right. I turned to look at Dennis and Norma. Instead, two other people were sitting close to each other staring at me.

"Oh, I'm sorry, wrong car," I said, as I opened the door to leave. Standing next to the car, I looked around the area. Someone turned their lights on and off. "There they are," I told myself. I walked to the car whose lights had flashed and stepped in again. There were five young people in this car, and I didn't know any of them.

"Hey, want a beer?" one of the guys asked.

"Yeah, I'll take one."

"Hey, Jack, give my friend a beer," he told the guy in the back seat. Jack handed me a beer. "Thanks, man."

"What are you on?" the guy sitting on the driver side asked.

"I don't know. I can't remember. Some kind of pill," I answered. "Well, thanks for the beer; but I got to go now."

"All right, guy. I hope you find whoever you're with."

Again I stepped out of the car and looked around me. The car that was two parking spaces away looked like Dennis' car. Then I saw Dennis and Phil in the back seat waving to me, laughing. "There they are!"

I took a few steps, and the driver opened his window. "Yes?" an older white guy asked.

"Never mind," I said as I looked around, really lost. I didn't know what I was going to do. I felt like running, running to the large fence and jumping over it. "That's what I'll do!"

I was just about to start running when someone grabbed my arm. "Art, are you OK?" I turned; it was Yolanda.

"Hi, Yolanda. Where did you come from?"

She pointed to the section behind this row of cars and said, "Right there. Come on, let's go there. We were waving to you and thought you were coming, but you went to this car instead. Are you OK?"

"I don't think so," I replied.

Once back in the car, I told my friends I had to leave the drive-in. They agreed, realizing I was having a bad trip.

We drove to a park and stayed for a few hours. It turned out to be a really hard night. I didn't like the feeling, and I thought I would stick to beer the next time.

ROLLS ROYCE

The following Monday morning, I called Yolanda; we spent two hours on the telephone. My mother even became upset with me for tying up our telephone line so long. "What if someone was trying to call me, and you were on the phone for so long?" she questioned.

At 10 o'clock I went back to the unemployment office to check the large board on the wall with all the job openings. The building wasn't very wide; however, it was deep. It went far to the back and had offices at the other end. Many women on typewriters were working away at their desks. I approached a desk with an older lady who was hand writing something. "Excuse me," I interrupted.

"Yes, young man. What can I do for you?"

"I was wondering, are those all the jobs you have here? I came last week, and today it looks like they are all the same kind of jobs."

"No, if you want another job, you'll have to fill out a form. Would you like to do that?"

I thought about it for a second. I wasn't good about filling out forms. In fact, I couldn't complete a form because I lacked reading and writing skills. The lady noticed it by my expression and seemed to know I didn't know how to read or write very well.

"I can help you. Why don't you take a seat? As soon as I'm done with this, I'll call you up."

I thought it was cool of her to offer. There were six chairs against the wall, with three guys sitting on them. I sat next to one of them.

On the walls of this unemployment office there were many posters of people working. The floor was a linoleum brown tile. It was shiny, as if it was well-maintained; however, it seemed very old.

I listened to the noise in the office. Typewriters were clanging away. Two more people entered the building and went to the boards to check the jobs.

One of the guys who sat next to me appeared to be the same type of person as I was, someone who liked to party. He reminded me of one of the guys who was also imprisoned with me in Preston. He had short, straight, black hair and a tattoo of a cross on his forearm. He was thin and wore a T-shirt and khaki pants.

The other guy next to me was a stocky white guy, wearing a dress shirt and slacks. He didn't turn to look at any of us; his eyes seemed to be looking straight ahead, as if he were watching T.V.

The last guy, who was sitting next to him by the entrance of the front office doors, had brown, wavy hair. He also appeared as old as we were.

I heard someone speaking loudly and looked up to see who it was. The voices were coming from the back part of the office. There was a lady who was very nicely dressed who was talking to a large, bald man. At first it seemed as if they were having an argument. All the office workers turned and looked at them. The discussion was getting louder. She turned her body around and pointed toward us. She said very loudly, "What do you mean, you don't have any boys?"

The man to whom she was speaking answered in a very low tone.

She answered whatever he said. "No! I am not! I'm not going to keep it down. I called last week and told you I was coming. You should have had boys waiting for me!" she cried out, sounding as if she was getting angrier.

I remembered that before I entered through the front doors there was a Rolls Royce parked outside of the office in the yellow zone. Now, as she was speaking and stepping toward us, I realized it was probably hers because of the way she was dressed and was acting. She sounded as if she were somebody special. As she came closer to us, she appeared very beautiful. She wore a black, shear dress and a very colorful, big scarf around her neck. Her hair was black, and she wore a straw hat with a large feather extending from the top, as well as bright red lipstick. She appeared to be Spanish (from Spain) from the way she spoke.

"See! I see boys over here! I bet they would like to go to school to make a lot of money!" She kept marching toward us.

As she approached, she looked at the guy who was sitting next to me and asked, "Do you want to be an operating engineer?"

"Yes," he answered.

"Do you?" she asked me.

I answered, "What is an operating engineer?"

"Someone who makes a lot of money!"

"I thought, "Heck, yeah!" I answered, "Yes!"

"Do you?" she questioned the white guy.

"Yeah, I guess," he answered.

She asked the last guy, and he answered the same.

"OK, all of you, go home and kiss your mamas goodbye. Tell them you will be back in two weeks. But in two weeks you will return for only the weekend and then go back."

I asked, "Where are we going and for what?"

"I'm taking you to a school to be operating engineers."

The guy sitting next to me asked, "Don't you need a high school diploma for that?"

"You will be crane operators, heavy equipment and things like that. You will make the best kind of money there is. If you don't have a high school diploma, then we will get you ready for a G.E.D. test. Don't worry. They will take care of you and make sure you pass. Now go home. Get your clothes, and give your mamas kisses. I will be waiting for you for two hours. Now hurry!"

All four of us stood from our chairs. I thought, "Sounds like a good idea, but I'm sure going to miss Yolanda. But heck, I'll have a good job; that's what I need."

"OK, lady, I'll be back. I need a job bad," I replied.

"Sounds good to me," the guy next to me added. The other two said they wanted to go also and would be back in two hours.

I arrived home to find Mom in the kitchen heating up her lunch. She was home from work for an hour.

"Hi, Mijo."

"Hi, Mom. Mom, I'm leaving for two weeks."

"What? What do you mean you're leaving? I think you better find a job," she said with her hands on her hips.

"Mom, this is kind of like work. It's a school. A lady at the unemployment office with a Rolls Royce is trying to get guys to go to a school. I think they really need more people there. I'll make a lot of money."

"How do you know this lady?"

"I don't. I just met her. She's taking other guys and asked me if I wanted to go. It's really a good deal. If I learn there, I'll be making good money all my life."

"Where are you going, and who do I call if I want to know where you are?"

"I don't know. I'll call or write and tell you when I find out." Even though I didn't know how to write properly, I sounded out my words and spelled them according to their sounds. My mother, sister, and girl-friends were the only ones who could read my writing.

During this time my mother and father were already divorced. My mother was working for a business that helped people get their immigration papers to live in the United States.

When I told my mother I was going to a school, she changed her demeanor and thought it was a good plan for me. My mother was always so easy to convince; she believed everything I told her. Sometimes I lied, and she would believe what I told her.

I took some paper bags from the cabinet and went to my bedroom, sticking the only other pair of pants I had in the bag, besides the ones I was wearing. Four pairs of underwear and socks also went into the bag. I had three shirts, not counting the one I was wearing; I put them into the bag. From the bathroom I took my toothbrush and a couple of personal items. I then stepped back into the living room where my mother was waiting.

I really didn't want to leave; but I knew it was the best thing to do at the moment, not being able to find a job. I was going to miss my brothers and sister.

"I have to call the girl I have been seeing, Mom." She knew I was talking to the same girl a lot; however, she hadn't met her as of yet. I picked up the phone and pulled the cord all the way to the washroom.

I dialed Yolanda's phone number. "Hello, Yolanda?"

"No, this is Loretta. I'll get her. Hold on one second."

Loretta was her younger sister. I waited for thirty seconds. "Hello?"

"Yolanda, hi. I'm going away for two weeks."

"Where are you going, Art?"

"To a school where I will learn how to be an operating engineer, operating heavy equipment and things like that."

"Oh, that's really good. I'm happy for you."

"Yeah, I think it's going to be good, too. You know I'm really going to miss you."

"I'm going to miss you, too. When you're there, mail me your address. I will write you."

"OK, I will." I thought to myself, "I don't even have any money to buy stamps."

"Art, I feel in my heart that I really care for you. Be careful, OK? Take care of yourself."

"OK, I have to go. The lady told me and the other guys to be back in two hours. I think I'll make it if I leave right now."

"All right, you better go. I'll miss you. Bye!"

"Bye. I'll miss you, too."

I hung up and took the phone back to the living room. My mother was sitting on the sofa waiting for me.

"OK, Mom. I have to leave now."

"Now where are you going? Explain this to me."

"I don't really know; she said to a school. The lady just said we were leaving in two hours, to go home and kiss our mothers good-bye."

"You are going with a lady you don't know? And you don't know where you are going? That doesn't sound right, Arthur."

"It's OK, Mom. The lady is all right. If you want to know where I went, just call the unemployment office on Alum Rock Avenue and ask the manager. I think he's the manager, a heavy, bald guy. That's the guy she was talking to. It'll be all right, Mom," I said as I bent down to give her a tight hug and kiss.

"All right, Mijo. Don't get into any trouble. I'll call your parole officer for you." I had to report to my parole officer once a week or else he would bust me and send me back to Preston.

"Thanks, Mom. I forgot all about him."

My mother wanted me to be good; however, for me that was hard to do. I had a difficult time behaving myself, especially when I was with my friends. I was always ready to do whatever they wanted to do. Even though I knew it was difficult, I was sure going to try, for Mom's and Yolanda's sake. I knew I didn't want to go back to jail again.

"Mom, do you have any money? Not a lot, just a little." I hated to ask her for money. I knew she was having a hard time making ends meet. She had a boyfriend who was living at the house and worked, but I didn't know how much he helped her financially.

"Pass me my purse," she answered. I did. It was sitting on one of the end tables. She looked inside one of the compartments and took out $10. "Here, Mijo. That's all I can give you. Maybe I can give you more later. You have to let me know where you are when you call. When you can, write me and let me know your address right away."

Again, I gave my mother a kiss and hug and left.

Arriving back at the unemployment office, I noticed the lady's Rolls Royce wasn't parked in front in the yellow zone. I entered the building, hoping I wasn't late. Glancing at the chairs to see if the other guys were back, I determined I was the only one who returned. The lady at the desk who offered to help me complete the form was concentrating on her typing; she didn't lift her eyes to look at me. I stepped to her desk and stood quietly until she stopped typing. She noticed me standing by her desk, stopped typing, and looked at me. Smiling, she asked, "Yes?"

"Do you know if the lady and the other guys left yet?"

"No, they have not returned as of yet. The woman went to lunch with my boss. You are the first one back."

At that moment the front door opened, and one of the other guys stepped into the building.

"OK, I'll have a seat and wait." I took a few steps to the chairs, carrying my bags, and sat down. "Hey, man, ready?" I asked the guy who had just entered.

"Yeah, I think. My name is Louie, ese."

"I'm Art," I answered as I reached out to shake his hand.

"Órale. Good to meet you, ese," he greeted as he took a seat.

"Same here. What do you think about going with this lady?"

"I don't know. But the way I see it, I don't have anything to lose."

"Yeah, I know what you mean. There're not a lot of jobs around. Where do you live, Louie?"

"On the westside. You?"

"Right now I'm on the northside, a few houses down from Coleman Avenue, on Emory. I grew up on the eastside, on Virginia Place. When I was locked up, my mother moved to the northside."

"Yeah, Emory Street, I know where that is."

"Hey, I think the lady is here," I said as I lifted my chin, indicating to look out the front window. You could see the top of the Rolls Royce.

We waited for a few seconds until the bald man and the lady stepped in through the front glass doors. The lady looked at us and asked, "Ready? Are you ready to go to school?"

"Yeah," I answered.

"Where are your friends? Are they coming?" she asked as she

looked at me.

"I don't know. They aren't my friends. I don't know them."

"Do you know them, Louie?" I asked as I turned to look at him.

"No, not me. This is the first time I ever saw them."

Just then the other Latino guy walked into the building. He seemed out of breath.

"Good, another one! Where is your other friend?"

The guy shrugged his shoulders.

"I'm ready to leave. Are you boys ready to go?"

Louie and the other guy nodded their heads affirmatively. I answered, "Yeah, I'm ready."

"OK, bring your things out to my car."

When we stepped outside to her car, she opened the trunk. We put all of our things inside. She closed the trunk and told us to get into her car.

Once we were in, she said, "Make yourselves comfortable. I will be right back. I have to sign some papers."

I stepped into the front of the car on the passenger side. Louie and the other guy sat in the back seat. She closed my door and went into the building.

"Hey, man, what's your name?" I asked the other guy.

"I'm Jerry, esa." He used the word "esa" with an "a," instead of an "e" because he couldn't pronounce it correctly.

"Cool, man. I'm Art, and this is Louie."

Louie put his hand out to shake Jerry's hand. "Where you from, Jerry?"

"From here, San Jose. How about you, Louie?" Jerry asked.

"From here, ese, San Jo."

San Jo was how we young Latinos referred to San Jose for short. East, west, north and south sides of San Jose were considered different parts of town to us. Sometimes we fought with each other, and sometimes we were friends.

"I never thought I would be going away to school," I commented.

"Me either," Jerry agreed.

"Hey, man," Louie commented, "this is a cool car. I wish I had one of these. I'll bet I could pick up a lot of girls with it."

"Yeah, man." I turned and saw the lady through the window, walking toward the door. "Here she comes. She sure looks good." I meant really pretty.

Louie looked out of his window and commented, "Yeah, ese, she sure does. But she is a little old." She appeared thirty to thirty-five years old. To young adults, as we were, she was very old.

She was walking fast, looking to make sure the street was clear, and coming around into the car. "How are you boys doing?" she asked as she stepped into the car and pulled out her keys.

"Nice car," I commented. "By the way, what is your name?"

"Oh, I'm sorry. I didn't tell you. Forgive me! I have been rushing all day. My name is Blanca. It means white or very light. My parents named me Blanca because they thought I was going to be very light complected like them. But as you can see, I'm not. I love my name. What are your names?" she asked as she made a u-turn.

I answered first because I was sitting in the front seat with her. "My name is Art Rodriguez. The guy behind you is Jerry, and the one behind me is Louie."

"Nice to meet all of you," she said as she pulled onto the ramp of Highway 101. "We will get all your information when we arrive at our destination."

To me it seemed strange that she was taking us without knowing who we were. She also signed papers with the bald guy who didn't know us either.

"Do we need a high school diploma for this school?" Louie asked. "I think I have my credits, but I never got my diploma."

"And you, Art? Do you have yours?" she asked.

"Yeah, I got mine. But I can't read or write."

"Oh? How did you get it if you cannot read or write?"

"It's a long story. I got it when I was locked up. One of these days I'll write a book about it." We all laughed.

"That's OK. This school is for this reason, to help boys like you. They will help you get a G.E.D; and, Art, they will test you so they can see where you are. Jerry, what about you? Did you get your G.E.D. or diploma?"

"No."

"They will prepare you to begin studying to be an operating engineer."

"So, Blanca, what do you do? Go to the unemployment offices and pick up guys like us all day long in your Rolls Royce?" Louie asked.

Blanca threw her head back and laughed. I looked at her when she laughed out loud. I thought, "She has a lucky husband to have such a beautiful wife." She had straight, white, clean teeth; and her eyes shined, indicating a happy state of mind.

"No, just today. My husband is a politician in Sacramento. He started this school for minorities. But it seems there are only Black boys there, which is all right; but he wants to include more boys of color in the school."

Jerry remarked, "So we will be the only Mexican-Americans there?"

"Yes, I believe so. You will be the only ones of any race besides Black. So that means you will have to behave. We don't want you to get into any fights. I do not know what kind of boys you are; but remember, you are going to this school to learn and to be trained to do something with your life," she said, with one finger pointing up as if she was really trying to get her message across.

Louie spoke up, "We won't get into any fights as long as no one starts anything with us."

I nodded my head in agreement when he said this. When he was done, I followed up, "Yeah, I can't promise anything because I'm not going to let anyone push me around." I looked back at Jerry, "Right, Jerry?" I wanted to see if he was going to back us up if anything happened.

I waited for Jerry to answer. He paused for a moment, not sure what he wanted to say. Finally, he said, "Yeah, that's right." Jerry didn't sound enthusiastic about it.

At this time in my life, fighting was a fun and exciting thing to do.

I asked, "So how many people go to this school?"

"I am not really sure, but there are a lot of them. Not all of them are studying to be operating engineers. Some are studying to be chefs; others are studying to be stewards."

Jerry asked, "What are stewards?"

"They are like waiters at first-class restaurants or on a cruise ship."

I chuckled and said, "I've never been on a cruise ship before and think I never will."

Louie also said, "Nope, me either. Never even saw one."

"What about you, Jerry?"

"No, I wish, but no."

"Well, just think. If you go to this school and finish, you are going to make so much money that you will be able to do anything you want!"

I said, "Yeah, right. I don't think so."

"Why?" Blanca asked.

"Well, in the first place, I hope I get through this school without no one messing with me. And knowing what I do about life, there will always be someone who won't like me; and then I'll have to defend myself. I have always had a hard time in school. I don't think so, lady."

"No, no, no. You have it all wrong. You can do it. This school will make you learn. They will not stop trying until you have your degree in operating engineering. You will see. All you have to do is stick it out, and do your best. That will do it, really!"

Jerry cut in, "Hey, Blanca, where is this place or school we're going to anyway?"

"Oh, about 100 or maybe 150 miles or so, I think. A few miles from Santa Rosa, up on Highway 120, not too far from the Petrified Forest."

Louie remarked, "Never heard of it and don't even know what petrified means."

"Me either," I agreed.

Blanca threw her head back and laughed again. She said, "You boys are funny. A petrified forest is a very old forest. The wood is so old that it turns into stone. The trees in this forest have turned to stone."

As we continued, we passed San Francisco and drove over the Golden Gate Bridge. We talked about other things besides the school, our families and where our parents were born.

ⅢA
PARTY

Soon we were climbing mountains and passing a pine forest. After a while she slowed down as we entered a small gravel road. I saw a sign by the road but was unable to make out what it said.

"Well, boys, here we are."

We were driving toward a one-story, newer building. We went over a slope on the road, and then I saw the tops of many more buildings. Some were two stories, and others were one story.

"This is it. I will walk you in and introduce you to the lady who is going to take care of you. Then I have to leave."

I asked, "Are you coming back?"

"No, this is it. My job is done. I probably will never see you again. I'm leaving for Spain tomorrow and then going to other places. I told you I was doing this for my husband."

I really liked her in a romantic way, feelings that developed in the few hours that I had known her. "Too bad," I remarked.

"Blanca," Louie asked, "are you just going to dump us here and leave? We don't know anyone here." I think he felt the same way I did. It was her personality.

"Oh, you will be OK. They like boys like you here. Don't worry!" she said happily, feeling good that we grew to like her in a little while.

Even though she was a lot older than we were, I found her really attractive. I thought, "I sure would like to meet her when I'm older."

She came to a stop, and we all opened our doors. Jerry asked, "Should we bring our stuff?"

"Of course, I am not going to take it with me," she said as she threw her head back, laughing again. I loved the way she gestured when she laughed; she looked very beautiful. She was a fun person.

We took our bags and suitcases out of her trunk and followed her inside the office. She went to the front counter and said to the African-

American lady who was sitting there, "OK, I brought some more boys."
The lady answered, "OK, Ms. Jordan, I'll take them from here."

"Blanca looked at us and said, "You boys take care of yourselves. Be good, and study hard!"

Louie stepped up to her and shook her hand. Jerry followed and did the same. I went up to her; but, instead of shaking her hand, I embraced her tightly. I felt like telling her I wanted to meet her again when I was older. She also held me tightly. It seemed as if she was attracted to me in the same manner; however, in reality she was just being friendly. She had a very nice scent. I thought, "Man, I wish I were older!"

She turned and said good-bye one last time and went out the door. The lady at the counter stood up and approached us. She said, "All right, boys. First of all, welcome. I'm glad you were able to make it to our school, and I hope you like your stay."

She started to write on a paper on the counter. Just then we heard Blanca's car start. There were no front windows to this office. On the back side there were large windows showing that we were on a ledge overlooking a pine forest. "I'm sure Ms. Jordan told you all about our school."

"Aw," I interrupted, "She didn't tell us anything. All she told us was that we were going to come to this school to be operating engineers. That's it." Jerry and Louie both were nodding their heads, agreeing with me.

"Oh, I see. Where are the papers she gave you? The ones you signed?"

Jerry answered, "No, we didn't sign any papers. All we know is that she was going to bring us here. She told us to go home and get enough clothes to stay a few days."

"Is that so? And you didn't sign any papers from where she picked you up? Anything?"

Louie answered, "Nope, should we leave?"

"Where are you boys from?"

"San Jose," I answered.

"That is really strange. She should have had you sign some documents before leaving. No one had you sign anything? Where did she pick you up? Oh, I asked you that already."

I answered, clarifying where we met her, "From an unemployment office in San Jose, the one on Alum Rock Avenue."

"I see. San Jose. Let me think. That's not far from Redwood City, right?"

"Louie answered, "Heck, lady, we don't know. All we know is she said we were coming to a school, and we were all game to come."

"OK, let me think how I'm going to do this. I don't have the consent forms for you to fill out. Maybe I can have you fill out these other forms," she said, deep in thought, looking down at some papers.

I knew I didn't want to complete any forms. I just couldn't do it. "I don't know about filling out any forms, lady. I'm not too good at that."

"All right. I'll have you come in tomorrow. All of us will sit down and fill them out together. Right now I will get you situated in your cottages, so you can settle in. How does that sound?" she asked. It appeared as if she knew about our education. "By the way, my name is Miss Johnson."

"That sounds good to me," Louie answered.

She called to someone in the other office, "David, would you please come here."

A young African-American guy appeared and answered, "Yes?"

She was writing something on a paper. "Can you please show these young men to their cottages?"

"Sure."

"Good. Let me get some information first. What are your names?"

Once she took our names down, she asked other questions, such as what grade we had completed in school, our addresses, home phone number, and a contact person in case of an emergency.

Once she was done, the young African-American guy led us away, out the door and down a walkway. The school was very hilly. There were many pine trees, from very tall ones to little ones growing in some areas as if they were grass. They grew wild.

When we arrived with Blanca, it appeared to be a resort; however, now it appeared as if there were not very many buildings. We were now walking on a paved road, coming over a hill. I could see the roofs to many buildings.

I asked the guy who was escorting us, "Hey, does this place have a pool?"

"I wish, but no, no swimming pools around here," he answered.

Louie asked David, "Is there anything to do here? You know, like partying?"

"Almost every night someone is having something. Whenever you hear the music, come on over. We all get together somewhere in the evening."

"Cool," Jerry acknowledged. "Are you inviting us?"

"Hey, no one has to invite you here. Everyone is always welcomed here."

We walked to one of the apartments the lady in the office called cottages. The building was two stories and appeared as any apartment building would in San Jose. It had ten units, five on the second floor and five on the first.

David stated, "All right, here you are. Here are your keys. Each one of you will have your own cottage. There is Number 7 over there, almost to the end; Number 6, next door; and right here is Number 5." He handed me the keys. He didn't explain anything to us as he started walking away. Turning, in a loud voice he said, "Dinner is at five. If you have any questions, call the office."

We decided that I would take the cottage closest to me, and they would take the end ones.

Louie and Jerry walked toward their cottages, and I went to mine. I unlocked the door and stepped into the room. I looked around and said to myself, "This isn't an apartment; it's a studio." There was only a large living room that was also a bedroom. The kitchen was also part of the living room, with one small bathroom and a little shower. There was a small T.V. on a stand, a sofa, a chair, and a small desk. All the windows in front and in the back had long, hanging beige drapes. The floor was covered with ugly, green carpet. There was a large picture of a ship with sails hanging over the bed. An odor indicated the room had just been painted. The cottage was small, but it was good enough for me.

I thought, "I hope they don't get more people. They might want me to share this little place with someone else. This room isn't big enough for two of us.

I turned on the television. There was only one channel, a station located in Santa Rosa. The news had just started. I turned it off because I didn't like watching the news. The only thing I heard was the beginning of the reports; the anchor said something about someone being shot, a shooting he said.

I stepped out of my apartment and went to Louie's room and knocked. He yelled out, "Come in!"

"Hey, man, what's going on in here?"

"Nothing much. But, I'll tell you this. I'm hungry! I wonder when dinner is going to be ready."

"The guy said it'll be ready at 5 o'clock. What time is it?"

There was a small clock on the desk. Louie glanced at it at the same time I did. He answered, "Twenty 'til."

Jerry must have seen me walk by his window. He also came to Louie's room and knocked. "Come in. The door's open."

All three of us sat and talked about people we knew. Louie knew some of my enemies. He also knew some of the guys whom I hung with.

The phone rang. Louie reached for it and answered, "Hello? OK, OK." Hanging up the telephone, he said, "Time to eat! Let's go!"

"Cool, man. I'm ready."

"Me, too!" Jerry agreed.

We walked to the cafeteria. There was no problem finding it because everyone was walking in that direction. It was a large building that had many tables. Most were filled. One of the men who was standing by the door as we stepped into the dining room looked at us and yelled, "There is a free table over there." He pointed to the center of the cafeteria.

We stepped to our table. We were the only Latino guys in the room. Everyone else was African-American, just as Blanca said.

A waiter came to our table, a young guy about our age. He had a red napkin over his arm and asked if we wanted anything to drink.

"Yes, I'll have milk," I answered.

Louie and Jerry both asked for Cokes. The waiter replied, "Yes, sirs," and left the dining room.

"Hey, man, this is pretty good. Seems like we're in an expensive restaurant," Louie said.

"Yeah, it does," Jerry added.

In five minutes the waiter came back with our drinks and placed them on our table. "Are you ready to order, sir?" he asked me.

"No, where is the, oh, here it is." I picked up the menu to look at it. There were only two things on it, chicken and steak. I looked at it and said, "This is a big menu for only two things. I'll have a steak."

The waiter wrote it down and asked, "How would you like that cooked, sir?"

"Heck, I don't know. I want it cooked so there is no red left."

"That's well done, sir."

"Oh, OK," I answered, not accustomed to this type of service. When

I was in jail, they cooked our food the way they wanted. If we didn't like it, it was too bad.

The waiter looked at Jerry and asked, "Sir?"

"I'll have chicken."

"Yes, sir. Today we have Chicken ala King; will that be OK, sir?"

"What is Chicken ala King?"

I cut in, "It's chicken with cream on toast. I used to have that once a week when I was locked up. It's good, man."

"OK, I'll have that," Jerry answered.

"So will I," Louie added.

The waiter took our menus and left our table.

"Hey, man, I think I'm going to like this school," I commented.

"Yeah, if it's going to be like this, so am I. I think we're going to gain weight being served like this."

"Yeah, if they serve us enough food," I added.

We ate Chicken ala King and steak as we talked. When we were done, we stepped out of the building. I saw telephone booths on the outside of the cafeteria. "Hey, anyone have change? I have ten bucks but no change."

"Who you going to call, ese? Momma?" Louie asked and laughed.

"No. Got any change?"

"Yeah, I have about a dollar's worth of coins."

"Lend it to me. I'll pay you back later when I break my ten."

"Sure, ese." Louie took out his money and gave it to me.

I stepped to the phone booth and closed the door, so no one could hear. I took out my wallet to look up Yolanda's number. I dialed. The phone rang.

"Soup kitchen, can I help you?"

"Oh, hey, I got the wrong number."

"No, you didn't. It's me, Juan, Yolanda's father. Is this Art?"

He recognized me because I have one of those voices everyone recognizes right away.

"Yeah, it's me. How are you, Juan?"

"I don't know. It depends on how you are going to treat my mija."

I could tell Yolanda's father had been drinking a little. He had a slight slur in his voice.

"I'm treating her good. Why are you asking?"

"What do you mean, why am asking asking? Because she's my

daughter, stupid!"

I didn't know what to say. I hated being called stupid. That was a really negative word. My father used to call me stupid when I was a kid.

"Is Yolanda home?"

"First, you tell me how you are going to treat my baby."

"I'm going to treat her fine, like I am right now, sir."

"Don't call me sir! I'm not your parole officer!"

I knew his tone meant trouble. He must have found out something about me and was worried about his daughter.

I kept my cool and spoke politely, "Is it OK if I talk to her; or should I call back later, Juan?" I didn't want to make the mistake of calling him sir again.

"Wait, I'll call her!" he answered angrily. He yelled out, "Yolanda! Pick up the phone!"

Yolanda answered another telephone, "Hello."

"Hi, Yolanda, how you doing?"

"I thought it might be you! I'm glad you called. How did it go? Are you at the school yet?" As she asked this, I didn't hear her father hang up the other phone. I felt he was listening.

"Yeah, I'm here. I'm fine. Just a little tired from the long ride. I know I just talked to you a few hours ago, but it feels like it has been a long time."

"Yes, it seems that way. I miss you already. I wish you were back in San Jose. It would be nice. I know you have to go to school so that you can earn a good living later."

The other phone was placed on the receiver at this time.

"What's wrong with your father? I just spoke to him, and he sounded kind of upset. He even called me stupid."

"Oh, someone at work told him who you are and that the school you went to was jail. He was really upset with me for picking you as my friend. But don't worry about it. My mother told me not to worry either. She said not to worry because my father was a wild guy when he was young, so he shouldn't make a big deal about it. She said it all depends on what you do with your life from now on. I'm so sorry he called you that."

Yolanda had told me her parents didn't get along very well. She loved them both, but her father drank too much. When he did, he said things he shouldn't. Sometimes her parents would stay upset with each other for weeks and not speak. Yolanda had told me she didn't think her father and mother were going to be together very long from the way her father had been acting.

Answering her I said, "That's all right. I'm used to being called names. That's what my father did a lot when I was a kid. Man, I'm sorry he was upset with you because of me."

"Don't worry; it's OK. I know the way he gets when he's drinking. I've lived with him all my life. He is a good father, and he loves me. I know he wants me to have a good life. By tomorrow he'll get over it."

"Well, I'm really going to try to make this school work. Time will go fast. I know time. I spent some of it locked up, so I know it'll go by fast. And besides, if I know this school isn't going to work out for me, then I'll leave in a few days."

"Oh, I hope you do. You can find work here. And, you know, there are a lot of schools you can go to in San Jose. You know, like a painter school, a carpenter or sheet metal, and even an electrician school."

"Yeah, I know. You're right. I don't have to stay here. I'll let you know in a few days what I decide to do."

"I'm glad you called. It's nice to hear your voice. I thought I wouldn't be able to talk to you for a few days."

"Yeah, me too. They gave us these little apartments here. But it's fine with me. At least I'm alone in my room. If they have anyone else share my room, I'll leave!"

"If you leave, come over here first. I want to see you!"

"I will! I miss you, too. That's why I'm calling you."

"I have $10. I'll try to break it tomorrow and call you again."

"Oh, that will be nice. I won't go anywhere. I'll wait for your call."

"All right. I'll call you. Well, I'll try to call you. But if you don't hear from me, don't get worried. That will mean they have me too busy, or I don't have the money. OK?"

"OK, Art. I'll dream about you."

"So will I," I answered.

"Art, you know I really care for you, don't you?"

"Yeah, I can tell. I care for you, too. All right, have a good night."

"Good night and I'll wait for you tomorrow."

"Bye," I said as I hung up the phone and opened the door to the phone booth.

Louie and Jerry both looked at me. Louie asked, "Was it good?"

"It's always good, man."

Jerry looked in his pocket and found coins. "I want to call my mother, too."

Jerry stepped into the phone booth. In a few minutes he came out and asked, "What do you guys want to do? Go back to our rooms?"

I answered, "Yeah, I think that's what we'll do, go back to our rooms. Later we can take a walk to see if anything is happening around here."

"I'm cool with that," Louie answered.

We went to our rooms for a while and watched television. Louie flipped through the channels a few times. His T.V. received more channels than mine did. The news was on some stations; again, the announcer talked about a shooting. It was on all three channels. We didn't like to watch the news, so we turned off the television.

At 8 p.m. we took a walk. First, we went upstairs and walked to the offices. No one was around. The offices were dark; everything was quiet. If it were not for the lights on the narrow streets, we would not have been able to see a thing. The place was kept up well. There was grass throughout the school. Next to the small, paved road were plants and bushes with large pine trees next to them. As we came over one of the small hills on the road, we heard loud music. "Hey, man, there's a party here," I said.

"Cool," Louie acknowledged. "Just like David said."

Jerry didn't say anything. I didn't think he really wanted to go. He asked, "Do you think we should go?"

Louie answered, "Sure, why not? The guy said we were invited to whatever was going on. I say let's go for it."

We started our walk toward the sound of the music. As we approached, we saw three guys standing on the first few steps of the stairs leading to the music.

Louie asked, "You think they'll let us in?"

The area was well lit. As we approached, I felt the nice breeze. Even the tops of the trees were making rustling sounds.

"I don't know why they wouldn't. Like you said, that guy David said for us to go; so really we were invited by David."

Jerry was silent. He seemed as if he was nervous about going to the party.

As we came to the bottom of the stairs, Louie asked one of the guys if there was a party taking place.

"Yeah, there is. You are welcome to go up, but something bad happened today. I don't know if it's a good idea for you to be here tonight." The guy was tall and on the thin side. His friend and the other guy were short, as tall as Louie, a little shorter than I.

"Oh, yeah?" Louie asked. "Why?"

"Because you aren't brothers. But hey, if you want, go on up. That's up to you."

Louie turned to look at Jerry and me. He looked as if he really didn't like the remark about us not being brothers. He asked Jerry and me, "Want to go?"

Jerry took a step back and didn't say anything. We could tell he wanted to go back to his room. I looked at Louie and nodded my head saying, "Sure, no problem here." Besides, this guy asked if we heard the news. As far as I knew, I had not heard anything.

Louie started walking up the stairs, passing the guy. Louie said, "If anyone wants us to leave, we will just leave."

"Yeah, no big deal," I agreed.

I followed and turned back to look at Jerry. Jerry saw me look down at him and said, "I'm going back to my apartment, you guys."

"What's wrong with that guy?" Louie asked.

"Heck if I know."

11   MR. KING

We went upstairs and entered the party through a large glass sliding door. There were whiskey bottles all over the place. It was wall-to-wall guys. This apartment had two large rooms. I asked a guy standing where the whiskey was being served, "Hey, can we have a drink?"

"Sure, help yourself."

We stepped to where the whiskey bottles were and filled two paper cups. I took a gulp out of the cup I served myself.

I felt as if many eyes were looking at us. We were accustomed to parties that were open, and everyone helped themselves. Because of this it wasn't out of place to serve our own drinks.

Louie stared at me and asked, "How is it?"

"A little strong but good. As good as it should be." Louie also took a swallow. I thought back to the second day I was released from jail. Eddie, my brother, and I bought a fifth of Seagram's Seven and drank it right out of the bottle. It was a little strong, but we liked it.

"Ese, I think there's going to be a fight here."

"Oh yeah, who with who?" I asked as I looked around to see if I could see anything. I took another small drink from my paper cup.

"Between them and us," he said, almost in a whisper.

"Between them and us, really? What makes you think that?"

"Can't you tell, ese? There're all staring at us, and the noise really went down when we came in."

"Be cool, Louie. I think everything is going to be all right. Just be cool."

"Yeah, right. I am cool. You be cool. I think I know you well enough already. I know you won't take anything from anyone."

"You're right about that, Louie. But let's see who will be the first one to try anything," I said seriously but at the same time playing around with him.

Louie was behind me as I started to step into the other room where the music was playing. A large guy, twice my size, bumped into me and spilled a little of my drink. I turned and said, "Hey, man, watch where you're going."

He turned, looked at me, and replied, "Oh, man, esa!"

I took my eyes off him only for a second, noticing everyone was circling around us. At that instant I saw a beer bottle flying from his hand toward my head. It hit me right between the eyes. BOOM! I went flying back and down and then rolled on the floor. Everything was spinning, and there was so much pain. I had both my hands up to my face as I tried to regain my thoughts. It happened so fast that I didn't know what hit me. In a minute I saw Louie pulling my hands away from my face.

"You OK, Art? Hey, let me look at you. Are you all right, man?"

I answered, "I don't know. I don't know if I am. Am I bleeding?"

Louie pulled my hands away and looked at me. He said, "No, man, you're not. Just little spots here and there from the glass but I think you're going to be all right."

I could feel the effects of the alcohol I had been drinking. It soothed the pain. I sat up and shook my head, feeling awake. "Come on, ese. Get up. I think you'll be all right."

Everyone who was standing around wouldn't lift a hand to see if I was OK. It occurred to me that some of them really didn't like our being there, or they would have tried to help or would have said something. I stood on my feet. Louie asked, "Hey, should we leave?"

I looked at Louie and asked in a very low voice, "Who is the guy who hit me?"

"He's standing at the doorway looking into the other room. He's a big guy. I think you better pass on this one."

I went over and served myself another drink, taking a big shot, and answered, "I'm ready, man." Louie thought I was saying I was ready to leave. I stepped over to the big guy. "Hey, man." This time I was ready if he was going to hit me again. He turned and faced me. Just as our eyes made contact, I hit him as hard as I could! He didn't move with my punch. In fact, it looked as if he became angrier. I took two more swings and hit him both times in the face. He dropped his beer and charged at me. I thought, "Man, I'm sure not going to box with this guy." I then grabbed him, and we both fell to the floor. As we were rolling around, I heard glass break. Louie jumped on top of the end table with a broken whiskey bottle and yelled out, "No one jump in! Whoever jumps in is the first one to get this bottle in the gut!" Louie was moving the bottle around just as they show on the movies.

The guy I was fighting was strong and big. Maybe this was a mistake! I wondered if I were going to win this one. I didn't lose very many fights. In fact, I couldn't remember any fights that I had lost.

As we rolled on the floor again, I held him in a headlock. As he moved, I knew I was never going to keep him there. I let go of the headlock and stuck my pointer finger into his mouth, on the inside of his cheek, still holding him in a headlock position. I pulled hard. He moaned. I told him not to move. He started to move again, and I pulled harder. We were in a position where no one could see that I had my finger in his mouth. I pulled really hard and told him to behave himself.

He said, "OK, OK, I will!"

One of the guys standing nearby said, "Hey, brother, don't let that guy tell you what to do!"

I whispered into his ear, "If you move too much and if you don't do what I tell you, you're really going to feel pain and have a bigger mouth than the last time you looked at yourself!"

"Hey, Blood, get that guy off of you!" one guy yelled, as he turned around as if he were not wanting to watch. It appeared he and his friends wanted to jump in to help their friend.

Louie was on top of the table, waving his bottle and yelling, "Fair fight! No one jump in! If anyone wants to jump in, I'm going to jump in with this baby I have here!" He kept moving the bottle.

"All right, everyone, here it goes!" I yelled. Then I talked to the guy who was on the floor with me, "I want you to repeat after me, all right?" He didn't answer. "All right?" I repeated as I pulled harder. I felt a little wetness from where I was pulling and didn't know if it was saliva or blood.

"I'm an Uncle Tom! Got that? Say it!" Identifying as an Uncle Tom was when an African-American conformed to the Whiteman's ways and was submissive to him. No Black guy ever wanted to say that. Some would even die before repeating this statement. To me African-Americans were like everyone else. I had no prejudice feelings toward other races, but I wanted to avenge myself really bad with this guy!

"Hey, brother, don't you do that now!" one of them demanded.

"Come on! Say it!" I insisted.

"I'm not going to say that!" he exclaimed, mumbling because I had my finger inside his mouth. Everyone thought I had him only in a head-lock.

"Come on, say it!" I demanded, thinking I would really get even for breaking that beer bottle on my head.

"No way!"

I pulled hard on his cheek. He was making sounds because it hurt so badly. I could feel the wetness getting worse.

"Come on! All you have to say is what I told you! That's all!" I pulled harder.

"All right! All right! I'll say it!" All of a sudden I felt him really try to get up and push me away, but I didn't released him. I pulled really hard. He yelled out, "OK, OK, I won't move!"

"Say it! I'm an Uncle Tom!"

He was breathing really hard as if he were angry, really angry, ready to get up and flatten me like a pancake.

"He exclaimed, "I'm an Uncle Tom! Now get off, so I can kill you!"

All the guys in the apartment were upset because he did what I demanded of him. He repeated in a low voice, "I'm going to kill you!"

I looked up at Louie. He looked down as if he were saying, "Ready, ese, to get out of here?"

I nodded my head, indicating I was ready.

Louie jumped off the table as if he were going to attack someone with his bottle. He opened the sliding door and stood inside next to it. I released the guy and made a dash through the open sliding door. He charged toward me. As I went out the sliding door, Louie followed. I pulled the door shut as fast as I could and kept moving away without looking back. We heard the shattering sound of glass as if someone had gone through the door. Not looking back, we ran down the stairs and down the small street, heading for our apartments. During that time they didn't have the safety glass as they do today. We had to get out of there fast before we were killed. I knew we were out numbered. If we stayed to fight all of them, we didn't have a chance.

When we arrived at Louie's apartment, we entered. We didn't turn on the lights, but we closed and locked the door. We could hear people yelling and making a lot of noise. It was only around 10 p.m. As we were peeking out the large front window, we saw a mob of guys marching toward us. Louie expressed, "Man, ese, what are we going to do? I think we're going to be killed tonight."

"I know, man! I think we are too!"

In my mind it appeared they were holding torches and carrying a rope to hang us. In reality they were holding flashlights. I could see their flashlights moving around as we were peeking out the window. They kicked the door down to my apartment. A light went on, and then crashing noises sounded as if they were throwing things. In a few minutes they were out of my apartment and were banging on Jerry's door. I heard them yelling. Someone kicked the door. It flew open. As they entered, I could hear Jerry yelling as if they were beating him.

I said in a low voice, "I think we better go and help Jerry, man."

"I don't know, Art. Think so? I'm ready if you are."

Just then we saw more guys running around the side of another building toward Jerry's room. By now there seemed to be about 20 of them.

"Hey, Louie, I think we'd better get out of here because I think they're going to be coming here next!"

"Yeah, ese, I think you're right! Let's go out the back window and go to your place because they already checked it."

"Yeah, let's go right now," I added. "Hey, Louie, if you are up to it, we could stay here and fight. I'm ready."

"Hey, Art, there are about 20 of them out there. I don't think we stand a chance!"

Just then we saw them kicking Jerry around on the grass. One of the guys looked toward where we were and yelled, "They must be in there!"

Louie hit me on the side and whispered, "Let's go, ese."

He left the room crawling on all fours, and I followed. We went out the back window. Everything was dark and quiet in back. We started to make our way to my apartment; but just before entering, I told Louie, "Hey, man, I think we should go behind those bushes over there and wait it out for a while." The bushes were 20 feet away from the building. Behind them were pine trees. It was dark. No one would be able to see us there.

"I'm game, ese."

We went to the large bushes and lay on the ground. From where we were, we could see the lights go on in Louie's apartment. The guys were throwing everything around the room. Through the window I saw someone get the TV and throw it against the wall. They were yelling. Then in a few seconds, one of them stuck his head out the back window. He yelled out, "Let's go back and check the other guy's room again!" He added, "Someone is going to die tonight!"

"Hey, Louie, I think we better stay here for awhile. What do you think?"

"Yeah, ese, I think you're right. It's not a good time to go back indoors. Hey, you must be a really strong guy to hold that big guy down like that."

"I had my finger in his mouth and was stretching his check. If I hadn't done that, the guy would have thrown me off and stepped on me, man!"

Louie laughed. In a few minutes Louie said, "Hey, look over there. Doesn't that look like Jerry?"

I looked down the row of bushes about 150 feet away. It was Jerry standing under one of the street lights with his hands in his pockets. "I'll go get him. I'll be right back," I said as I lifted myself up and stepped back under the cover of the trees. It was very dark. I made my way to Jerry without being seen because it was so dark.

Yelling could be heard from a distance. When I was 20 feet from where Jerry stood, I stopped. I didn't want to be seen from the street light. I would probably be killed. "Jerry!"

Jerry turned when he heard his name called. He stared into the darkness. "Jerry! Over here!"

He placed his hand over the top of his eyes to deflect the shine from the light. "Yeah, is that you, Art?"

"Yeah, it's me. Don't let anyone see you, but come here."

Jerry looked around and then dashed into the tall trees where I was hiding. "What happened? Did you guys kill someone?"

I was surprised that he asked the question. "What do you mean, did we kill someone? What did you hear? Did someone die?"

"No, those Black guys said they think you killed him. They took him to the hospital."

"Man, I hope I didn't kill him. Hey, man, he hit me with a bottle first. What happened to him is what he gets!"

"Yeah, but hey, everyone in this place is looking for you and Louie. I think they're going to kill you guys if they find you. They almost wanted to kill me. I thought they were when they first caught me, but they let me go because I wasn't in there with you guys."

"Why are you out here?"

"I'm looking for you guys. Man, they're looking in every apartment, even other Black guys' places. I think they want to kill someone tonight. Where's Louie?"

"He's over there. Come on. I'll take you. Follow me."

We made our way to where Louie was waiting. This was a big thing. I felt a lot of excitement and felt as if I were hiding from the cops, trying not to be caught. I knew one thing, however. If they were to find me, I was going to give them a good fight.

"Hey, ese, what's happening? Those guys are really mad at us, huh?" Louie asked Jerry.

"Yeah, esa. They said they were going to kill you guys. What did you do?"

"Not me, ese. Art here. He cut some guy up pretty bad. I don't know why they want me too," Louie said, kidding.

"Yeah, right man. You were right there backing me up. You're my crime partner! If one of us is going to die, we both are!"

"What did they tell you, Jerry?" Jerry told Louie what he told me.

We were there for a few hours. Later we had no idea what time it was, but we were getting tired of hiding. I suggested we just walk in and do our best fighting. I told them I thought we would win. They both thought I was crazy.

We were silent for a few minutes as we listened to all the yelling. Someone hollered that they found us, and everyone was making their way to where we were supposed to be. In a little while we heard them yelling out that we should come out because they were going to find us sooner or later.

Jerry said, "Hey, I know what we can do. They'll probably go to your room a few times through the night, but I don't think they'll come to mine. Why don't we go to my room and hide there till the morning?"

I replied, "Hey that sounds good to me. Heck, I don't want to stay out here all night. What do you think, Louie?"

"If you think it's OK, then I'm with you. Whatever you want to do."

"Yeah, hey, if they catch us in there, we'll fight it out and then come back here to wait. Let's go."

"Wait," Jerry said, looking really hard toward the buildings. "I thought I saw someone out there."

I looked really well, and so did Louie. We all decided there was no one in the distance.

"Should we go? Ready? I think it'll be all right. If not, we'll do what we have to do."

"Are you sure?" Jerry asked. Jerry was scared we might get caught and would have to fight. At this point I knew Jerry wasn't accustomed to fighting. To Louie and me it was fun; however, we knew if we were going to fight here, it wasn't going to be something enjoyable with so many guys looking for us.

We all stood and headed to Jerry's back window. Jerry had left it open just in case we returned to his place. We crawled in and left the lights off so we would not be seen. I went to the front window and moved the drapes over slightly to look outside. There were four groups of guys who were walking toward each other. They had flashlights in their hands; but to me it seemed as if they had long, burning torches.

One group of six guys started to go to Louie's room again. "Hey, man, they're going to your room, Louie. They might go to mine next and then come here. We better be ready."

"What should we do?" Jerry asked, sounding really scared.

Louie answered, "Ese, I'm not going out there and hiding again. I say we stand our ground and have it out. I know I can knock out at least two of them."

"Yeah, I know I can handle three of them. That's the most I've ever fought and won." When I was going to high school, I fought three guys and did really well.

Jerry appeared very frightened. Louie said, "Hey, ese, Jerry, that means if there are 20 of them, Art takes three, I take two, and you take fifteen!" Louie and I both laughed nervously!

Jerry didn't say anything to that. He did say, "Why don't you hide under the bed? If they do find you, we'll have to fight."

I looked at Louie and replied, "That sounds like a good idea. We'll get under the bed. If they look under there, we'll come out fighting. But if they don't, we'll just sleep there in case they come back later."

"Sounds cool to me," Louie answered. "But if they start beating up Jerry again, we'll come out fighting."

"No," Jerry answered, "you don't have to do that. I don't care if they beat me up a little. If you guys come out fighting, they might kill all three of us!"

That is what we did. It was a queen-size bed. We crawled under it.

Jerry fixed his blankets, so no one could see under the bed without first moving the blankets.

As we hid under the bed for the next few minutes, we didn't hear anything. In five minutes we could hear voices in Louie's room next door. In two minutes there were bangs on Jerry's door. "Hey, boy! Let us in, or we'll break the door down!"

Louie and I were hiding under the bed when Jerry opened the door. Six African-American guys stomped inside. "Where are they? Have they come back? Have you seen them, boy?"

"No, I haven't. I told you last time they aren't here. I don't know where they are. I'm trying to go to sleep."

Another one of the guys said, "Heck, we should hang you anyways, just for knowing them."

I was waiting to see if they were going to start to beat up Jerry again. If they did, I was going to come out fighting. I wasn't going to let them beat Jerry when we were hiding under the bed. I knew Louie was going to do the same.

"I told you. I really don't know them. I just came here with them."

Louie and I didn't move a muscle; we knew better. If we were to fight just the guys who were in the room, we were outnumbered. From where I was, I could see a lot of shoes. Seemed to me there were 25 guys in the room.

"You know, boy, if we find out they were here, you've had it!"

"OK, I know. You told me that the last time you were here."

"Let's go!" one of them yelled as they all started to leave.

We hid under the bed until we dozed off, sleeping the rest of the night.

The following morning when I awoke, Louie was next to me. Everything seemed quiet. I crawled from under the bed and approached the window. I looked out; the surroundings looked the same as the day when we arrived. I wondered what time it was. I looked at the small clock on Jerry's table next to the bed. It was 7:30 a.m.

"Hey, Jerry, Louie. Hey, man, time to get up. We have to go eat."

Jerry rolled over on his bed, his arm over his eyes. At that moment he remembered what had happened and sat up quickly. "Hey, is anyone around here? Did you look?" Jerry got out of his bed as if there were a fire.

"Calm down, Jerry. Everything is cool. No one is around."

Louie pulled himself out from under the bed. "Hey, ese, how does it look out there?"

"Looks OK. No one around. Hey, I'm hungry, man. Let's go get some chow," I said.

"I'm ready, ese. Just let me go and wash up."

Jerry still looked worried. He was peeping out the front window when he said, "What if they find us?"

"Hey, Jerry," I said as Louie went into the bathroom. "Don't worry, man. If they find us, Louie and I will handle them."

In a few minutes we were all washed up and dressed. Louie and I went to our rooms to change our clothes. We walked out and started to the cafeteria. I thought I would see people on the way, but there wasn't one person. We arrived at the large dining room. As we entered, guys were saying, "There they are! There they are!" The entire place went silent. There were 300 guys, and every eye was on us. It felt cool to walk in with everyone looking at us. We were ready to fight. I felt important.

"Right here," I told Louie and Jerry. I looked around as everyone stared, looking as if they wanted to kill us. I didn't care. The night before we were hiding out because it looked like a mob was after us; they were going to hang us right on the spot. We were really outnumbered. Now it didn't bother us. If we were attacked, we were ready and willing. It wasn't the same scary night anymore; it was day. If they wanted anything with us, we were ready.

Just as a waiter came to our table to ask what we wanted to eat, a supervisor approached us. "Gentlemen, the dean would like to speak to you at his office. Can you come with me?"

I looked at Louie and Jerry, saying with my eyes, "Oh, man, busted!" They acknowledged my expression as we arose from our seats.

As we approached the offices, there was a guy standing in front next to the building. His arm, chest, thigh, and forehead were all bandaged; and he was using crutches. The side of his lips had three stitches where I had stretched his cheek.

The supervisor asked us to wait outside with the guy. He was the one who went through the glass window, the guy I had down. The supervisor indicated he would call us in shortly. We stood there, waiting.

The big, Black guy was staring at me as if he wanted to kill me right on the spot. "What are you looking at, man?" I asked.

"I'm looking at you. Where are you from?"

"I'm from San Jose. Why?"

"Because I'm coming to San Jose, and I'm going to get you!"

I thought, "This guy is brave. He hasn't had enough."

I didn't feel sorry for his being all bandaged up because he had broken a bottle on my head for no reason, and he wanted to kill me. I stepped up to him and said, "You want to get me later? Do it right now!" With my open hand, I hit him on the shoulder, as if I were starting a fight. It really was more like a push.

"Ay, man!" he said in pain. I had hit him on his bad arm.

"Come on, man, right now!" I knew he couldn't fight. He was too hurt.

"I'm going to kill you!"

"Hey, come to San Jose anytime. Come to the eastside and ask for Art Rodriguez. I'll meet you." I wasn't scared of this guy. If he was to come to San Jose later, I would win another fight with him. I was sure of it.

I was well known in the eastside. I had both African-American and Latino friends. He thought I fought him and made him say Uncle Tom because of his race, but it was because he broke the bottle on my head.

The door to the dean's office opened. A man called in the bandaged guy. "We will be with you boys in just a few minutes," he said.

The bandaged guy entered, and we waited. In fifteen minutes the door opened, and the man and the guy appeared. Now it was our turn.

"You boys can come in now."

We stepped in. I thought, "Man, I hope they don't call the cops on us. I don't want to get locked up again." I didn't look back at the bandaged guy as we entered. I didn't want to give him any satisfaction.

As we walked into the large office, there were two Baptist ministers, three other well-dressed men, and two men dressed in clothes as if they were priests. All of them were African-American. We sat down on a sofa that was against the wall, as the man behind the desk spoke. I thought he was going to say, "Who in the heck do you guys think you are?"

The man introduced us to everyone in the room. He clasped his hands and looked down at his desk. Looking up at us with a sad expression, he said, "What can I tell you, boys? I'm really sorry that everyone took everything out on you."

One of the ministers added, "We are sorry. When tragic things like this happen, many go out of control. We know it wasn't your fault. It's a sad situation for all of us."

I didn't know what they meant. Why wasn't it our fault? Why are they saying they were sorry? Louie, Jerry, and I didn't understand.

Louie was just as stunned as I was. He asked, "Why do you think this happened?" He was trying to find out why they were feeling sorry for us.

One of the men who was wearing a suit answered, "We don't know. Martin Luther King was a good man, and there was no reason why this should happen."

I quickly recalled the day before, just as I was turning off the T.V., the news anchor said something about someone being shot. I wondered if this was what they were talking about when I wasn't paying attention.

Louie asked, "You mean Mr. King? Reverend King, right, the preacher?"

"Yes, Martin Luther King. He was killed yesterday."

I didn't understand what had happened. I had never heard of Mr. King. I didn't know who he was or what he represented.

The guy behind the desk continued, "I think it will be better if you boys leave our school. I mean, for your own safety. We do not want anything to happen to you with the way things are. We can only watch you so much. If things do not settle down really fast, we might even close the school for right now. We do not want anyone else to get hurt."

"Leave here? We just got here," I replied, knowing there were no two ways about it. We were leaving.

"Yes, I know. If you would like, you may come back next year for our second-year program. If that is all right with everyone," he said as he looked at the other men wearing suits.

One of them answered, "Sure. I think if the boys are willing to give it another try then, we will be happy to accept them back."

Louie asked, "So when are we going to leave? Who's taking us home?"

"We will arrange that for you. I know you boys have not eaten breakfast yet; our driver will stop and get you something. He will drive you to your rooms. You can pick up your things, the sooner the better."

All three of us agreed. We didn't like the school anyway, being that we were the only Latinos enrolled. We knew it was going to be a problem as time passed.

12 A HERO

"Hello, is Yolanda home?"

"Yeah, hold on," Juan answered. I then heard him yell out Yolanda's name.

"Hello?"

"Hey! How are you?"

"Art! Hey, where are you, at the school?"

"No, I'm home. I left there. It was no good, so I didn't want to waste my time. Are you going to be there? I want to come to see you."

"Yeah, I'll be here. When are you coming?"

"Right now. I'm going to use my mother's car. I'll be over in a few minutes. She told me I could use it for a little while."

"Oh, it's going to be nice to see you."

"Do you want to come out to the car, or should I knock? I don't think your father likes me very much."

"He's been in one of his moods because he and my mother haven't spoken for awhile. But it's not you, Art. Come over. I'll go out to your car, if that makes you feel better." We said bye and hung up the phone.

"Mom, thanks for you car. I'll be back in a little while."

"OK, Mijo, but be careful. You don't have your driver's license yet. I don't want you to get caught or get in an accident. Call me when you get there."

"Sure, I'll call you. Thanks, Mom," I said as I kissed her and left.

I arrived and parked in front of Yolanda's house, hoping she would look out to see me. I didn't want to knock on the door because I didn't know if her father Juan had been drinking. If he was, I knew he was going to tell me something I didn't like. So far he hadn't told me I couldn't see his daughter; but if he had, I would have snuck around to see her anyway.

It was a nice day. Her house looked the same as the last time I visited. The lawn appeared to have been mowed recently. There were rose bushes up against the house and small flowers along the walkway coming out to the sidewalk.

The front door opened, and Yolanda appeared. She smiled when she looked at me sitting in the car. As she walked to my car, I saw her beauty. I knew she was going to be the girl with whom I was going to spend the rest of my life. She carried herself very nicely as she walked. Her right arm swung back and forth. She was wearing tight pants, medium high heels, and was very attractive. She opened the door and stepped into the car. Yolanda moved close to me and kissed me, while giving me a nice hug. "Hi, I really missed you. I'm so glad you came back," she said as she brushed my hair back with her hand.

I returned her kiss and hug. She smelled like roses. "Hi, and I'm glad to be home. Well, I'm glad I'm here."

"I hope I know you for the rest of my life, Art," she said as she kissed me again.

"Yeah, but what about your father. Do you think we can make it even if he doesn't like me very much? What if he's looking out at us right now?"

"It's OK. We're not doing anything bad. He knows I care for you."

"So, Yolanda, how have you been? I hope you missed me a lot," I commented, even though I knew what she was going to say.

"You're funny. You know how I've been. And you know I missed you a lot. How have you been? What happened at your school? What did you tell them was the reason you were leaving?" she asked, even though she knew I was only gone for a day.

"I didn't give them a reason. They gave me one. They said that because there were all African-American guys at the school it was better that we—me and the other two Latino guys—left because they shot and killed Mr. King."

"Oh, yeah, I know. That was really a tragedy. It's been on T.V. all day and yesterday. What do you think about it?" Yolanda asked, worriedly.

"I don't know. I never heard of him. Did he do good things? Some one said he was a church guy, right?"

"Not just a church. He was really a good man. He helped all the Black people, even Hispanics. Because of the things he did, it's affecting us also."

"Really, I didn't know that." I wasn't into news and the world around me at this time in my life.

"Hey, Yolanda, want to go out with me again this weekend? It'll be fun."

"I want to, but let's see if my father will let me. The way he has been lately, I don't think he will let me go anywhere. Things are not well at all right now with him and my mother."

"That's strange; I thought your family was doing really good."

"Yeah, most people have a lot of problems at home. But to everyone else it just looks like things are nice and dandy."

Yolanda and I sat in the car for more than two hours and talked about her family, my family, and what we had been through in the past. I told her about my father in Mexico. At this time I really didn't know him as an adult; but while I was growing up, I had many difficult times with him. He was a harsh man; however, we had some nice memories of him, not many, though.

That following weekend we went out on both Saturday and Sunday. On Sunday we went to our regular hangout, the Jose Theater. That's how our relationship developed for the next year. At times we saw each other a lot, and sometimes we couldn't. For a year, however, we had a really good time together. Everyone knew us as a pair. I loved being with Yolanda. Not only was she fun to be with, but also she made me look good because she was such a fun and pretty girl.

The next year her parents filed for divorce, and she and her mother moved to San Diego. I told her I would call and write to her and asked that she do the same for me. I really cared for her and wanted our relationship to keep going well.

For the next year Yolanda and I called each other and wrote letters. She learned how to read my letters because I still didn't know how to spell or write very well. Almost every word I wrote was wrong. Not very many people could read my letters. She came to San Jose every four months to see her father, uncles, and aunts. However, as the months continued, we didn't keep in contact as much as we had been doing. A few months followed when I didn't hear anything from her.

During this time I was working at a chrome plating shop. I was a helper, carrying things that needed to be plated from one large room to another.

Eighteen months after Yolanda moved away, my sister Tita was in the kitchen when the phone rang. I was in my bedroom. She called me, "Arthur, phone!"

"Who is it?" I asked as I entered the living room, stepping toward her. I thought it was a girl I was going out with that night; her name was Lucille.

"I'm not sure, but I think it's your other girlfriend, Yolanda."

I gave an ay, ay, ay expression and in a low voice said, "Tita!!! Shhh, don't say that so loud! She might hear you."

"I didn't say it loud. I have the phone covered up with my hand."

"Yeah, but sometimes you can hear even if you have the phone covered," I answered. Overall, Tita and I had a good relationship, but every so often we had our skirmishes. When we were younger, we were always fighting.

"Hello?" I answered, nervously.

"Hi! Guess who?"

"Oh, man," I thought. "I need more words to recognize the person I was speaking to."

"I don't know. You tell me."

"It's me, Yolanda! How are you? I haven't heard from you for three months. I was wondering what happened."

"I'm here. How are you? When are you going to move back? I've been waiting."

Yolanda had told me a few months before that when she could she was going to move back to San Jose. I had been looking forward to it.

"Art, do you still feel the same about me? It's been a long time since we've been together. I really miss you. You don't have another girlfriend, do you?" I did care about Yolanda, but I felt a little hurt with her for being so far away. I was the last one to make a long distance phone call and the last one to write.

I wondered if she heard my sister.

I answered, "No, of course I don't have another girlfriend. You know you are the only girl I care for. Now let me say this, do I go out? Yeah. And do girls go out? Yeah, they do. But I don't have another girlfriend who I care about the way I care for you." In other words, I was trying to tell her I did go out with other girls. However, I didn't care for the girls I dated. They were just friends. Yolanda was the only one for whom I had feelings.

"Oh, yeah, well, I go out, too. And there are guys in San Diego, too."

I cut in, "What are you saying? Are you going out with other guys?" I could feel myself becoming upset.

"Well, that's what you said. So I'm saying it, too."

I raised my voice a little, "That's not the same. I don't want you going out with anyone else!"

"Then you don't go out with anyone else."

Now I was really upset. "What? Don't tell me what to do! Who do you think you are?"

"I'm just telling you that if you can do it so can I." Yolanda was talking calmly and didn't sound upset whatsoever.

"You know what, man! Forget it!" I slammed down the receiver, and it made a hard noise.

Tita was in the kitchen and didn't say anything right away. I yelled out, "Man!"

Tita said sadly, "I'm sorry if she heard me. I didn't think she did."

"Tita, it's not your fault. This is what happens when two people live so far apart." I really felt bad that I became so upset. I wanted to call Yolanda back and tell her I was sorry. Instead, I decided I would call in a little while or later that evening.

In five minutes the phone rang again. Tita answered it. She said, "Hold on." She looked at me and said, "Arthur, it's her again."

I still felt a little upset. "Tell her I can't talk right now. I'll call her a little later."

I went to my bedroom and lay on my bed, hearing the phone ring again. Tita yelled out, "Arthur! It's for you, and it's not who you think!"

I returned to the living room and picked up the phone, "Hello?"

"Hey, ready for a good time?" It was Lucille. She was a very pretty girl and was fun to have around me. I liked going out with her because she was always ready to have a good time.

"Hey, how are you? Heck yeah I'm ready. Are you ready?"

She laughed and answered, "Yeah, I'm ready! You could pick me up right now if you want. What time are you going to pick me up?"

"I'll go by there later. I'm not sure, maybe 8 or 9 o'clock."

"OK. My sister and her friends are having a little party at our house, but I'll be looking for you. I'll be ready."

"OK, Lucille. I look forward to having a good time with you."

Months before this I bought a 1960 Pontiac. It was an all-right car, but it wasn't as cool as my brother's 1959 lowered, gray Chevy.

Later that evening Eddie was home. Sometimes when he went out, he went in someone else's car. "Eddie," I asked, wanting to borrow my brother's car for the evening, "are you using your car tonight?"

"I don't know, why?" he asked, knowing what I had in mind.

"If you're not, can I use it?"

"Where you going tonight?"

"I don't know. I was going to pick up Lucille and go do something." Tina was Lucille's younger sister, and Tina was Eddie's girlfriend at that time.

"Sure, but be careful with my car. Don't wreck it."

"I won't. I'll take care of it."

"If you see Tina there, tell her I'm waiting for her call."

"OK," I said as I stepped out of our bedroom.

Later that evening I was driving up East Hills Drive toward Lucille's street and saw a lot of cars. There was no parking. I stopped and doubled parked. I felt good driving my brother's lowered 59 Chevy; it was so cool looking. I stepped out of the car while the engine was still running and the lights were on. There were so many people at the party. "Why go look for another party when there was one here?" I asked myself. There were ten girls out in front of the house, as well as some guys. Someone yelled, "Are you looking for Lucille?"

"Yeah, is she around?" I answered, standing next to the car.

"Yeah, she told us to watch for you. Are you Art?"

"Yeah, that's what they call me," I said loudly so the girl could hear me. It was already dark outside; but the street light was right there, making it bright. Lucille stepped out as if she were rushing. "Man," I thought, "she looks nice."

"Bye, Lucille!" one of the girls called.

"Bye, Lucille," someone else said.

"Have a good time, Lucille," another added.

When Lucille was almost to the car, a guy stepped out of the house, also rushing. He yelled out, "Hey, Lucille!" It seemed as if he had been drinking. I didn't know Billy. I heard that he was a guy she was seeing in the past.

Lucille said, "Oh, man!"

"Lucille, come back here!" he cried.

"Hi, Art. I'm glad you are on time. Let's go!" she said, still rushing.

I looked at her, smiled, then looked at the guy coming toward us. He looked at me and yelled, "She isn't going with you, buddy!"

I stepped around to open Lucille's door as she was telling Billy to get lost. Billy was telling her how much he loved her and not to go. Standing with the door open and waiting for her to get in, I prepared to shut the door for her. In the meantime most of the people from inside the house came out to see what was happening, to see if Lucille was going to make her getaway. I heard later that Billy had been there for a while pestering her. Lucille didn't like him at this time, but they had previously been boyfriend and girlfriend. I stood smiling, thinking this guy was crazy. If it were me, and my girl wanted to go with some other guy, I would say good-bye, face the sun, and follow it. In other words, I would forget about her.

Lucille came around to my side to get into the car. Billy was trying to block her way. Waiting for him to put his hands on her, I was prepared to take care of him. She couldn't get by Billy. I walked to where they were struggling and stepped in between them, asking, "Lucille, do you want to come with me or stay with this guy?"

"No, I'm not staying; I'm leaving with you, Art." I could tell Lucille liked me very much.

"All right, let's go." She started toward the car.

The guy was holding a beer can and looked at me, stating, "You . . ." and threw his beer can at me. I moved sideways; the beer continued flying without hitting me. Billy was a well-built guy but short. He looked at me and said something. He started coming at me like a bull, swinging both his arms to get me. I held my arm out and held him back, holding his head. It was easy to control him because he had already been drinking a lot. Then I pushed him with my hand; he fell back and tripped over his own feet.

Billy really seemed as if he were an annoying kind of person. Lucille jumped in the car; and I shut the door, starting my way around to the other side of the vehicle. Billy stood from where he was and yelled out, "Art!" I turned. Again, he charged like a bull, punching in a big-round-circles way. I let go with a right blow and then a left, trying to protect myself. He went down to the ground again. I thought that was it, but then he stood up and came at me a third time. This time I held his head and pushed hard; he fell to the ground once more. Everyone on the porch and the front grass clapped and hoorayed as I stepped into the car. I felt like a hero. Lucille and I drove away. I really felt good.

Lucille was happy being with me, and I felt as if I had rescued her. That night we had a really good time. We joined other friends and found a party to spend the rest of the evening.

The next day Eddie came home from visiting Tina. He walked into our bedroom, where I was, and asked, "Hey, Art, do you know a Billy?"

"Well, I met him last night. Why?"

"Because as I was going to leave Tina's house, a guy came to my car with a bat and told me to get out of the car. I told him I didn't mind fighting him, but I wanted to know why he wanted to fight me. He thought I was you because he called me Art and told me I knew why. He thought it was me who took him down last night. I told him he was wrong, that I am Eddie, your brother. He told me you beat him up last night when he was drunk, and he wanted to fight you when he is sober."

"Oh, yeah, then what?"

"I told him you love fighting, that I'd let you know, and that you will go looking for him."

"That's right," I answered.

"He gave me a message to give to you."

"Oh, yeah? What's the message?"

"He said to tell you he will fight you anytime. Also, he said you can have Lucille. He doesn't care for her anymore after last night."

I laughed and said, "Yeah? Well, next time I see him, I'll see if that's true. He said I could have Lucille?"

"Yeah, do you love her?"

"No, I like her a lot. She's really nice and fun to be with, but that's it. I'm sure she feels the same way."

Eddie agreed, "I know."

13 UNCLE WILLIE

My mother, Uncle Ben, Uncle Willy, and Uncle Frank had started Bonus Polishing and Plating, a chrome plating business. I was told that once their business was off the ground and running they would hire me; and I could work in the family shop, polishing large car bumpers. It was hard work. I would have to wear four pairs of gloves and hold a very large steel bumper to a giant lathe, buffing it on a big wheel, moving my whole body up and down with the bumper.

I quit my other job the day they told me I could now work for them. My friend Phil wanted to use my car to take care of some business that day. I told him, "Sure, man. Drop me off at work, and pick me up when I get out." He agreed.

That morning, as we were driving to my mother and her brothers' new business, we pulled over because an ambulance came from behind on 13th Street. As it passed, I told Phil, "Man, I wonder how it would feel to take a ride in one of those."

"I don't know, man. I've never been in one, but it would probably be fun."

"Yeah, hey, if you go first in one, let me know how it feels," he said as he laughed.

I also laughed and added, "If you go first, let me know. Why do I have to find out if you go first?"

The shop was on Maybury Road as the road runs next to Highway 101. It was one property away from 13th Street. There was a line of large bays where other businesses existed. We had to drive all the way back to the last bay on the long building.

When we arrived at the shop, my uncle Willie yelled out, "Hey, our new employee is here! Let's put him to work!" Uncle Willie was my mother's younger brother. Uncle Ben was next in line from my mother, and Uncle Willie followed. He was a good guy, thin, and spoke as if he knew everything there was to know about anything. When he lived in New Mexico, he was a cop.

Once during their lunch at the shop, I was higher than a kite on drugs. He told my other uncles and me that because he was a cop for so long he could smell anyone on drugs a mile away. I thought to myself that he really didn't know everything. He would have known I had just smoked a joint, but he couldn't even tell.

My Uncle Frank was my favorite uncle. He is the one who hired me for the job at Bonus Polishing and Plating. He was the kind of uncle who paid attention to me, always wanting to see me do well and to be happy in whatever I did.

Uncle Frank worked the large tanks in the plating shop. Long electros, about two feet long and four inches in diameter, were placed in tanks. One electro was of nickel, and it was placed in it's own tank; another copper and chrome, in it's individual tank. They also had one small bar or electro of gold and a small tank to do gold plating. They plated everything from bumpers to motorcycle parts. One large bay was where the plating was done, and the other was where the polishing was completed.

Once I changed my clothes, Uncle Willie told me it was time to go to work. "Come in here, Arthur. I'll show you how to polish."

The lathes stood four feet high and were big. The wheels on which we polished were a foot in diameter; the large nut that held the large wheel was four inches in diameter. It looked huge. The bay had four lathes and many wheels and large sanding belts hanging on the back wall. Things were very dusty because of all the polishing that was done in that large bay. They cleaned up everyday; however, it was still dirty from all the work they did.

Phil was in the office in the other bay talking with my uncle Frank. My Uncle Willie and I were standing in front of the lathe. "All right, Arthur, first I'm going to show you how to change the wheels."

"OK, Uncle Willie." I stood there, wanting to learn everything there was to learn, feeling I was going to enjoy working with my family.

Uncle Willie held a large, red, pipe wrench tight in his hand. "This is the way you do it. First, you put the pipe wrench in the nut to take it off." He hit the "on" button and hit "red" to turn it off; however, all I saw was his hitting the "on" button, not the "off". He held the wrench tight, and the nut disengaged. The lathe stopped, as if he did it with his might. "Got that?" he asked.

"Yeah, looks pretty easy to me." I also noticed he had a red rag wrapped around the handle of the pipe wench.

Uncle Willie took off the wheel and replaced it with another one, hand screwed the large nut, and asked, "OK, now you can tighten it just the way I showed you; but use the reverse button. Do you think you can do that?"

"Sure, no big deal. Looks easy." Before turning the machine on, I took the large pipe wrench from him with the red rag wrapped around the handle, placed it on the large nut, and held it tight. I hit the "on" button only. BOOM! The motor that turned the lathe was so strong that it took the wench right out of my hand. All I saw was a circle of red flying around me. It came back over the top of the lathe toward me! It was the red wrench! BOOM! It hit me in the chest, and I went flying back 15 feet! I bounced off the wall behind me and landed on the floor, all taking place in a split second. I didn't know what happened or where I was. I couldn't breathe and thought I was going to die that second.

I was gasping for air and couldn't get any. Uncle Willie was yelling at the top of his lungs, "Arthur is dying! Oh, my God! He's dying!" Everyone was running into the bay where we were. My arms were crossed on my chest as I was trying to breathe. Uncle Willie kept yelling, saying, "His chest is tore open! He is bleeding to death! What did I do?"

As I looked up from the floor, almost at the point of passing out because of my inability to breathe, I saw my mother, Uncle Ben, Uncle Frank, and my friend Phil. Uncle Willie was screaming and scaring the heck out of me, making me really feel this was it. Surely I was a goner. I thought my chest was torn open. I was dying more from Uncle Willie's panic and his saying I was going to die than from being out of breath.

"Someone call the ambulance, hurry!" someone hollered.

Uncle Frank asked, "Arthur, are you all right? Arthur, can you breathe?"

I shook my head that I couldn't. I was trying to breathe but wasn't able. At that point I noticed if I took very short breaths, I could breathe a little. So I started doing this. Really suffering because I needed a lot of air, I felt everything start to go black; however, I stayed conscious.

In a few more minutes, I could hear the ambulance. Uncle Willie was still running around as if he were a chicken with his head cut off. I was breathing, but my breaths were very shallow. I was having a difficult time. Once the ambulance arrived, I heard them turn off the siren as they approached the front of the building. The ambulance attendants came in with their gurney. By this time I was catching my breath; however, I was in a lot of pain. My chest hurt enormously. I was lifted onto the gurney and taken to the ambulance. As I was lying inside the vehicle, I saw everyone talking, debating who was going to ride with me and who was staying to take care of the shop.

There was a part of the ambulance window that had gray tape on it. I thought it was in the event that the ambulance crashed the window wouldn't shatter. I could see out at everyone, but they couldn't see in very well. Phil's face then appeared. He looked in at me. Everything went silent in my head, and I saw Phil's expression telling me, "Hey, you lucky bum, you get to find out how it feels to ride in one of these things first." He had a slight nod and had a mild smile.

I returned the same smile, one that said, "Yeah, good friend, I am." Phil was a good guy. I cared for him a lot as a trusted partner.

My mother stepped into the ambulance and told me Uncle Frank was following in the company truck. She sat on a small stool as the ambulance attendant asked me questions. We backed out of the long driveway and passed all the other bays and businesses. On the road I heard the siren as we were moving. I was thinking of the report I had to give to my friend Phil.

"Arthur, how do you feel?" my mother asked, with her worried expression.

I answered with my first low words, "It hurts, but I'm OK. At first I thought I was going to die, the way Uncle Willie was acting."

"Yes, Mijo, he thought the red rag was blood. But you know how he is. I'm glad you are all right. You got me worried. I think you are going to be all right."

By this time we were approaching San Jose Hospital Emergency. The ambulance pulled up to the large doors. The doors of the ambulance were opened, the gurney was pulled out, and I was taken out of the ambulance. As soon as I was pulled through the large doors, Uncle Frank appeared. He looked worried. My mother told him I looked a lot better now. She told him that it wasn't as bad as it seemed.

They took me into a room for only a minute; then I was taken to the x-ray department. I waited in the hallway for a few minutes. A young, beautiful girl approached me; she was thin and really attractive. Her hair seemed to be long. It was black and was put up in a bun. She had big, black eyes. "Hi, are you hurt?" she asked. She was about my age.

"Yeah, I am," I answered, still in a lot of pain.

She pulled me into the x-ray room. "Well, we're going to see what's wrong with you. What happened?" she asked as she was getting the room set for me.

Uncle Frank had asked me to say I was hurt at home, so it wouldn't make their insurance increase. "I was doing something at home and got hit in the chest."

"Oh, well, let's see what you did." She called out the back door where the x-ray techs moved around from one room to another and said, "I need someone to help me." Another lady came in to help her pull me onto the x-ray table. As she was trying to put me in different positions, she handled me very gently. She took four different x-rays. Once they were done, she told me she was going to check them and would be right back.

"Hey," I called before she left the room.

"Yes?"

"What's your name?"

"Oh, my name is Flora," she said and left. I really liked her mannerisms and the way she looked.

I tried to talk to her more, but she was busy. She had me taken back to the emergency department. I was in the room with Uncle Frank and my mother. In a short while the doctor entered and said I had two broken ribs and was really bruised. He said I should be laid up for awhile. Uncle Frank thought that my disability wouldn't start unless I spent the night in the hospital. He tried to talk the doctor into keeping me overnight. The doctor said that the hospital was full, and he didn't think it was necessary to keep me.

They put a large brace around my chest and directed me to stay in bed for a few days. I was young and didn't think I could stay in bed that long, but told the doctor I would try.

Uncle Frank took me home. Once he was gone, I was already bored. I wanted to do something, even though I couldn't move my body very well. I thought about Yolanda and felt like calling her. I picked up the phone and dialed her number. "Hello?"

"Hey! How are you?"

"Not too good. I had an accident today."

"You had an accident? What happened?" she asked, sounding worried.

"I fractured two ribs; but I'm all right, just have a hard time moving around and breathing."

"Oh, I'm sorry. I wish I was there with you. Does it hurt a lot? How did you do it?"

I went on to tell her the story. She thought the part relating to Phil, about riding in the ambulance, was funny. Once I told her the story, she asked, "Art, I was wondering how long you were going to stay mad at me from the last time we talked."

"I wasn't mad. I was just a little hurt with you."

"Well, it sure sounded like you were mad."

"I wasn't mad. I might have been a little upset."

"Well, that's mad."

"No, that's not mad. Mad is when I'm really mad and throwing things around and hitting people."

"Guess what?"

"What, you're moving back to San Jose?" I answered, thinking I was wrong.

"That's right, I am."

"Really? When?" This was good news to me.

"In about a month or two. I'm going to be moving with Aunt Rachel. She lives off White Road on East Hills Drive, where we used to live. My sister Jessica already lives there. She said I could also come."

That was just a few blocks from where Lucille lived. "Oh yeah, cool. I'm glad. I'll be able to see you again all the time. Do you look the same?"

She laughed, "Of course I look the same! What do you think? I'm fat already?"

I didn't think she was going to get fat when she became older because her mother was still thin. "No, I know you won't get fat. It's not in the cards."

"What do you mean it's not in the cards?"

"Well, look at your mother and father. They're not fat, so you probably won't be. I read that somewhere."

"Art, can I tell you something that I never told you before?"

"Sure, go ahead."

"I think I love you."

"Really? Are you sure? That's a big word to use just like that." I had a feeling she felt that way for awhile; but after not talking to her for a few days, I thought maybe she wasn't in love with me after all.

"Yeah, I think I do. I thought so a long time ago. But I wasn't sure, so I never told you. I remember one of the times we were together you told me you don't like to express that word because you said it was a very important word, and people use it too freely. I never told you before because of what you said, but I feel safe saying it now."

I felt good she said she loved me; however, I didn't want to say it myself. Even though I thought I felt the same as she did, I didn't really know yet.

"How do you feel, Art?" she asked.

Now I felt on the spot. "I don't know. Yeah, I love you, too," I answered. I thought, "What the heck." I hoped I would feel the same when I saw her again.

She didn't say anything for a few seconds. I knew she felt bad because I didn't answer her right away. Then she asked, "How do you feel?"

"How do I feel? Not too good. I was hurt today at work, remember?"

"No, I know that. I mean tell me more how you feel about me."

"I told you I loved you. I know I do because I really care for you. Why do you think I call you all the time and try to write letters to you? Because I care!" She was trying to get me to say more to her; however, I didn't think the phone was a good place to express all my feelings.

We started talking again about what happened to me at work; I told her a little more about Phil and me and who was going to ride in the ambulance first. She thought it was really funny. When I made her laugh, I liked it. Whenever I told her something that was supposed to be funny, she always laughed. Sometimes I thought she was faking the laugh just to make me happy. We talked some more, and I told her I would call in two days. We agreed and hung up the telephone.

I had to get up from where I was sitting, but the pain was really great. I wanted to turn on the T.V. to see what was showing.

I took my wallet out and looked for Lucille's phone number and dialed it.

"Hello," her mother answered.

"Yes, is Lucille home?"

"Yes, hold on. Lucille!" she called out.

In a minute Lucille came to the phone, "Yes?"

"Hey, it's me. How are you?"

"I'm fine. Are you sick? You don't sound good."

"I broke two ribs today at work."

"Really, what happened? How did you do that?"

I went on to tell her the entire story. After telling her, I asked, "Lucille, want to go cruising?"

"You can't go. You're hurt. How are you going to drive?"

"Come on, I'm not going to drive with my ribs. My arms are OK! Want to go?"

"Yeah, I could go; but I have my friend Mary here with me. Can she come?"

"Sure she can. I'll pick you up in a little while."

"Are you sure you feel like driving? I mean, you just went to the hospital today; and now you're going to be driving around."

"Yeah, I know. Maybe we can go to a park or something. I can't stay home and do nothing. This is no fun."

"All right. We'll be ready," she answered. We said good-bye and hung up the telephone.

I picked up Lucille and Mary. Mary was a nice girl. She liked to rat her hair high, and it attracted attention from the guys. After going to Alum Rock Park, we drove through the flats. No one was there because it was a weekday. We drove past the main part of the park to the swimming pool and the playground area. It was a very quiet day, and not too many people were present. We decided to get out of the car, cross the stone bridge, and sit on the grass under the trees for a little while. The park was as nice as it always was. We used to visit often as kids.

Mary and I talked about things in our lives. She was telling us about her life and how she had been messing up because her father was always beating her. I told her she should move away from home. She replied that she had nowhere to go. No one in her family knew what was really going on in her life. If she told her aunts and uncles, they wouldn't believe her because everyone liked her father. Mary hinted that there was more she wasn't telling us, but we couldn't get her to tell us. We tried to tell her what to do to get out of the situation. I knew how she felt because I had a father like her's; however, all he did was beat me. I didn't know if more was going on with Mary because she was a girl.

Even though my father had left a long time ago to Mexico, I still felt the same negative feelings when I heard about fathers talking down to their children negatively or beating them.

In two hours we left the park. I was really starting to feel bad from the injury to my ribs. The shot and pill they gave me at the hospital started to fade. I could barely walk to the car and now felt as if I couldn't breathe very well. I wanted to cough, but it was difficult. Once we made it to the car, Lucille asked if I wanted her to drive. I told her I could still drive. I just had to move my arms, hands, and feet.

As we drove down Alum Rock Avenue, I looked for a cheap gas station and pulled over to a Hudson station on Alum Rock right by Jackson Avenue. The gas was $.24 a gallon.

I didn't know it at the time, but I was being followed by Billy and his friends. Billy was the guy who confronted my brother with the bat. They saw me coming down from the park. I pulled into the station and next to the pump. The attendant came up to the window. He was wearing a T-shirt.

"I'll take $3.00 of regular," I requested, not being able to see the guy's face. I moved my head to look at him but couldn't bend my body to get a good look.

All I saw was an arm and fist flying through the open window, a blow that connected to my face. BOOM! I fell to the side onto Lucille's lap. The punch didn't hurt; however, it felt as if, instead of striking me in the face, his blow hit me in the ribs! I was out of breath. I could barely talk! I said, "I'm going to kill you, man!" The gas attendant, who was really Billy, stood in the same spot, waiting for me to get out of the car. I had no intention of getting out of the car. I was trying to deal with the pain in my ribs. I reached under the seat of the car, looking for a very large crescent wrench I kept in case I was in a fight and was outnumbered.

Billy started running toward another car. He went in where his friends were and yelled out, "He has a gun! He has a gun!"

The car they were in was parked in the street. Billy ran to it. I was still looking for my wrench. I couldn't reach it because of the pain I was feeling. Their car started moving and almost drove away without Billy because they were scared, thinking I had a gun. The door flew open, and Billy dove in as the car was moving.

I was still in pain. Lucille said, "Don't look for your gun. They're gone." I was trying to catch my breath.

"I'm going to kill that guy!" I uttered strongly, getting angrier.

Now I was sorer than earlier. Once I recouped I took the girls home and decided to play it cool the rest of the day at home. I couldn't go out for a while until I was better, knowing that if I ended up in a fight and wasn't recovered I would surely lose.

Two weeks later I was feeling much better. I was up and around and went out a few times with my friends. They told me not to worry. If anything went down, they would take care of me. I knew I could trust them.

Yolanda called me and said she was in San Jose. I went to see her at her aunt Rachel's house. It was really nice seeing her. She hadn't changed one bit, still the same nice looking girl I knew. She told me she was making the move back to San Jose for me. I had decided that once she returned the other girls who I was seeing would be out of my life.

Yolanda told me that in two more months, when school was out, she was moving back for good. She had a job waiting for her when she moved to San Jose. I told her I was really happy and that I really missed her, which I did. When it was time for her to leave, I didn't want her to go. I told her we should just go and get married. She could stay at my mother's house.

"You want to marry me?"

"Of course I do," I answered.

"Then you must love me."

"Yeah, why do you ask? That's what I told you on the phone, right?"

"I don't think you really told me on the phone."

"Yes, I did. Maybe you weren't listening. I'll tell you again. I love you. Now will you stay?"

"I can't. I have to wait and tell my mother and father that I'm coming to live here first."

"How are they doing?"

"Oh, not too good. My father is always drunk now. He's living with a lady that doesn't like me. That's why I come and stay at my aunt Rachel's place. My mother has a boyfriend who I don't like."

"Why not? Why don't you like him?"

"Because."

"Because why?"

"I would rather not say."

"You could tell me. You could tell me anything."

"Because he is a lot younger than my mother. He looks at me weird."

I didn't like the sound of what Yolanda had just said. "What do you mean he looks at you weird? In what way?"

"You know. How a man looks at a girl, and it gives the girl the creeps."

"No, I don't know. You mean in a bad way? He's looking at you in a bad way?"

"Yeah, that's what I mean."

I was really upset. I could feel the steam about to blow. "You know what? I'm going to go over there on the bus. And I'm going to get that guy! I'm going to get him and . . . ."

Yolanda knew when I said something like this that I meant it. I was ready to go and to take care of business with that guy, and I didn't care how old he was.

"No, you can't," she insisted.

"What do you mean I can't? Why can't I?"

"Because he's my mother's boyfriend."

"Yeah, but that doesn't give him any right to look at you that way! He just can't do that!"

"Well, I really don't know if he's looking at me that way. I know I feel he is. But if he means it, I don't know."

"He better not be!" I declared, still irritated.

"I don't want this to really get out of hand. I should not have told you anything."

"Yeah, you should have. I don't want that guy to do anything to you!"

"He didn't. If he does do anything, I'll tell my father. He'll take care of it."

"If that was to happen, I want you to tell me, too."

"OK, I will."

"Promise?"

"Yes, I promise."

That's where it stayed. Yolanda went back home that night.

In four weeks I returned to work at my mother and uncle's shop. I didn't like it. The work was dirty and hard. I wanted to find a good job where I didn't have to work so hard, and it wouldn't be so dirty.

In two months Yolanda moved back to San Jose. I asked her if she would marry me. I went to Kay Jewelers and bought her an engagement ring and a wedding ring. I wanted her to stay home and not date other guys or even go out with her girlfriends, which she did.

14 A DEAL

had told some people who knew Billy that it wasn't over until it was over, planning to pay him back for what happened at the gas station. I found out where he lived and went to his house to take care of business. I parked my car a block away from where he stayed and walked to his place. I carried a weapon under my shirt in the back of my belt. My plan was to knock at this front door. As soon as he came to the doorway, I was going to take out my weapon and end the problem.

I knocked on the door with one hand, keeping my other hand behind me to reach for my weapon at the first sight of Billy. I held the screen door open in order to have a clear view of him. I heard someone coming to open the door and felt excited, the same exciting feeling I had when I was running from the cops or trying to get away with something. The door opened. An older lady stood in front of me.

"Yes, may I help you?" she asked.

"Yes. Is Billy home?" I answered as I peeked behind her to see if he was visible.

"Oh, no, I'm sorry; but he isn't home. He isn't here very much anymore." She had a Spanish accent.

"Oh, OK. I'll come back another time. Tell him Art Rodriguez came looking for him."

"OK, I will. Do you know Billy well?" she asked as if she was really concerned about my answer.

"Well, I know him, not really well, but well enough."

"Can you do something for me?"

"If I can, I'll see what I can do," I answered. She was such a sweet lady that I hated to turn her down.

"If you see Billy out there, talk to him about being good. I want him to have a good life, and he is going the other way. Billy has a good heart and needs a friend to talk to him."

I thought about this, knowing I would never be a friend of his and would never be able to say these things to him; however, I wanted to help his mother feel good about her hopes. "Sure, I'll talk to him about that. Thank you, Señora. Don't forget, if you see him first, tell him I came by."

"OK, Mijo. I'll tell him. Thank you."

"You're welcome," I answered. The lady's comments made me rethink my plans to take revenge. I didn't want to ruin the lady's life by attacking her son for what he did. Billy is the only person with whom I can remember not taking care of unfinished business. In fact, years later Billy did become a good friend of mine.

In time my mother's father moved out of the back house. Eddie and I moved into it and had a lot of parties. We had a group of people who hung out with us, guys and girls, always enjoying each other's company. Sometimes we played records all night long and awoke in the morning with them still playing. Every time I hear a song by Jimmy Reed, I think about those days.

There was one girl in the group who really liked me. At first she was just like everyone else, doing what we all did, having fun. After a while she would sit there and not do anything. She changed the music when it needed to be done, and that was about all. I asked my brother Eddie, "Hey, what's wrong with Olivia? She doesn't like to party anymore."

"You know why she doesn't like to do drugs and drink anymore?"

"No, why?"

"Because she likes you, and she knows you like good girls who don't get loaded and drink. She is trying to be good for you." I had no idea that Olivia liked me. The next time we went out as a group together, she sat next to me and stood by me as if she were my girlfriend; however, I didn't like her the way she liked me. Besides, I felt I was in love with Yolanda. I wanted things to be good between Yolanda and me, but I still liked being around girls.

A week later we all went out in two car groups to a few parties. Olivia was next to me most of the time, but I didn't hold her hand or kiss her. I really didn't enjoy being with her. Now that she liked me, she was really quiet; she wouldn't talk or laugh as she did previously. All it seemed that she did was stare at me, which I didn't like. Later that night we were ready to call it an evening. We stopped at our usual late-night hangout, Tico's Tacos. There were two of them, but this Tico's Tacos place was on the corner of Fourth and St. James streets. Later it was moved to the corner of Julian and Fourth Street.

Eddie parked in front of Tico's Tacos. There weren't many parking spots; however, everyone parked behind each other or in the street. Just as we arrived at the taco bar, other people were also arriving. I asked Olivia to stay outside with me. I didn't want be seen by all those people with her next to me. Someone here might know Yolanda and tell her I was with another girl. We stood in front of the car and talked. I had no intentions of even kissing her because of Yolanda.

In a few minutes someone in one of the cars honked a horn. At first I thought it was someone greeting us. Then I looked inside the car and saw that it was Yolanda's older sister. "Oh, man!" I thought to myself.

"What?" Olivia asked.

"Oh, it's nothing. Let's go inside." We went inside with everyone else.

The restaurant was small; but there were a lot of young people, some sitting and some standing. I kept looking outside through the large windows of the restaurant. In a few minutes I saw Yolanda's sister leave with the people who were with her.

The following morning I thought I had better call Yolanda. "Hello," she said sadly when she answered the telephone.

"Hi, babe, how are you?"

"Where were you last night?"

"I went out with my brother. Why?"

"Who were you with?"

"I was with the cuates (twins) Rudy and Joe, Richard Perez, Eddie, and Eddie's girlfriend, Tina. Why?" I asked innocently.

"You were with a girl. Who is she?"

"What girl? I wasn't with any girl. Who told you that?" This was something I learned from my father. He would answer his friends in this manner. Dad would never ever confess to anything.

"Art, you know who. Art, my sister saw you last night. She said she saw you kissing her."

"I wasn't kissing anyone. I'm telling you the truth! Your sister didn't see me kissing anyone."

"She said she saw you at Tico's Tacos. She said she even honked at you when you were kissing her."

"I don't know what you're talking about. I wasn't with any girl. What girl? Yolanda, you know I wouldn't do anything like that. You are my only girl."

"Art, how can you lie? She saw you. She said she saw you, and I don't think my sister is going to lie to me."

I knew one thing for sure. I wasn't going to admit to anything, not even standing with Olivia. "Yolanda, can you ask her again if she is sure it was me? Ask her what I told you, that it wasn't me and that I wasn't kissing another girl."

"What did you tell my sister last night?"

"I didn't tell her anything. I didn't talk to her. I don't know what you're talking about."

"You mean you didn't talk to her? I'm sure. I know if you saw my sister you would have spoken to her."

"That's what I mean. I didn't talk to her. Ask her again."

"All right then, I'll ask her. But she did see you."

"She's getting me mixed up with someone else. I know I wasn't that drunk not to know who I was with or if I spoke to your sister. Yolanda, you know you are the only one. Why would I want to marry you if you weren't? I care for you, and I wouldn't go out with any other girl."

Even though Olivia was with our group all the time, I acknowledged to myself that I shouldn't have sat with her in the car or stayed outside of Tico's Tacos. It was a mistake; however, it wasn't my fault.

Yolanda was now silent. She now doubted what her sister told her. She asked in a softer tone, "Are you sure it wasn't you?"

"Yeah, I'm sure." During this time in my life, I was young and dumb. I wasn't man enough yet to tell the truth.

After that night I didn't want to see Olivia anymore. I didn't want to have anymore problems. The following weekend I went out with Yolanda on Saturday.

The following Sunday I sold my Pontiac and bought a cool, lowered 1964 Ford. It was yellow and white. The inside and outside were really clean. I liked driving that car. Every time I hear the song, "I'm a Girl Watcher," I think of my lowered Ford. Once I was playing the song really loud while I was cruising up Alum Rock by Capital Avenue. Three girls were walking and turned to look at me. One of them yelled out, "How about a ride?" I smiled and thought, "No, I'm just girl watching."

The following week Phil, Yolanda, and I went to a party. We had too much to drink. I asked Phil and Yolanda if they wanted to go with me to Los Angeles to meet my grandparents, uncles, and aunts. They felt it would be cool, so we started down Highway 101 to Los Angeles. It was fun when we started. We were singing along with the tapes and having a great time. At 2 a.m. we were approaching King City, about 100 miles south of San Jose. We started sobering up. I didn't feel very well and neither did Phil and Yolanda.

"Hey, man," Phil asked, "Don't you want to go back home?"

"Yeah, I don't feel very well myself," Yolanda added. She said she was going to fall asleep. Now that I was sobering up, I thought about Yolanda's aunt. She must be upset because Yolanda wasn't home yet. I turned around and headed back to San Jose.

I told the others, "It should take us two hours to get back home." It was dark and foggy. After turning around, I drove for ten minutes before my car started to conk out, requiring that we pull over to the side of the highway. I was out of gas!

Phil asked, "Do you have a gas can or something?"

"No, I don't."

We sat there in the fog as the cars drove by us. I blinked my lights at them. Finally, in an hour someone stopped.

I stepped out of the car. It was colder outside, more than inside of the car. A young guy asked, "What's the problem?"

"I ran out of gas. Do you happen to have any?"

"As a matter of fact, I carry a gallon with me all the time."

I wanted to pay the guy, but he wouldn't accept any money. He told me the way I could pay him back was to carry around a gallon from this day forward. When someone was in need, I could help them. I've done that throughout my life.

Once the car was started, we were on our away again. The nearest gas station was 15 miles up the road. In 2 miles the engine light went on, and we had to pull over one more time. "Man, what's wrong now?" The car didn't want to start up again. I opened the hood to see if I could see the problem. It was 4 a.m. I checked the crank case for oil; and it was empty, nothing marked on the dip stick. I stepped back in the car. Yolanda was wrapped in her big coat and was asleep. Phil was in the back seat, freezing with his light jacket.

"What's wrong now, Art?"

"Oil, I don't have any oil in the car."

"Do you have any in the trunk?"

"No, who is going to carry oil in the trunk? I could see carrying gas in the trunk, but not oil."

Phil wanted to know, "What are we going to do?"

"Wait. That's all we can do. Wait."

"Wait for what?"

"I don't know."

Again, each time a car came by, I blinked my lights. There was less visibility now; the fog was worse. There weren't too many cars passing during that hour; three cars drove by in an hour. In another half hour an old van pulled up beside us. "Cool," I thought. I stepped out of my car and walked to the driver's side of the vehicle. A hippie was behind the wheel. He opened his van window and asked, "Peace. What's wrong?"

"I ran out of oil." I knew he wasn't going to be able to help me. If I could get a ride to the gas station up ahead, I might be able to get a ride back. I was really tired at this point; however, I couldn't sleep in the cold.

"I think I have oil," he said, as he opened his door and stepped out of the van.

"Cool," I replied, not believing someone would carry oil with them. The hippie stepped around the van and opened the large door on the side. There were a lot of people sleeping inside the van. He tapped one guy and asked if he could move. The guy did. The hippie who was driving moved some boxes from under his driver's seat and pulled out a gallon of used oil.

"I have this. It's used, but I think it'll work."

"Heck yeah, that'll work. Thanks a lot, man!"

I poured it into my engine case and brought the empty can to the hippie, thanking him. I asked him if I could pay for it. He didn't want any money. He said if he took money then he wouldn't feel good about himself. He felt everyone should feel love and peace for one another and help each other.

He said he wouldn't leave until my car was started. I went back to my car, and it started right up. He waved and honked as he drove away.

Phil opened his eyes in the back seat and said, "Got oil, huh?"

"Yeah, I did. Some hippies turned me on to it."

I heard him say in a low voice, "Cool."

The gas station was coming up soon. I kept my eyes open for it and knew it would just be a little way ahead. All of a sudden the car started shaking. I pulled over and came to a stop.

Yolanda woke up and asked, "What happened? Are we almost home yet? I want to go to bed."

Phil picked up his head and asked, "Where are we?"

I answered, "I don't know. I think we're in Greenley." Greenley was a very small town.

Stepping out of the car and walking around to see if I had run over something, I came to the back part of the car and saw that I had a flat tire. "Man! Everything is going wrong tonight." I opened the trunk and moved things around, taking out my spare tire. I looked around for the jack. No jack!

I then went back into the car and sat there. Phil asked, "What's wrong."

"Flat tire."

"You going to fix it?"

"No jack."

"Oh man, I'm cold," he said as he closed his eyes again.

I felt sick from the drinking and from the long night and tried to go to sleep for a little while. I couldn't. I looked over at Yolanda and thought, "She looks pretty even when she is asleep."

In two hours six cars passed; I blinked my lights at all of them. Two of the cars blinked back but kept right on going. Finally, one car passed and pulled over beside us; he backed up to my car.

The guy stepped out of his car and came up to mine. He asked, "What's the problem?"

"I got a flat, and I don't have a jack."

"No problem. I have a jack you can use. Let me get it for you." The guy was so cool that he helped me change the tire. When we were done, the sun was rising. It was daybreak.

I thanked the man, and he went on his way. In ten minutes we found a gas station. I filled my tank with gas and bought extra oil, just in case. In another hour we stopped and had breakfast. I was tired, as were Yolanda and Phil. Both of them slept most of the night.

After breakfast I continued driving. No one was talking. I thought about how nice these people were to stop and to help us. I would never forget their assistance. Whenever I hear "Like a Rolling Stone" by Bob Dylan, it reminds me of this event.

After this night my car never ran properly. It wouldn't go over 45 miles per hour. It felt as if it were dying from old age.

A month later I went to Dennis' house on Virginia Place. Next door lived the Lopez girls. Stella's boyfriend Richard had a really cool low-rider 1956 Cadillac. It was light green, a two-door. It was really clean on both the inside and outside.

As I pulled into Virginia Place, Richard stopped in the middle of the street to greet me. His car door and my car door were next to each other.

Richard greeted, "Hey, Art, how's it going, man?"

"Everything's cool, Richard. How about you?"

"I'm doing well, guy. How are things?"

"Well, let me think. I'm trying to keep out of trouble, but you know how hard that is."

"Yeah, tell me about it. Hey, Art, cool short." We called our cars a short. It was a slang word.

"Thanks, man. I like your Caddie."

"Oh, yeah, want to trade?"

"Sure. Do you have your pink slip?"

"Yeah, I do. Do you have yours?"

"Yeah, man, let's trade." Without parking or turning off our engines, we both stepped out of our cars. I opened my trunk, and he opened his. I threw a few things of mine in his trunk. He took a few things out of his Caddie's trunk and threw them into my Ford. I reached in through the window, opened the glove compartment, and took out my pink slip. Richard did the same. We both signed them on the hood of the Ford; I handed mine to him; and he handed his to me.

"Deal, Richard."

"Yeah, man, sounds good."

As he was looking over my Ford, he said, "And looks good!" I felt Richard thought he had the better end of the deal; however, I thought the opposite.

"Take care of my car, man."

"Yeah," he laughed. "You take care of mine, too."

I stepped into the Caddie; and he entered my Ford, which was now his. We both drove away. The Cadillac was a very nice, smooth running car. I couldn't believe I made such a good deal. No bumps could be felt as I drove it. It ran like a top.

I turned left on King Road, making my way to the entrance of the freeway on Alum Rock. Once on the ramp I stepped on the gas. The Caddie took off really nicely and quickly.

"Man!" I said to myself when I saw all the smoke behind me. I thought perhaps a car had blown up in back of my Caddie. Then I saw it was my car. It smoked like a train! I thought, "Man, maybe it isn't a good trade after all."

When I arrived home, I parked in front of our house on Emory Street. Tita came out and asked why I had Richard's car. I told her about the trade. She told me I got a good deal. "Yeah, it looks good; but I don't think it is," I responded.

As she was giving the car a once over, she asked, "Well, it looks really nice. How does it ride?"

"It rides really smooth. Want to go around the block?"

"Yeah, I do." She stepped into the passenger side of the Caddie and closed the door. I got back inside and started the engine. She commented, "I can't even hear the engine."

"Can you see it?" I asked.

She laughed, "What do you mean, can I see it? Of course I can't!"

I took her around the block. Our neighborhood had houses that were built in the 1940's. Once I was back on my street, I punched the gas pedal. "Look behind us," I said as I looked in the mirror.

She turned and stared. "Wow! I can't see anything with all that smoke. Can you fix it?"

"I don't think so. I think it's in the motor, and it'll cost too much. I think I got the short end of the stick on this deal."

"Yeah," she answered, still in wonderment. "That's bad."

The next day I took the car to two shops. Both of them told me it was probably a ring and would require pulling the engine apart. I didn't have the money to fix the Caddie; therefore, I decided to wait a while before repairing it.

That evening I picked up Phil and Dennis to go cruising. Both were surprised that I had Richard's car. They said they saw him driving by in my Ford and wondered what he was doing with it. I told them the story.

We were preparing to leave when Dennis told us it was too early for him to buy beer at the Alum Rock gas station. The guy that sold him beer wasn't at work until 7 p.m. I told him that maybe my buddy Rudy was home. Rudy was my brother's friend whom I had known for years. He was twenty-one. I didn't think he would have a problem buying us beer.

We drove down Virginia Place to the next block where my mother owned our house. Rudy lived on that block, as well. We parked and I knocked on his front door. Rudy's sister came to the doorway.

"Hi, is Rudy home?"

The girl who answered the door was Rudy's younger sister.

"Yeah. Hold on, Art. I'll get him," she answered as she stepped away.

In ten seconds Rudy came to the door. "Hey, Art, how are you, kid?"

"I'm cool, Rudy. Hey, I was wondering if you can do me a favor." I saw Rudy often. When I would go out with my brother, Rudy was there most of the time.

"I don't know. Depends what it is. Want me to beat someone up for you again?" I had asked him to do that when I was younger.

"No, not anymore, Rudy. If I need someone beat up, I'll do it myself now. Can you go and buy us some beer? Dennis usually gets beer from some guy at a small store, but it's too early right now."

"Hey, why don't you do what you used to when you were a kid?"

"What's that, Rudy?"

"Go and steal a bottle of whiskey and sell it to me cheap, and then go buy beer with that money?"

I laughed. Phil and I used to do that when we were younger.

Rudy added, "Sure. Give me the money, and tell me what kind you want."

We waited for Rudy in the car until he returned. In twenty minutes he arrived with our beer. We took our case and put it on the back floor of the Caddie.

"Hey, I saw this car around the neighborhood. Where did you get it?"

"I traded it for my Ford."

"Yeah. You had a cool Ford, but I think this one is classier." Rudy liked Fords. He still had his old 1951 Ford that he had owned for years.

15 SAY BYE FOR ME

e left to pick up Yolanda at her aunt Rachel's house off East Hills Drive. Opening a beer and taking a drink, I turned on King Road and made a left on Story Road, leaving a trail of white smoke. A few cars honked to let me know something was wrong with my car. Then I saw something in my rear view mirror. At first I couldn't make out what it was because of the smoke. Then I heard a sound. It was a siren, a motorcycle cop. I pulled over not far from Hopkins Avenue.

"Hey, man, cover the beer with something," I said.

Phil had his jacket and covered the beer. "All right. It's covered. Everything is cool. Don't worry, Art. Act normal," Phil insisted.

The cop stepped off his motorcycle and came to my opened window. As the cop was removing his gloves and looking down at me, standing tall, he said, "I think you have a problem."

"I do? Did I do anything wrong, Officer?"

He laughed. "Well, you didn't do anything wrong; but you definitely have a problem."

"I do?" I asked, acting dumb.

"Don't tell me you don't know what your problem is?"

"Ah," I said not wishing to tell him in the event there was something else wrong with the car.

"You are going to have to get that fixed. This car should be calling all the fire departments out with all that smoke."

"Oh that, OK. I just bought this car from a guy, and he didn't tell me it smoked until after I bought it."

"Can I see your registration and driver's license?"

I removed them from the glove compartment and my wallet and handed them to the officer. I also showed him the pink slip, so he would know I just became the owner of the car. Maybe he would give me a break. Dennis and Phil sat there, not saying anything, hoping the cop didn't check for beer, which cops almost always did.

"Son, I'm going to have to give you a ticket. If it wasn't this bad, I would just tell you to fix it and let you go. However, this is just too much smoke."

"Officer, if you let me slide, I'll give it back to the other owner. He'll have to fix it," I stated, trying to persuade the cop.

"Sorry, I can't do that. Wait here. I'll be right back."

In a few seconds he came back to the car. "All right. Maybe I'll let you slide if you promise to take care of this problem this next week. Where are you boys going?" he asked as he looked around the interior of the car. I saw his eyes scanning the back floor where the beer was covered.

"I'm going to pick up my girlfriend and to see another friend," I answered, trying to sound like a nice school boy.

"Are you boys up to anything you shouldn't be doing?"

"Oh, no, Officer. We're just trying to keep busy. That's all."

The cop looked to the back seat where Phil was sitting and asked, "You OK back there?"

"Yes, Officer, I'm fine," Phil answered.

The cop then looked to the floor. He saw the jacket and asked, "Do you mind lifting that jacket so I can look under it?"

"What jacket, Officer?"

"Young man," he asked Phil, "please pick up that coat."

Phil had no choice. He picked up the jacket. The cop then looked at me. "I thought I smelled beer."

"Officer, we weren't going to drink it in here. We were going to drink it at our friend's house." This was a lie because each of us had already opened our cans.

"I will only ask you once," the cop said, stoned face. "Depending on how you answer will tell me how I will handle this. Do you have any open containers in this car right now?"

Phil and Dennis didn't say anything. I knew I couldn't lie to this cop. He wasn't a dumb cop, so I took my chances and told him the truth. "Yes, Officer. We do."

The cop took a deep breath, trying to decide what he was going to do. In those days it wasn't a big thing to have beer unless a cop wanted to make a big deal out of it. "Is anyone here over twenty-one years old?"

"No, Officer. None of us are."

"Where did you get the beer?"

"We stood by a liquor store and waited for someone to buy it for us."

"Do you know the person you asked? Get his license number or anything?"

"No, Officer. We just asked. He went in and got it. He left and we left." I sure wasn't going to put the finger on Rudy.

"OK, here is what I'm going to do about it. I'm not going to give you a ticket for an open container. The beer you'll have to dump out in the gutter, every one of the cans. Then take your empty cans and throw them in the trash over there," he said as he pointed to a trash can at a store on the corner. "I'm not going to take any of you to jail. So I'm giving you a big break today. However, I am going to give you a ticket for the smoke."

"Come on, boys. I don't have all day to spend with you. Start dumping." The cop went to his motorcycle as we stepped out of mine. I stepped around our vehicle and went to the passenger side, where Phil and Dennis were standing. We squatted down and poured the beer in the gutter.

"Hey, Art," Phil said, "we should only dump half of it and hide the other cans under the seat. He can't see us from there."

"Man, you're crazy! If we get this cop upset at us, he'll take us in. He's already giving us a break. I think we should just do what he says and go to find more money to buy more beer."

"Yeah, that's right, Phil," Dennis agreed. "I don't want to get busted today. I'd rather go back home and get more money."

"Yeah, Rudy will buy us more beer anyway. He might not want to, but he will."

"OK, that was just a thought on saving some money." We stood in the same place when we were done dumping all the cans. The cop came back and looked at the cans, the beer was flowing down the gutter. He then stooped down to look under the seat. I looked at Phil and he at me. I'm glad I told him not to do what he suggested.

"Done?" he asked.

"Yeah, I think we're done. It's a waste, Officer," I said.

"Oh well, that's the way it goes. You think that's a waste. If I was to give you a ticket, you would really see what a waste is. You are saving a lot of money by my pulling you over instead of someone else."

"How much do you think it would have cost?"

"Oh, a lot, but I don't want to scare you."

The cop had me sign the ticket for the smoke. Before leaving, he told us to behave.

We drove back to Virginia Place. Dennis went into his house to get more money. We drove down the street to Rudy's house once again. I stepped out of the car and knocked on Rudy's front door. His sister Mary Helen answered. Mary Helen was my age, and she was very pretty. I always thought she was a very attractive girl; however, she was in love with someone I knew. She ended up getting married very young.

"Hi, Art."

"Hi, Mary Helen. Is Rudy here?"

"Yeah, let me get him." She turned around and said in a loud voice, "Rudy, the door. It's Arthur." Everyone who knew me when I was very young knew me as Arthur.

In a minute Rudy came to the door. "Hey, what happened? Didn't I buy you enough? Don't tell me you drank all that already and that you want more?"

"Yeah, for sure! A cop stopped us on Story Road and took it away from us."

"What do you mean he took it away from you. Man, that cop is going to drink all your beer!"

"No, he didn't take it away from us. He made us dump it all on the ground. But at least he didn't give me a ticket for an open container."

"Man, that's a mean ticket. You would have had to pay a lot of money for that."

"Yeah, I know. That's what the cop said. Hey, do you think you can go and get us some more beer?"

"Again, haven't you and your friends learned your lesson? Maybe that was a sign not to drink today." Rudy was a cool guy; he just liked to play around with me.

"Yeah, we want more beer, Rudy. Hey, you'll be back fast."

"OK, I'll go. But you guys wait here. I don't want to get caught buying you kids beer."

"All right. No problem."

I gave Rudy the money, and he left in his Ford again. I returned to my car with Dennis and Phil. "All right. He went to get our beer, man."

"Cool, Art."

"Yeah," Dennis agreed.

I commented, "Yeah, Rudy is all right. Dennis, do you remember Ray Hernandez?"

"Yeah, I remember him. I didn't really know him. When he used to come around was a long time ago, right?"

"Yeah, it was. Let me tell you a story about him."

Ray Hernandez was a good guy when I met him. He was a lot older than Phil and I. I was fifteen years old; he was twenty-three. We hung out at the Lopez girls' house. He was a large guy with a round face. At first we got along with him really well. In fact, once he even saved my life.

One day he invited me to go with him. "Hey, Art, let's go to Alum Rock Park to fool around."

"Sounds good to me, Ray."

Ray had a convertible MGB, an English car. It was very small; these cars only had one front seat. Sometimes we would fill it up with five persons, two in bucket seats in front and three people sitting on the trunk part of the car with their feet stuck in behind the front seats. The car wasn't cool looking as far as having a cool paint job, but it sure ran nicely. Because it was so small, I would jump in his car without opening the door. On this day he arrived at my house. When I saw him drive up, I came out and jumped into his car. "Ready, Art?"

"Yeah, man, I'm ready. What do you want to do at Alum Rock Park? It'll probably rain on us."

Ray didn't have a top for his car. When it rained, the inside of his car became all wet. We covered everything with plastic and sat on the plastic if it rained hard, sometimes covering ourselves with the plastic. Everything still became wet.

"I don't know, fool around? I haven't been there for a long time."

We had just had a week of straight rain. The ground was so waterlogged that the water just ran off, creating puddles and small floods. Usually the creek at this time of year turned into a violent river.

"OK, man, I'm game. Whatever you want to do, I'm OK with it."

We entered the park. Sure enough the creek wasn't the gentle calm creek we knew in the summer. Ray parked toward the back of the park. He jumped over the door and out of the car. I followed him.

"Hey, Art, let's go for a hike back there."

"That's cool with me, man. I've been back there years ago but not all the way." Alum Rock Park is in the Diablo Mountain Range.

We started walking. The day was overcast, and every little while we felt rain drops. It was cold; however, I had not brought a jacket. I knew if it really became cold, I would just have to deal with it.

We walked along the creek for a long time. The creek had so much water rushing through it that it was roaring. The ground was wet and cool. I thought that I would stop being so brave when it was so cold. I decided that from now on I would bring a coat. We walked a few miles back until we arrived at the fork in the creek. On the way we had fun; sometimes we even ran.

"OK, Art, which way do you want to go? Right or left?"

I looked at the creeks as they merged together. It really didn't matter which way we went because I had never been this far back. Both seemed to be exciting.

"I don't care. Right I guess."

"All right, let's go."

"Hey, Ray," I asked wanting to get to know Ray better. Ray was a guy who hung out with us only once in a while. Lately we had been hitting it off well. I told Ray things about my home life; and he gave me good advice, as if he knew all about life and what I was experiencing.

"Yeah, Art, what can I do for you?"

"I just wanted to know, where are your parents from?"

"Well, my father told me he was from a little town; and he used to be a gangster."

"Really, he was a gangster? What kind of gangster, the real kind or the want-to-be kind?"

"Hey, wait, you didn't ask me that. You asked me where my father was from."

Now Ray changed the subject. "I think we need to take this trail. It looks like it goes up. Maybe if we go up, we will be able to get a better view. And you know what they say about a good view."

"No, what do they say?"

The trail disappeared, and we started making our own path up the side of the mountain. Most of the trails were made by animals such as deer. "They say the better the view you can get in life, the better and the wiser you'll become if you pay attention to the view of life and see what it is telling you," Ray expressed in a matter-of-fact way. At my age Ray really seemed smart. He always showed his wisdom, I thought.

"So, was your father a gangster?"

"No, I really didn't say that. I never knew him, but there is a possibility he was."

"Oh, you never knew him," I repeated, feeling out of breath.

We were climbing higher and higher by the minute. The creek now looked as if it was far below us. There was another hill on the opposite side of the creek. "What about your mother, Ray?"

"What about her?" Ray answered. He was in front of me, and I was following him.

"What does she do? I mean for work?"

"I don't talk about my mother."

The hills were full of oak trees and grass. There was grass from the year before that was now dry. New green blades of grass were growing because of all the rain we had been getting. Every 25, 50, or 100 feet, there was an oak tree. The air was fresh, and it felt cool being up in the hills.

As we walked, we could feel the softness of the soil, unless we were walking on rocks. We were going higher by the second and had traveled quite far from Ray's car, maybe 5 to 7 miles. Brief showers started to fall. I took cover under a tree when it really started to rain hard. Ray said he was going to keep moving and that I could catch up with him. The showers stopped as fast as they started, and the downpour was finished.

I started hiking again. By this time we were really far up the mountain. I looked down at the creek; it appeared like a crooked line because it was so far below us. I caught up with Ray, who was now 100 feet ahead of me. Walking close to the edge of the mountain, I suddenly slipped on the soft ground and started to fall because the mountain was very steep. I was falling almost straight down and yelled, "Help!"

I was done for it, I thought; and I was going to keep falling. I grabbed some large bushes that stopped my fall. Not a muscle in my body moved.

"Art! Where are you?" Ray yelled. He had just seen me behind him. All of a sudden I was gone.

I yelled back, "Over here, Ray! I fell!"

Ray was 100 feet ahead of me. He made his way to the edge of the mountain. Once he did this, he was able to see where I was. Ray clasped his hands around his lips in order to be heard better. He yelled, "Can you climb back up?"

I looked down. It was steep and far. I froze. "I don't know."

"Don't look down. If you look down, you're not going to be able to do anything. We're too far to go for help."

"All right, I won't look down anymore!"

I tried to reach up to grab a tree root that was sticking out of the ground, but I couldn't move. The root was a good 3 feet higher from where my hands clasped the bush. I was really nervous. The bush moved a bit, as if I were pulling it out of the ground, because it had all of my weight to support. It felt as if I was going to fall.

"I don't think I'm going to get out of here, Ray!" I shouted.

"Take your time. Don't move for a few minutes. I know once you get a hold of yourself you'll be all right, Art," Ray expressed confidently. He was trying to be encouraging.

I tried to move upward again trying to grab a large rock in the ground. When I did, the rock came out and fell off the cliff. I turned to see it go down, seeming as if it took forever to reach the bottom to the creek. The ground was very moist.

At that moment I saw and felt everything around me moving, and I believed Ray saw it as well. He started to run back to where he had been walking and was now out of sight. In two minutes he appeared over me, looking down.

"Don't move, Art! Don't move! I think if you move the whole hillside is going to go!"

I wondered if he saw anything move from the position where he was standing a few minutes ago. "Ray, do you think this part of the hill will fall?" I asked, feeling very worried.

"Maybe, just maybe. For right now don't move at all!"

There was a small tree right above me, but it was too high. It was 6 feet or so above me. If I had been closer, I would have tried to grab the roots that were hanging from the cliff.

As I was hanging on, I felt the earth move. "Ray, I'm moving! I can feel it! I think this hillside is going to go. I'm going down with it! Tell my mother that I love her. Tell everyone bye for me!"

In just a few seconds, I was going to die. I couldn't move up or down. If I did, I was going to make the hill slide down. From where I was, it seemed as if 15 feet of the mountain was going to go down with me. I thought of my mother and hoped she wouldn't grieve too much once I was gone. I wondered if my brothers and sister were going to miss me. I knew I wasn't going to survive this fall. It was too long, and there was nothing but rocks at the bottom. Thinking of my friends and the time I was locked up, I wondered if I would ever see any of them again. This was it; I was sure.

Ray saw bits and pieces of dirt and rock starting to fall. He saw a large crack on top of the hill where it was starting to break loose. Ray ran in the other direction, turned around, and started to run back toward me. I felt everything around me starting to give way. Ray started to gain speed as he moved toward me. I thought he was going to jump toward me and that we were going to fly away. I didn't know what Ray's plan was.

He jumped toward me, reaching up, and caught a tree branch above me. He let his feet dangle back and forth until they stopped a foot above me. Ray was a hero. He took a chance on missing that branch and almost fell himself.

"Grab my legs!" he yelled.

I didn't want to; however, I let one arm go as fast as I could and reached for his leg. Once I grabbed Ray's leg, I released my other hand and grabbed his other leg. Just at that instant a landslide started, and everything under me went down the hill.

Ray yelled, "Art, climb up to me!"

I started climbing. Once I reached the top of his hands, I grabbed the tree limb and climbed the tree. When I was up and free of the landslide area, Ray pulled himself up and over the branch. He was strong for being such a big and heavy guy. We both made our way to the center of the large tree, finally feeling safe.

"Ray, thanks, man! Thanks for saving my life! Thanks, man. You could have died there too!"

Out of breath, Ray answered, "Well, Art, sometimes you have to do what you have to do, even if it means your own life." We both appeared as if we had been rolling around in the mud. I was full of mud from the cliff.

All the way back to Ray's car, I still couldn't believe he had put his own life on the line to save mine. I thanked Ray a thousand times.

16 POOR GUY

udy drove up with our beer. "Cool story, Art," Phil acknowledged. "I never knew that about him."

"Yeah, man, cool story. That Ray was all right then," Dennis added.

"Yeah, Ray was a cool guy. He taught me a lesson. You have to do what you have to do for your friends." However, later that year Ray became a guy I ended up disliking.

"Whatever happened to him?" Phil asked.

"I heard he shot himself in the head because some girl didn't want to marry him."

"Man, that's too bad, Art."

I opened the door to get out of the car to get our beer. "Yeah, I was locked up when I heard about it."

I stepped to where Rudy parked his car; he stepped out of his car and closed the door. "OK, man, here's your beer. This time put it in your trunk just in case that same cop pulls you over. If I were you, I would play it safe. I don't want to go and have to buy more beer later."

"All right, Rudy. Thanks, man. If there is ever anything I can do for you, just let me know."

We left Rudy's house and returned to Story Road, headed to Yolanda's home.

"Man, I don't know why you guys don't want me to have a beer right now," Phil complained.

"Because Phil," I insisted, "that cop might be around. If he sees us around here, he'll know we went for more beer. Just wait a few minutes until we get to Yolanda's house. Then you can have one, man. Be patient, Phil."

When we arrived at Yolanda's house, I told Dennis and Phil to wait a minute, asking them to take only a six pack from the trunk. I asked them to hide it, so Yolanda's aunt wouldn't see it.

I knocked on the front door of the house. A little girl answered, "Hi, is Yolanda home?"

"Wait," she answered as she ran back inside.

In a few minutes Yolanda's aunt came to the door. "Oh, Art, it's you. Come in, come in. Have a seat." Instead of going and getting Yolanda, she sat down with me.

"So, are you planning to marry Yolanda?"

"Am I what?" I was shocked she would come straight out and ask me such a question.

"I'm asking if you're planning to marry Yolanda."

"Well, if we keep going out and seeing each other, yeah, I guess."

"I like you, Art; so I'm going to tell you this. If you have plans to marry her, if I were you, I would do it right away before you lose her," she recommended, as she stood from her chair.

I wondered what in the heck she trying to say. "Why?" I asked. It was the only thing I could think of asking.

She turned and looked down the hallway and said loud enough so Yolanda could hear her, "Yolanda, are you off the phone. I didn't call you because I was letting you finish. I was keeping Art company." I felt that Yolanda's aunt Rachel was trying to help me out with something; she liked me. Yolanda didn't notice that her aunt was giving me a message. I think she wanted me to straighten Yolanda out about having two boyfriends. She knew it wasn't right.

"Are you ready?" I asked as she entered the living room.

"Oh, I don't know if I'm going to go."

"Oh yeah, why?"

"Well, I have some things I want to do today."

"Didn't we have it planned that I was going to pick you up, and we were going to do something?"

"What are we going to do?"

I could tell Yolanda really didn't want to go with me, so I answered, "You know, if you don't want to come, I understand."

"OK, I'll go. Let me get a sweater just in case it gets cold later." She went to her bedroom for her sweater. Her aunt gave me an expression as if she were saying, "Be careful, Art. Be careful."

We said good-bye to her aunt Rachel and went out the door. When we were on the walkway headed to my car, I stopped and asked her, "Yolanda, who were you talking with on the phone?"

"To someone."

"I know that, but who?"

"To a friend, that's all. Just a friend."

"A guy?" I asked, hoping I was wrong.

"What are you, my boss now? It's none of your business who I was talking to!" I had never seen Yolanda become upset so fast and talk this way. Something wasn't right. We stayed on the walkway, our voices growing louder and louder, arguing about her telephone call. I didn't think it was right that I had stopped talking to other girls, and she was still talking to guys on the phone. The argument reached the point that Yolanda said she wasn't going to join me. She went back into the house. I went to my car and told the guys she wasn't joining me; however, they already concluded this from overhearing the fight we had on the walkway.

I spent that evening with my partners, but I didn't have a good time because of what happened between Yolanda and me. We cruised around trying to find parties. Once I had three beers, I felt a little better. I forgot about the big fight with Yolanda.

"Hey, Art, you were telling us about Ray earlier. What happened with him? I know he didn't come around anymore because there was a big problem."

"Yeah, man. It was too bad it turned out like that. You know, Ray was like an older man to me. He was OK, but he became too bossy. He wanted to be the leader of the crew. He even wanted to tell me what to wear and how to dress. I told him I had a strict father all my life, and I wasn't going to have another one. He said he wasn't my father but a good friend. I told him many times not to tell me what to do. Then he started pushing me around. I was young then and didn't want to fight with a man."

"He did that? I didn't know that. What happened then? What did you do about it?"

"Well, one day we were parked at the corner burger bar. Ray was really getting moody with me. He told me he was going to beat me up and make me look like I got beat up by three guys because he was a lot bigger than I was, and he could do it." The burger bar was at the corner of Virginia Place and King Road. At that time we lived at the end of Virginia Place.

"Oh, yeah. Then what happened?"

Dennis added, "Man, you should have knocked him out, Art." Dennis knew I was a good fighter and could probably have done it.

"Yeah, but man, he was a big guy. You know if that guy would have sat on me he would have killed me! I didn't want to fight him, not because I wasn't sure if I was going to win but because I knew I would win if we had a fight. I might lose the fight, but I would win the battle. Later I would get a bar or something and make sure I won! But you know, I didn't want to do that because Ray used to be OK with me. I had to find a way to get him but I didn't want to get him too hard."

"Yeah, that was cool," Phil expressed. "But how were you going to do that?"

"I asked Ray if he felt like fighting someone and if that was why he was acting the way he was toward me. He said, 'Yeah, I feel like fighting; and you're the only one here.'"

"Really," Phil commented as he laughed.

"Yeah. So I told him I would be right back. I left on foot and walked to Rudy's house. Rudy was home when I got to his house; his car was parked outside. I knocked on his door; he was inside watching T.V. I asked Rudy if he could do something for me. You know, Rudy is a good fighter. He was really tough. I remember when I was young he started a fight at school. He tore up some guy bad, man! I asked Rudy if he could go to the corner and scare some guy for me, telling him I liked Ray and that he was OK with me. However, lately Ray wanted to fight with me. Because he was a lot older than I was, I didn't feel right about fighting with him."

"Rudy said this was no problem. But I stressed to him not to beat Ray up, just push him around a little. This way he wouldn't think he was the toughest one around. Rudy said all right."

Phil expressed, "Man, this is getting good!"

"He started putting on his shoes, even as he came hopping out the front door. He seemed as if he was in a hurry to have a good time. Rudy told me he wasn't going to take his car. If something really happened, he didn't want the cops to tow it away."

"We walked back to where Ray was. I pointed out Ray to Rudy before we approached Ray's car. Ray glanced at us, wondering what I was doing with this guy. I felt bad for Ray because he had a worried expression."

"Oh yeah, funny, man," Phil said.

"Well, it wasn't really funny. I really felt bad about this. I hurt over it for years. Even when I was in jail and heard Ray had killed himself, I wished I could have been there for him."

"Why?" Dennis asked.

"Because Rudy went up to him and said, 'I heard you have a problem with my friend Art?' Rudy shoved him in the shoulder. Ray didn't say anything. Then Rudy did it again with his other hand in a fist. Rudy told Ray that if he thought he was tough he would show him otherwise. I wanted to tell Rudy, 'OK, Rudy, that's enough. I think you got the point across.' But I didn't say anything. Ray was quiet, as if he was really scared of Rudy. Then Rudy, with both hands, grabbed Ray by the shirt, up by his collar, and told him that if he continued to push me around he was going to go looking for him. I really felt bad because Ray's eyes started to form tears. I didn't know if it was because he was scared of Rudy or if he felt bad that I was involved."

Phil stated, "Art, hey, I would feel bad, too. Poor guy."

"Yeah, man. That's why I say I have always felt bad about what happened with Rudy and Ray. At the time I didn't even think about Ray saving my life, but I felt like kicking myself later. But, you know, Ray was really pushing me around. He had to be stopped."

"What if you just didn't hang out with him?"

"I tried; but he always showed up where I was, as if he wanted a punching bag to push around. So really, I almost had no choice but to ask for help."

"Then what happened," Dennis asked.

"Well, Rudy left; and Ray was silent and wouldn't talk to me. I tried to talk to him, telling him I was sorry, which I was. I think, in truth, he was hurt with me and just didn't come around anymore."

"Never?" Phil asked.

"I saw him around here and there, but he always gave me the cold shoulder. I think he was embarrassed that he didn't fight back. Rudy was younger than he was. Also, Rudy was a fighter; and now I know Ray wasn't."

"Poor guy, man," Phil said after hearing the whole story, making me feel worse.

"Yeah, that's why when I heard he killed himself while I was locked up I really felt bad. Sometimes in life you make big mistakes that you can't fix. That's what I did, and I'll have to live with it all of my life."

We kept cruising and telling stories that night, returning home later. The following Thursday I received a call from Uncle Ray in Wilmington, California. "Hello," I answered. Uncle Ray was a cool uncle. He was always good with me, even when I was a young kid. If Uncle Ray wasn't smiling or laughing, he really looked mean. He had major problems with drugs; however, he never told me about them or never encouraged me to use anything until this time. I knew about his drug use from all the family talk, but I didn't care because he was cool with me. He had been married to Aunt Connie for a long time, and they had one daughter at this time. Connie was my mother's youngest sister, the same age as Eddie.

"Yeah, Uncle Ray, what's up?"

"Hey, Art! What's going on? The Rams are going to be the champs this year!" During this time the Rams football team was in Los Angeles.

"I don't know, Uncle Ray. I think the Raiders are going to do them in!"

Ray laughed as he always did, and he giggled for everything. "Art, hey, man, when you coming down? You know, we have a lot of girls here in LA. Come down, and I'll fix you up with some! Come on down!" Uncle Ray stated in a persuasive manner.

Uncle Ray liked me a lot as I did him. I was nineteen and he was twenty-four. "Yeah, Uncle Ray. I've wanted to go. Maybe I'll go with my partner Phil. Can you find him a girl, too?"

Uncle Ray laughed again and answered, "Heck yeah. Come on down. We'll have a party for you. We have stuff waiting for you, man!"

I wondered what he had for me in Los Angeles. Uncle Ray, Uncle Joe, and Uncle Alfred were party guys. They were always doing something. I really enjoyed hanging out with them.

"All right, Uncle Ray. You talked me into it. I'm coming! Remember, you said you are going to give me a good time, right?"

"Heck, yeah!" he laughed out loud. "Come on over! Your aunt Connie said she will cook you a good dinner! Now that means you have to come!"

I was still upset with Yolanda, so I thought I might as well visit with my uncles and aunts in southern California. If she was talking to guys on the phone, I might as well go and be with someone else.

After hanging up the telephone with Uncle Ray, I dialed Phil's number. He answered, "Hello."

"Hey, man, what's up?"

"Nothing much. I just got home from work." Phil was working in the sheetrock trade because his brother was in the same business as were some of his uncles.

"Hey, can you take a day or two off from work?"

"For what?" Phil really didn't care; in his kind of work, it didn't matter if he was there or not. If his company really needed someone for the day, they would call the union. Someone was always sent out to take his place.

"My uncle Ray called and invited me to go to LA to visit. Want to come? I'm going; I think I'll leave in the morning."

"Yeah, that sounds like fun. I'm ready. I just need to throw a few things together. What are we going in?"

"I thought it would be cool if we went in your car because mine smokes too much." Phil had a 1953 Chevy. It was light green but nothing fancy. It wasn't a head turner.

"Yeah, that's fine with me. I think it'll make it there. I'll pick you up in the morning. What time do you want to leave?"

"Heck, I don't know. Let's say around 8:30. That sounds good."

"All right, cool. I'll be there about that time. I hope we have a good time."

"Yeah, I think we will. You know my uncle Ray. He's cool."

"Yeah, OK, Art. I'll see you in the morning." We hung up the telephone.

The following morning my sister Tita came into my bedroom. "Art, wake up. Phil is here. It's early for him to be here."

"What time is it, Tita?"

"7:30."

"Man, he's early." I got out of bed, put on my pants, and walked into the living room. "Hey, man, how's it going? You're here early. What's up?"

"Nothing. I thought I would come early. Maybe if we leave now, we'll get there earlier," Phil expressed, sounding excited.

"All right. Let me wash up. I'll throw some things in a bag, and we'll take off."

I heard my mother come out of the restroom. She stepped into the living room. "Mijo, what are you doing up so early? You didn't go to work today?"

"No, Mom. I asked for the day off. Phil and I are going to LA to visit the family." All my uncles and aunts lived either in the same apartment building or the same street. They all liked to be around each other and were always in each other's company.

"Hi, Phil. Are you going with Arthur?"

"Yeah. He's always talking about how much fun it is over there. I'm really looking forward to going with him."

"Oh, yeah. The boys are fun to be around. You just need to be careful not to get into trouble. My brother and brothers-in-law sometimes do things they shouldn't, so be careful."

"Oh, yeah, I'm always careful. I know better," Phil expressed, lying, knowing that if my uncles wanted to do something wrong he would be the first to go along with them.

"I just need to throw some clothes together, Mom. Then we're leaving."

My mother was on her way to work. "When are you coming back, mijo?"

"I think either Sunday evening or Monday morning. Depends how I feel."

"Depends how you feel? It's nice to be young and have no worries."

At my age I didn't know what she was talking about, not having any worries.

"OK, Mom," I said as I went up to embrace her good-bye. "Don't worry about me, Mom. I'll be all right."

"You know that is a mother's job, worrying about her children."

At that time I didn't know what that meant either. I went to my bedroom and gathered a few things to prepare to leave. I was going to wash up but decided to shower before leaving. Phil had to wait. That's what he deserved for arriving so early, I thought.

In twenty minutes I was ready. "All right, Phil. I'm ready. Let's go."

"Cool, let's go!" Phil repeated and started out the door. He opened the trunk; I placed my things inside and stepped into the car.

17 THICK
TORTILLAS

We left and started down Highway 101 heading to Los Angeles.
Once we traveled some distance, I asked Phil, "Hey, you remember Uncle Ray, right?"

"Yeah, I mean, not really good; but I know him. I remember he stayed with you guys with his wife."

"Yeah, you do remember him. Let me tell you a story about him."

"Cool, I like your stories."

"One time Aunt Connie and Uncle Ray got into a fight. Aunt Connie came from LA to stay with us to get away from Uncle Ray. She was in San Jose for about a month. Eddie's friends were Donald, Fernando, and Richard, his brother. Those guys, you know them, right?"

"Yeah, I know them, but not really good like you."

"Yeah, I know. Anyways Fernando met Connie; and they liked each other. My aunt is Eddie's age, only two years older than I was. She and Fernando were the same age. They went out a couple of times."

"In a month Ray called and said he was coming to San Jose. He wanted his wife to go back to him. She told him he had to straighten up if she did return. He said he would. A few days later Fernando came knocking on the door, asking for Aunt Connie, not knowing Uncle Ray was there."

"Oh, yeah, man, a fight!" Phil suspected, anticipating a confrontation.

"Yeah. I guess Aunt Connie didn't want Uncle Ray to know Fernando was coming by to see her. When my sister Tita said someone was at the door for her, Uncle Ray stepped to the door and asked Fernando what he wanted. Fernando said he wanted to see my aunt. Ray went out the door swinging; he was doing well."

"Oh, yeah? Man, then what happened?"

"Eddie and I stopped the fight. Fernando went home and came back with the other guys. This put Eddie and me in a bad position because Ray was our uncle, and all the guys were our good friends. Ray went outside where they jumped him, all of them. Eddie and I then went outside. All we really could do was try to stop them, which we did. Man, Uncle Ray was really upset. He wanted to get them one at a time, but after a few minutes he said he wasn't going after them because they were our friends. Uncle Ray is really a cool guy."

"That night Uncle Ray and Aunt Connie went into Tita's bedroom where they had been sleeping. They started talking. I think Uncle Ray wanted to know what happened between her and Fernando. The talking escalated to yelling. Later in the night they were fighting, and I mean fighting. My aunt was a fighter; no one messed with her. When she and Uncle Ray started fighting, it sounded as if the walls were going to collapse. I told my mother I was going to see what was going on in their room. I opened the door to look, and the mattress and blankets were all over the floor. Uncle Ray had Aunt Connie in a headlock. She had his thick hair in her hand and was pulling it back hard. My uncle couldn't do anything. Their bodies stopped moving when I opened the door. They were out of breath. 'Are you guys all right in here?' I asked."

"Ray answered, 'It's OK, Arthur. Close the door and let us talk.' As soon as I closed the door, they went at it for another hour. During the night everyone woke up when they started to go at it again. The next morning my aunt had one big, nasty black eye."

"Oh yeah," Phil cut in, "what about your uncle. Did anything happen to him?"

"Just a little. He had scratches and scrapes and was a little bruised up, as you would look if you had been in a fight, but nothing compared to Aunt Connie. Let me tell you, my aunt Connie could fight. I saw her in action before this battle. The next morning her eye was swollen so bad that it looked like a peach, with the slit being as much as her eye would open."

We kept driving all day down highway 101. Driving normally took eight hours before Interstate 5 was built. We stopped for gas in San Luis Obispo and had something to eat.

"Hey, Phil, did I tell you the story of when Eddie, my friend Richard, and I went to LA?" I told Phil the story, how much fun it was.

Later in the afternoon we arrived in Wilmington in Los Angeles County. My family lived on Golf Avenue. My grandparents and Aunt

Maryann and Uncle Alfred lived in the upstairs apartment. Uncle Ray and Aunt Connie lived one apartment over but downstairs. Behind that building was a long building that had small apartments where Uncle Joe and Aunt Linda lived. Uncle Joe was older than Aunt Maryann and Aunt Connie. Two years separated all of them.

We drove into the parking lot that was in between the two apartment buildings. As we parked, Aunt Connie came out the side door. She stood with her hands on her hips until we turned off the engine. I stepped out of the car and closed the door behind me. "Aunt Connie! Hi, nice to see you."

"Well, hello stranger!" she said as she stepped up to embrace me.

"You remember my friend Phil, right?" I asked as Phil was stepping up to join us.

"Yeah, I remember you. How are you, and how was the trip?"

Phil reached out to shake her hand. "Hello, it was fine. I like traveling with Art; he keeps me going with his stories."

Just then the door opened again. Uncle Ray stepped out and yelled, "Hey! You are in Ram's country!" He stepped forward and put his arm around me. Uncle Ray was 5'6" and had black, short hair. He had a dark complexion. He was a good guy to get along with unless someone upset him.

"Hey, Art, it's nice to see you. I'm glad you made it. We were giving up on you. We have everything lined up for you. Man, we got some fine chicks to come to visit. We're going to have a dancing party at Alfred and Maryann's place upstairs!"

"Cool, Uncle Ray. Sounds good to me. I know I'm going to have fun."

Uncle Ray answered, "You better believe it. You're really going to have fun tonight."

Aunt Connie stated, "Now don't get the wrong idea about these girls Ray keeps talking about. They are nice girls. We told them you and your friend were coming from San Jose and needed female company. They said they would come over. I know you are going to like Mercy and Janet."

"I'm sure we will. Hey, Phil and I love all girls. Right, Phil?"

"Yeah, you can say that again!"

"Hey, Art!" someone called.

I turned in the direction of the apartments on the other side of the parking lot. It was Uncle Joe coming out the door of his small apartment. He was wearing a white tank top and khakis. He was güero, blonde looking. His nickname in the streets was Güero. He carried himself similarly to one of the guys in the old movies, such as in the movie, "Born to Be Wild," a guy who wrapped his cigarettes around his short sleeve shirt. When he laughed, it was usually with a half a smile. This was his natural smile; his baby pictures also showed it.

"Hey, Uncle Joe, how are you?" I asked as I went to meet him half way through the parking lot.

"I'm good. Just trying to lie low. But you know, that's hard to do in LA."

Uncle Joe loved fighting. After two beers he didn't care whom he fought. "Oh, yeah, well, you look good, Uncle Joe. How are Linda and little Linda?" Linda was his wife, and little Linda was his three-year-old daughter.

"Art!" Linda yelled, flying out of her apartment door. "How are you?"

"Hey, Aunt Linda! I'm good. Nice to see you!"

She held her arms up in the air, waving, wanting to hug me. Aunt Linda grew up in Wilmington also. She had sisters our ages. They also liked to party. The last time my brother Eddie and our friend Richard went to LA, we went out with my aunt's sisters. We had a good time and spent most of the weekend with them.

She reached me in no time, embracing me. She was really nice; I liked her. She also really loved my uncle. "How is the little girl?"

"Oh, she is just fine. She is taking a nap right now, but you'll see her in a little while."

"That's good. This is my friend Phil. He came with me this time. Uncle Ray said he was going to show us a good time."

"Oh, Ray!" she said as she patted Ray's shoulder. "You are going to mess these kids up with your good times!" she expressed, laughing.

"Yeah, I want them to grow up to be just like me!" Uncle Ray said.

Uncle Joe laughed with his crooked smile and said, "Yeah, right!"

"I want to go up and see Grandma and Grandpo. Are they up there?" Most people called their grandfathers grandpa, but we were raised to call our's grandpo. I still don't know where that name came from or who started calling him grandpo. He didn't seem to mind it because he always answered to the name.

"Yeah, let's go up there," Connie said. Let me get my baby. She went into her apartment and picked up her daughter Rita.

We all started walking. Aunt Linda said she couldn't go because her baby was sleeping, and she couldn't leave her alone.

Once we were in the quad of the apartments where they lived, we started upstairs. The door was open to their apartment, but the screen was closed. I heard the T.V. and someone speaking in the apartment.

I knocked and opened the screen door. "Hey!" I said to Grandma who was standing in the small kitchen making her thick tortillas.

"Arthur! How good it is to see you, Mijo!" My grandmother appeared very old and sickly. Her heart and stroke problems surfaced early in life, requiring that she stop teaching school many years ago. She had long hair down past her hips; it was gray and white with a little black in it.

The apartment was normal size. On the wall over the television was a large picture of the Last Supper. The rest of the walls held pictures of all our family. The kitchen had three small walls with windows, which made it appear larger than it actually was. There was a metal table and chairs. My grandparents weren't interested in anything fancy; they were happy with whatever they had.

"Grandma, it's nice to see you! How are you?" I asked as I stepped into the living room and up to her in the kitchen threshold. I gave her a big hug. My grandfather was sitting in his chair next to the door. He wasn't an affectionate man. He greeted me, "Hello, muchacho. Good to see you."

"Hi, Grandpo. How are you? What's new?"

Grandpo answered, "I've been working a lot. I have to work if I'm going to pay the rent."

My grandfather was a steel worker. In San Pedro, California, there is a bridge that resembles the Golden Gate Bridge. Not long before this he was working at the high point of the bridge when he fell. As he was falling, by the street level of the bridge, his large suspenders caught a piece of steel and saved his life. He was off work for a few weeks from the soreness he developed. He liked to wear big hats and large cowboy belt buckles, along with a lot of turquoise stones from New Mexico.

"That's right, Grandpo," I answered.

One of the bedroom doors opened. Aunt Maryann and Uncle Alfred came out; Uncle Alfred was combing his hair with his hand. As he was stepping out into the living room, he said in a very deep voice, "Hey, Art, good to see you, kid." Uncle Alfred was very thin and had long, black, straight hair. He had an acne problem and was still dealing with it. This created many scares on his face.

"Hey, Uncle Alfred, how are you? You look good," I commented as I embraced him. He wasn't my blood relative. Aunt Maryann was; but he was always good to me, even when I was younger.

"Well, look who the cat dragged in!" Aunt Maryann exclaimed when it was her turn to hug me. She was very thin, with a thin face and a thin nose. She had long, light brown hair.

"Hi, Aunt Maryann. It's really nice to see you!" I turned my attention to Phil. "Everyone, this is my very good friend Phil. He came with me."

Phil raised his hand and greeted everyone. "Yeah, I felt I had to come to visit you, since Art talks about all of you. He told me I would love all of you, and now I can see why. You all seem to be good people."

"Art," Uncle Ray called from outside the screen door. "Come on. Connie put together a meal for the guys. It's hot, man!" Uncle Ray said as he rubbed his hands together, indicating I was going to love her cooking.

"OK, Uncle Ray, we're coming."

It seemed as if Uncle Alfred's thin body couldn't produce such a deep and powerful voice. He reminded Phil and me to come back shortly, "Don't forget to come back. This is where we're having the party for you guys. We invited some people over." Uncle Alfred was well known; his family name was Nieto.

"Arthur," Grandma stated, "take some of my tortillas down with you."

I loved her thick tortillas; no one could make them as good as she did. She wrapped ten of them in a kitchen towel and handed them to me to take downstairs with us. As thick as they were, a person could only eat so many of them.

We told everyone good-bye but added that we would be back in a little while. Phil and I went downstairs to Uncle Ray and Aunt Connie's place. "I hope you guys like spaghetti. That's what your aunt made."

"Yeah, I like it. What about you, Phil?"

I really wasn't crazy about spaghetti. I would eat it if I had no choice, and I had no choice here. I sure wasn't going to tell them that I really didn't care for spaghetti.

"Heck, I'll eat anything! I'm hungry, man." Phil expressed.

We sat at the kitchen table and had our meal, talking during the entire time. Ray kept reminding us that we were going to have a great time later that evening.

After supper I took a shower. Once I was done, Phil took his. I didn't want to be smelly when I met the girls they invited. I was really looking forward to meeting new girls that night.

I went back upstairs for a while. Uncle Joe was waiting for me. He was all dressed up with his long shirt, buttoned all the way to the top, and his khaki pants, which were nicely pressed. "Hey, Art, how is the family in San Jose? How is my sister and your brothers and sister?

"They are all fine as far as I know. My mom is fine; she is working. Uncle Willie is doing well. Aunt Annabelle and Uncle Bob are fine, too."

"Good, I'm glad. Anyway, if they weren't doing well, we would have heard about it already. But I thought I'd ask anyhow," Uncle Joe stated as he laughed.

"Yeah, they are all doing fine."

Just then someone knocked at the front screen door.

t was a very nice looking girl with long, black hair. She was dressed up as if she was going to a party.

Aunt Maryann called, "Come in, Judy. Come in!" Judy was wearing red high heels, bright red lipstick, and a black leather coat. She was an attractive girl.

Judy stepped in and looked at me. "Hi," she said as she smiled.

"Hi," I answered and also smiled.

Uncle Alfred introduced us. "Art, this is Judy. Judy, this is my nephew Art. There, now you both know each other."

"Well, I know I'm really early. I didn't have anything to do, so I thought I would come over to get to know your company."

"Hey," Aunt Maryann commented, "you're not early, girl. This is your house. You know what 'mi casa is tu casa' means, right?"

"Yeah, I know that, Maryann. You told me that before. So I wanted to come to be in my house then!" she expressed as she giggled.

From the bottom of the stairs, I heard my name called. "Is someone calling me?" I asked everyone.

Judy answered, "Yeah, I think so, if you are Art; and I know that's you because I just met you!" Judy was trying hard to be friendly with me, and I liked it.

Aunt Maryann expressed, "Sounds like your uncle Ray."

I stood and stepped out on the walkway that led to the stairs, standing by the guard rail. "Yeah, Uncle Ray."

"Come down here for a minute, Art."

"OK, coming," I answered as I stepped to the stairs and went down. "Yeah?" I asked as I approached where he was standing.

"Come into my apartment for a minute. I have something for you."

We walked to his front door and stepped inside. Phil was sitting on the sofa waiting for us. I sat next to Phil and asked, "What's up?"

"I don't know. Your uncle Ray said he wanted to give us something, but he wants both of us to be here."

Uncle Ray grabbed a chair and pulled it over to face us as he spoke. "OK, here is what I have for you guys." He had something clenched in his hand. He brought his arm up to about eye level and opened his hand. There were four red pills. Uncle Ray smiled and said, "Reds! You guys are going to have fun tonight!"

I asked, "What are Reds?" I had never heard of Reds; they weren't in the San Jose area at this time. LSD, Whites, Grass, and other drugs. I had taken these, but never Reds.

"Reds are Reds, what can I say?"

"Yeah, but how are they supposed to make us feel?"

Uncle Ray laughed and answered, "Good!"

"I know. But like LSD? Are we going to trip out or what?"

"I don't know. I never tried LSD. All I know is they make you feel good. Do you want them or not?"

Phil answered right away, "Heck, yeah!"

Then I followed, "Yeah, I'll try them; but I wish I knew what they're going to do to me."

"Here are two for you, Phil; and here are two for you, Art. That should do the job for you."

I walked into the kitchen and took them with a glass of water. Phil did the same. From the window I saw my grandfather walk toward his car. On the weekends he would never stay home. He had a girlfriend and even had children with his girlfriend. Everyone knew about his relationship with her, even my grandmother; however, she never said anything. She loved him so much she never wanted to bring up the subject.

"OK, Uncle Ray, let's see what happens. I hope I don't make a fool of myself tonight."

"No, you're going to have a good time."

The screen door was still open to his apartment. From where I was sitting, I saw more girls going upstairs.

"Hey, Uncle Ray, more girls. I met one already."

"Oh yeah, which one?"

"Her name is Judy."

Phil looked at me, surprised, and said, "You already met a girl? Where was I?"

"Just a while ago. You were here waiting for me."

Uncle Ray asked, "How did you like Judy?"

"She is nice, really nice. She's good looking and very friendly."

"Yeah, you think she is nice. Wait until you see the other girls who are coming."

"Did you invite other guys, or are we going to be the only ones with all the girls?" Phil asked.

"We invited other guys. But don't worry. They are bringing their girlfriends. I'm making sure you guys are going to have a good time, man!"

"Let's go upstairs, Phil, and meet some of these girls. I'll introduce you to Judy. You'll like her."

"Yeah, cool, I'm game for that!"

We started to walk upstairs. Uncle Ray told us he would be up in a little while. As we were making our way upstairs, we saw other people arriving. We stepped into Aunt Maryann and Uncle Alfred's place. "Hey, you're back. Did your uncle Ray fix you up?" Uncle Alfred asked.

"Yeah, he sure did," I answered and turned to Phil. "Hey, Phil, I want you to meet Judy." Judy had a very nice smile. "Judy, this is my buddy Phil. He's all right."

Judy was sitting on a large chair and extended her hand to shake Phil's. "Hi, nice to meet you, Phil. I'm glad you came to LA to see us. I've never met anyone from up north. I only know LA people."

Aunt Maryann introduced me to two more girls. "Art, this is Monica and Becky. They also came to meet guys from up north. I don't know why Judy said she didn't know anyone from up north," she said as she turned to look at Judy and continued. "You know, I'm from San Jose, too."

Judy laughed and answered, "Yeah, but. . . you know what I mean!"

Monica was very pretty; she was on the chunky side. She had a face that was alive with energy; her expressions and mannerisms made her really look pretty. She was wearing bright red lipstick; a white blouse; and a short, black skirt. Her hair was wavy and long. Becky wasn't as pretty, but I was sure by the way she carried herself that she was a fun person.

"Hi, Monica and Becky. It's nice to meet you both."

Phil followed my words, "Yeah, really nice to meet you. I didn't know they had such pretty girls here in Wilmington. And that goes for you too, Judy."

I looked at Phil and continued, "Phil, this is Judy. She's the one I was telling you about downstairs."

Phil and Judy both looked at me. Phil added, "Hey, we already met!"

"Yeah, we met already!" Judy answered as she giggled.

"OK, OK, I'm just trying to liven things up here!" I was playing around because I could tell by the way they were looking at each other that they were going to hit it off well.

Alfred handed Phil and me a beer.

My grandmother had gone to her bedroom. That's where she was going to spend the rest of the evening.

Connie stepped into the living room from outside. "Hey, how come there's no music. I think the party started when all these girls stepped in!" She went to the stereo and put on some nice sounds.

More young people arrived, and then some guy and his girlfriend started to dance. Phil was standing next to me. "Hey, Art, these Reds feel good, don't you think?"

"Feel good? I can't feel anything. They're not working for me. I'm going to go and see my uncle." I stood up and stepped across the room where Connie was sitting. "Aunt Connie, where is Uncle Ray?"

"He'll be up in a bit; he's downstairs at home."

"OK, I want to talk to him. I'll be right back," I said as I headed toward the door and downstairs. While I was down at the walkway, Phil was up at the balcony. He called, "Hey, where you going?" Judy was at his side. I thought. "Man, that guy is fast."

"I'll be right back; I'm going to go see my uncle. Don't let those girls go anywhere."

"He and Judy laughed, and I entered Uncle Ray's apartment. He was sitting on his sofa with his head back on the cushion. "Uncle Ray, you awake?"

"Yeah," he answered, groggily as he lifted his head. He smiled and asked, "Hey, how does it feel?"

"Man, Phil is feeling it. I don't feel anything. I think I need two more." Uncle Ray sounded as if he was also on something.

"Are you sure? Two is plenty for someone who has never dropped Reds before."

"Yeah, I don't know why I'm not; but I'm not. It's hitting Phil all right."

"OK, man, but I hope it's not too much for you." Uncle Ray took more out of his pocket.

"Man, Uncle Ray, were you going to take all of those?" I asked, thinking he was really hooked on Reds.

Ray laughed and answered, "No, they're not for me. I'm going to pass them out to other people who are coming. Here are two more for you."

"Cool," I answered, happy because I was given more. I drank them down with the beer I brought downstairs with me.

"Now go back up and meet some girls, Art!"

I went out the door and headed upstairs. As I stepped onto the balcony, I could see there were more people standing outside of the apartment. I walked by them and greeted them, "Hey, man." To another person I also greeted, "Hey, man, how's it going?"

One of the guys said, "You must be Art."

"Yeah, that's what they call me. Nice to meet you."

I met the few who were outside and entered the living room where I saw Phil dancing with Judy. I thought he was dancing well for someone who doesn't know how to boogie.

Two more girls were introduced to me; however, I was a little shy to talk to them. One of them was talking to me and was really trying to be friendly, asking me about San Jose and saying that she would like to visit one day. She said she has some cousins in the area whom she didn't know.

In forty-five minutes Phil was really having a good time. "Man, those pills Uncle Ray gave him worked really well," I thought. They had not, however, done anything for me.

Uncle Ray was in Aunt Maryann's kitchen talking to someone about football. I stepped into the small kitchen and waited a second until he was done expressing his thought. He turned my way and asked, "Hey, Art, how you feeling?"

"Nothing, Uncle Ray. Nothing."

"You're kidding? Really? Man, something must be wrong with your system. Let's go down to my office, so I can see what I can do." The people who were in the kitchen had no idea what we meant. Uncle Ray led the way downstairs, and I followed.

Once we were in his living room, he asked, "Nothing? Not even a little feeling, a buzz?"

"No, Uncle Ray. I don't feel anything. Just a little from the beer I'm drinking but nothing else."

"OK, man, here's two more. I don't think I have seen someone take so many for the first time, and nothing happens."

I swallowed the two Reds. Once they were down I commented, "I sure hope something happens." I immediately began to feel as if I were a little drunk. "Oh, man!" I said as I grabbed onto the wall.

There was a knock at the front screen door. Ray looked at me and asked, "You OK, Art?"

"Man, Uncle Ray, I think the first two just hit me!"

"Hello, we're here," the girls at the front door said.

"Oh, man, Art, don't tell me that!" Uncle Ray turned his attention to the girls outside. "Yeah, come in. Come in." Uncle Ray looked at me and asked, "Hey, Art, sit down for a minute." I made my way to the sofa with his help. I felt as if I was really drunk. I had no idea that this was the feeling I was supposed to feel. Maybe I was feeling it earlier but didn't know it.

Becky was one of the girls, and she wanted to know where I was. They both appeared high on something. "We came back to see where Art went. I want to dance with him!" Both of the girls came and sat down, one on each side of me.

I didn't know if I was now able to dance. I didn't even know if I could make it upstairs. These Reds didn't make me feel the same as the other stuff I had taken previously, but they made me feel really drunk.

"What the heck," I thought. "I'll do anything. I might as well have fun!"

"Art, ready?" one of the girls asked. It seemed as if she was dragging her voice, a record on the wrong speed.

"Yeah, let's go!" I stood and was ready to leave, wondering how long I had been sitting because it seemed as if the other two pills had now hit me. I could hardly stand. "Let's go." Both girls put my arms over their shoulders.

"Come on, we'll take care of you!" one of them said as she giggled.

The next thing I remembered, I was lying in Uncle Ray's living room with the two girls looking over me, as if they were wondering what in the heck happened.

To me it seemed very dark. I was lying on the floor looking up at the outline of the girls' hair. I couldn't see their faces. One of them asked, "Is he all right? Is he going to die? Did he OD?"

The sun was shining bright. I thought back to what had happened. All I could remember was one of the girls asking if I was all right and if I was going to die. "Man, I blew it! I missed a good party!"

I opened my eyes to make sure I wasn't in the hospital. I was in one of the bedrooms in Uncle Ray's apartment.

"I hope I didn't make a fool of myself!" I thought. Stepping out of bed and putting on my shirt and pants that were lying on a chair, I went to the living room where Aunt Connie was sitting with her baby daughter Rita.

"Art! Did you sleep it off? How do you feel?"

"I feel good. I'm not sick. No headache. Everything is fine, except I missed out on a good night."

"Yeah, for a while there we were going to take you to the hospital. We thought you overdosed. We were really worried."

"Really? I wouldn't think six Reds could kill anyone, can they?"

"You never know. Everyone's different. It seemed as if your heart stopped beating a few times. Ray wanted to take you to the hospital right away because he knows all about that stuff. Uncle Joe kept telling him you were going to be all right. He said you were tough. I guess he was right."

I saw my shoes and socks next to the couch and pulled them over to where I was sitting, starting to put them on. At that moment the screen door opened. It was Uncle Ray. "Art! My nephew! You are up and breathing! Man, I made a big mistake last night; and I'll never do it again!"

"What mistake, Uncle Ray?"

"What mistake? Giving you those Reds. I should not have given you any or at least no more than the first two."

"Heck, I would have bugged you until you gave them to me anyway."

"You had me scared, Art. You really did. I've seen a lot of guys OD in my days, and I sure didn't want you to be one more added to the list. Well, I guess you learned one thing last night."

"Oh, yeah, what's that?"

"If you are too loaded, you will lose with the girls."

"Yeah, Uncle Ray, you have a good point there. I really messed up last night."

I was finished putting on my shoes. "Well, I'm glad everything turned out, and I'm alive. I don't think I could have overdosed on only six Reds, but I did really miss out on a good time."

"Don't worry about that. Your partner made up for you. He just had a really good time."

"Oh, yeah, where is he?"

"We don't know. He danced all night; and the next thing we knew, he and Judy disappeared. We haven't seen them since."

Uncle Joe stepped into the living room. "Hey, Art, did you have a good time last night?" he asked and laughed, thinking the whole thing was a big joke.

"No, Uncle Joe. It was no fun not being able to have a good time with the girls."

"What do you mean, no fun? You were as high as a kite. Most people who get that high like it!" Again he laughed.

We talked about how much fun everyone had, and they shared with me all that I missed.

In a few minutes I could hear Phil's voice. There was also a girl talking, and I knew she had to be Judy.

Phil knocked on the door and stepped into the living room with Judy at his side. "Hey, everyone!"

I answered, "Hey, Phil and Judy. Where you guys been?"

Smiling, Phil answered, "Yeah, we left when everyone started to leave; and we ended up at another party."

Judy cut in, "Yeah, it was my friend Lydia. After that we went to my mother's place."

I looked at Phil and whispered, "Yeah, right."

Phil laughed and answered, "No, really. We went to her mom's house. It was almost morning when we arrived. Then she made a big breakfast for us. We haven't slept all night."

"Where did you go last night, Art? Did you take off, too? For a little while you were here, and the next thing I knew I didn't see you anymore."

Aunt Connie laughed and exclaimed, "He went to dreamland!" Uncle Ray and Uncle Joe both laughed.

"Really, Art?" Phil asked with his large jaw smiling from one side of his face to the other. "Were you with one of the girls?" He asked seriously.

Uncle Joe verified, "He overdosed on Reds. He really went to dreamland."

"Yeah, but I didn't have dreams. I wish at least I had."

"Don't worry, Art. There'll always be other parties. You are still young," Phil suggested, trying to make me feel better.

We stayed in the living room talking about other things. In a little while Uncle Alfred came down to Uncle Ray's apartment.

"Hey, Art," Uncle Alfred asked, "Do you remember when you were young and came to visit us? We took you out to teach you how to fight. And you got drunk and ended up getting sick all over my Ford!"

"Do I remember that? Heck! I spent the whole morning cleaning and washing that car. Let me tell you, it was no fun. I can't even remember everything that happened that night."

They all started laughing because they all remembered it clearly.

As the day continued, Uncle Joe kept giving us beer. In the afternoon we were drinking very slowly because we didn't want to over drink. I didn't want the same thing to happen to me that occurred the previous day. We had dinner upstairs at Grandma and Aunt Marryann's apartment.

Even though I missed the big party, I enjoyed being with my family that weekend. We left and drove back to San Jose on Sunday evening, arriving home at 3 a.m.

19 ROVING EYE

he next day I called Yolanda, and we talked for a long time. She told me she didn't intend to be mean with me. She also agreed not to be talking to other guys on the phone. I told her if she was going to be mine then she had to be mine all the time. "Yolanda, don't you want to marry me?" I asked.

"Yeah, but when?"

"I'm ready when you are."

I found a job at Owens Illinois, a company that manufactured plastic bottles in Santa Clara, a city that is next to San Jose. I made enough money to be able to support her.

The next day I went to Yolanda's house, and we made plans to get married in two weeks. I didn't want to wait again, only to find she might start dating someone else. We weren't going to have a large wedding because I couldn't afford it, and her parents and my mother couldn't afford it either. We weren't concerned with having a large wedding.

Yolanda and I were young, but we felt we were in love. That was good enough for us. Yolanda's aunt Rachel gave us permission to use her house for the reception. We were planning to have just a few good friends and our families at the reception.

The following week I went to Phil's house. We were on the way to the store when I saw my old Ford come around the corner. Richard slowed down when we met. My window was opened, and so was his. "Hey, Richard, how's everything?"

"I don't know, Art. I mean, this car, I can't get on the freeway with it. It doesn't go fast enough."

"Tell me about it. I already got a ticket in this car for smoking so much. I don't know how I'm going to take care of it."

"Oh, yeah. Are you telling me you want to trade it back?"

"Yeah, man, I'm game if you're game."

"Sure, why not," Richard agreed as he opened his car door. Phil and I stepped out of the car. I opened the trunk, and he opened his. I didn't have anything in mine, but he did. He threw his stuff into the Caddie's trunk. I took out the pink slip, the same one I received from him. He pulled out his pink slip and we traded. "Later," we both said as we drove our cars away.

Phil expressed, "Man, that was easy. I mean, you didn't even pull over or anything. That's funny."

"Yeah, that's how I got the Caddie in the first place, almost at the same spot."

In a few days I went to court on the ticket. Richard had signed a paper saying he was the owner of the car. I didn't have to pay or do anything about the smoking car.

In two weeks Yolanda and I were married at the courthouse. On a Friday we had made an appointment with a judge. He seemed like a really nice guy. I was a little nervous the first few seconds because the only times I ever stood before a judge wasn't for good things. He said what the State of California required him to say and pronounced us man and wife. Yolanda looked very pretty that day. She couldn't get her smile off her face.

The day went really well. That evening I had my good friends and our families together at the house of Yolanda's aunt. My mother was really happy for me because she felt I would now be forced to settle down. Yolanda appeared to be happy that day. We were going to make the best of our marriage, and I was determined to be happy.

I didn't have to buy any beer because all the older men paid for beer and drinks. Juan now appeared as if he loved me and as if I was his best son-in-law. I knew I was his only son-in-law; therefore, I was his best and worst.

For the most part the beginning of the party went well. Both Yolanda's mother Sandy and her father Juan were there. Once Juan had a few beers, he started to talk loudly. He didn't bring his girlfriend with whom he was living. Whenever Sandy stepped close to him, he really became overexcited. Sandy, Yolanda's mother, had brought her boyfriend with whom she was living. However, he didn't attend the party; he stayed at the hotel they rented. I was sure glad he didn't attend. If he had, I know Juan and he would have had a fight for sure.

One of Sandy's brothers stepped up to Juan and told him he needed to cool it. Yolanda's uncle told Juan that this was Yolanda's day; and he, Juan, shouldn't ruin it. Juan didn't like his comment at all and wanted to know if he or they, his brothers, were going to ask him to leave.

Yolanda's aunt Rachel was Sandy's sister, so the party really belonged to their side of the family.

All of these older guys were tough guys when they were young and continued to be the same, even as they became older. Yolanda told me stories about their getting into a lot of trouble when they were youngsters. Some of her uncles still got into fights and loved it. They reminded me of my uncles. It appeared they wanted to fight with Juan. Because of things Yolanda had told me, I didn't think they ever liked Juan.

I hated to say anything to Juan or Yolanda's uncles because I was only a young kid. Who was I to be counseling these "veteranos"? However, since I was the groom, I had to say something to stop any fights from ruining our wedding.

First, I went to Sandy's brother who was standing with two of his other brothers. I greeted them again and asked how they were doing. I asked him, while looking at the other brothers, if they could do me a favor. They said they would do anything for the king of the day. I asked if they could leave Juan alone. I reminded them he really loved Sandy. Today Juan was also losing a major part of his life, his daughter. The older men listened to me and agreed they were willing to say nothing, for Yolanda's sake. I then went to Juan and told him his ex-brothers-in-law weren't going to tell him anything because of his remarks against Sandy. I asked if he could hold it down, not for his or Sandy's sake, but for Yolanda's sake. I reminded him that this was her day. He agreed.

The rest of the evening went well. Everyone had a good time, and there were no fights. I danced with Yolanda all evening. We had a lot of fun.

Before this day I rented an apartment downtown on Seventh Street. It was a one bedroom apartment. After the reception Yolanda and I went to our new apartment. I had good feelings. Even though I was still too young to be married, I felt it was very nice being married. I felt like a man. I knew this was it, this was the way my life was going to be. I believed I was going to be all right and have a good life.

As the months went by, Yolanda and I developed our routine of being married. I still went out with my friends on the weekends and sometimes during the week; however, I knew other girls were off limits for me because I was now a married man.

I was nineteen years old, and I didn't know how to show my wife the proper respect. I was her boss and wanted her to ask permission for everything she did. I think I was that way because this was how my father treated my mother, and I learned from him. I was just too young and didn't know better. Yolanda also had her problems. I lightened up as time went by and became a better husband.

We lived in a very small apartment on the east side, off of King Road, a studio. It only had a small kitchen and a bedroom that was also a living room. It was good enough for us.

We were told the first year of marriage is the hardest. I thought after that first year we were not going to fight anymore, but that didn't happen. If a day went by and we didn't have a fight, it seemed as if something was wrong. We almost made it a point to have our daily arguments, many times more than once a day; we were having a really difficult time getting along. At times we would fight over small things. I had a temper that I could not control. She knew how to push the right buttons to trigger my anger. When I was a young kid, I had a bad example to follow, my father. He was always upset with my mother for one thing or another. I felt married life was supposed to be this way.

As time went by, Yolanda always seemed to be in bad moods. We tried to get along, but it was difficult. We both knew we married too young. If we had waited a few years, we could have avoided a lot of heartache, not only for ourselves but also for our children.

I would become upset with Yolanda for having a roving eye. She would stare at other guys, and I really didn't like this. This was something men would mostly do, but with us it was Yolanda who had a roving eye. Whether I was with her or not, this was wrong. She was married now; and that's the way it was, unless she was planning something about which I didn't know. She would deny it, and we were off into our daily fight.

Of course we also had our good times. We told each other we loved one another, but sometimes I wondered if that was really true. I knew I really cared for her because she was my wife.

Two years passed. I had been in a big fight with Yolanda, and I decided to move to Los Angeles County where my family lived.

Later Yolanda and I spoke on the telephone a few times, and we made up after two months. She decided to move to Wilmington, California, where I rented a place for the two of us. While we lived there, she became pregnant. We had our first child, whom we named Jorjito.

On the way home from the hospital, I looked at him in the back seat with Yolanda and could not believe that he was mine, that I had produced a real human being. I was thrilled that I was a father to a real baby. Before long, he was up and running. Time just moved along fast. I loved my first son very much.

After moving back to San Jose, I stopped going out with my friends. Whenever I went out dancing, I went with my wife. I learned this was the way it should be if I wanted to make our marriage work. I wanted to be a good husband and a good father. I really tried.

During this time our second son was born, David. He was really a cute baby. I felt he was the best looking baby in the ward. All the babies looked as if they were little old people, all wrinkled. He was handsome. Everyone said he looked like me. Both of my sons were good kids. They had a lot of energy and always liked to play.

When my son David was two, he would walk over to the next door neighbor. The house was only a few feet from our front door. I would go outside and call him back. The old lady next door, Miss Marty, was the kind of elderly person who always complained about everything. One day she called the police on my sons. The cop parked on the street in front of the house. My sons were playing cars right on the front porch. One of my sons was two, and the other was four years old. When the cop stepped to the front door, the boys were right there at his feet. When the officer approached the front door, I answered, "Yes?"

"We received a complaint about two boys here."

"Yes, Officer, I know. It was next door, Miss Marty."

"Yes, it was her. Are we talking about your sons?" he asked, looking a little confused because I wasn't that old myself.

"Yes, my sons."

"May I speak to them?"

"Sure, go ahead."

He waited a second and asked, "Can you call them?"

I laughed and told the cop that they were at his feet. He looked down and asked, "These are the boys she is complaining about?" Then he continued, "I'm sorry I'm bothering you, sir. I'll just go over to her house and speak with her." The cop walked a few feet to her home, knocked, and entered. He was embarrassed that he was called for two very young children.

I had a tree in the back yard about which Miss Marty always complained. She said the leaves would fall on her property, and I should cut the Chinese Elm down. "Mr. Rodriguez, when are you going to cut this tree down?"

"I don't know, Miss Marty. I don't know," I would answer.

One day my mother told me what my grandfather Ben did when he lived there years before; he had faced the same problem with her. One day Miss Marty was sitting in the shade. He looked over the fence and asked her if she could please move out of his tree's shade!

One day I saw Miss Marty and her sickly husband sitting on lawn chairs in their driveway, under my tree's shade. I looked over the fence and stated, "Oh, Miss Marty, can you please move over a little because you're in my tree's shade. You didn't ask if you could use it."

All she did was stare at me, as if I was out of my mind. I enjoyed doing this every so often to retaliate for all the complaints she made.

Yolanda and I had good times and bad times together. I didn't realize that married life was going to be so difficult, but it was.

My little boys also had a difficult time because Yolanda wasn't the type of mother to show affection, to hold her little boys and to cuddle them. I tried to take her place by showing my affection, but I knew it wasn't the same. I understood that it would mean so much more if Yolanda were to share her love with our sons.

I read to them at night before bed and told them stories. They really enjoyed these little stories. I really loved my boys and knew I would suffer any hardship for them. I also didn't want them to grow up having to spend part of their lives in jail, as I did. I had lived a hard life dealing with my father when I was young. Sometimes I would become angry with my sons. I tried to be balanced with my children and not treat them the way I was treated. However, being raised harshly by my father made it difficult. I had to learn on my own to show love and be reasonable with my children.

One thing I knew, I would never leave my boys. I wanted to be there for them all their lives.

After being married for five years to Yolanda, she learned how to drive a car and would often go to see her friends. Sometimes when I arrived home from work, she would be a little high from drinking.

"Yolanda, where were you? What have you been doing all day?"

"What do you care? You don't tell me what to do."

"And the boys, where were they when you were drinking?"

"Don't worry about them. They were all right! And don't worry about me!"

"What do you mean 'don't worry about you.' You're my wife, and I have to worry about you!"

"Shut up! Don't tell me if I can drink or not! I'll do whatever I want."

This situation and arguments occurred often. I had reached the point of not fighting with Yolanda anymore. I wanted things to work out because I was thinking about my little boys and wanted the best for them.

20 JUST LIKE THE OLD DAYS

(O)ne day I arrived home from work. I was now working for Owens Corning Fiberglas Company in Santa Clara. It was hard work, but I enjoyed having a job that allowed me to support my family. The phone rang; I answered it, "Hello?"

"Art, this is Eddie. Hey, can you help me out?" my older brother asked.

"Sure, what do you need, Ed?"

"Well, my car broke down on the freeway; and I need help getting it home. Maybe we can hook a chain to it and pull it here." Eddie lived at home with my mother on Virginia Place. He had a Lincoln, a nice running and good looking car; but it was really a big gas hog. Eddie was single and could afford it.

"Sure, Ed. I'll be over in a little bit."

"Man, Art, I'm telling you. If Tita's boyfriend Eli comes over again, I'm going to get him. I'm going to stick him with a knife. I'm going to stab that guy!"

"Eddie, what happened, man? Did something happen there?" I was worried because Eddie was the kind of person who meant what he said. If he said he was going to stab someone, these words were not talk. He was really going to do it. I didn't want my brother to go back to jail for killing someone.

"He came over here a little while ago. But if he comes back, man, I'm going to take care of him!"

"Ed, don't do anything until I get there. I'm leaving right now. Don't do anything until I get there, OK?"

"Man, Art, I'm going to get that guy!"

"Ed, I'm hanging up; and I'm on my way! Don't do anything!"

I hung up the phone. Yolanda was worried. She asked, "What happened? What's wrong with your brother?"

"I've got to go! I'll call you when I get there, and I'll tell you then. Bye," I dismissed myself and raced out the door.

I drove as fast as I could to the eastside. I looked in my rear view mirror to make sure no cops were in sight. I didn't want to get a ticket for speeding.

I arrived on Virginia thinking I traveled fast enough so that nothing could have happened in that short of a time period. I parked the car in front of the house, stepped out, and went to the front door. The door was open but not the screen door. Someone inside was walking around, but I wasn't sure I saw a person until I opened the screen door. Eddie was pacing back and forth in the living room. There was blood smeared all over the walls and all over the floor. Eddie kept repeating, "I got him, man! I got him!" Eddie was also covered with blood. Most of the furniture was knocked over and out of place.

"Eddie! Are you hurt? You OK?" I asked as I went up to him, worried. He wouldn't answer. He just kept repeating the same thing. "Eddie, you're full of blood. Are you all right? Did you get cut?"

He stopped pacing and looked at me, saying, "This isn't my blood. This is his blood."

From the amount of blood there was, I knew there had to be a body somewhere. I looked around on the floor, not believing someone could lose so much blood and still be alive. I stepped to the hallway and looked for a body, but there was none. "Eddie, where is he? Where did you put him?"

"He took off running. I don't know where he is. He might be at one of the houses in the neighborhood. I don't know."

"Ed, what happened? How did this happen?" I was wondering what my mother was going to say when she arrived and saw her living room so bloodied and torn apart. She always left for work making sure her house was in good order. Now it looked like a war zone.

"After I talked to you, I went in the kitchen and got the biggest knife out of the drawer, just in case he came over again. I put it under the cushion of the couch. He came back and just walked in. He said he wanted to know where my sister was. He went into the kitchen and took out one of Mom's small steak knifes and stepped up to me from behind. He put that little knife to my neck, demanding to know where Tita was. That's when I took out my big knife and let him have it. First, I cut his arm. Then I cut him somewhere on his side and other places. That little rat, I got him! That'll teach him!"

"Man, Ed, I hope he doesn't die," I stated, worried. I wasn't worried for Eli, but I was for my brother Eddie. Going back to jail would not be good. "We're going to have to clean up all this mess before Mom gets home."

"I don't know, but I got him." From the way he was speaking and pacing, Eddie seemed to be in a state of shock. He was still hyper from the fight.

"I'm going to go into Mom's room to call home," I said as I went into the room and closed the door behind me. As I stepped into the bedroom, I realized that being in my mother's room brought back a lot of memories. It was my mother and father's bedroom when we were kids. My mother still had the bedroom set my father bought for her when they were young; it was really nice. It was made from oak, and it had flowers carved all over each piece. The bed was in front of the window as if the window was the headboard. I stretched across the bed, reached for the phone, and dialed.

"Hello?" Yolanda answered.

"Hi, it's me."

"What happened?"

"Eddie cut up Tita's boyfriend. I think he probably died somewhere."

"Did someone take him to the hospital? Is he alive?"

"I don't know. But I know this. He has eight brothers in San Jose. And they are all like him. So if he called one of them, we're going to have a lot of company soon." Eli and his brothers were from somewhere in the Los Angeles area.

"Be careful. You don't want to go back to jail again."

"Yeah, I know. You know what? I better get off the phone because I have to call Victor. I've got to go. Bye."

She said good-bye, and I hung up the receiver. Victor only lived a few blocks away. I dialed his number. "Hello?"

"Yeah, is Victor there?"

"Hold on."

"Hey," Victor answered.

"Hey, Vic, we have trouble here at Mom's house. Eddie just stabbed Tita's boyfriend Eli."

"Oh, yeah, when did this happen?"

"Just a few minutes ago. I think you better come over right away. That guy has a lot of brothers!"

"OK, I'll be over right away." He hung up.

I dialed home again, "Hello?"

"Yeah, it's me again. I called Victor. He's on his way."

"What did he say?"

"He is on his way. He will be here in a few minutes because he doesn't live that far."

Just then I heard a car slamming its brakes, skidding on the street. Another car came to a screeching halt behind that one. Then another. I said, "Oh, man, it's time! Got to go!"

The door to the bedroom opened; Eddie stood in the doorway. "OK, Art, it's time. Just like the old days. Come on."

"I've got to go. I have to help my brother."

"Oh, be careful. Don't get killed, and remember you have a family."

"Yeah, I know," I said as I hung up, pausing and thinking. "I do have a family and little boys whom I love very much. I don't want to give up everything for one fight that was Eli's fault. But I can't leave my brother alone in this. He's my brother, and I have to do whatever I can to help him. I have to be by his side."

I was standing a few feet from the bed and then stepped into the hallway. Eddie and I were waiting for a few seconds for the guys to enter the house, but they were taking a long time. I went back into my mother's room and looked out the window. I saw Mike, Crooked Mouth, and another guy talking to Eli's older brother Juan. When Mike, Crooked Mouth, was a young boy he had a disease, which left him with a crooked mouth. Mike, Crooked Mouth, said, "Man, I told you. We can't go in that house. This is where Eddie and Art live. We know them. I have known them all of my life. I can't go and fight with them with you vatos (guys)."

"Yeah, but ese, you said you were going to back us up here."

"Yeah, I know I said that; but that was before I knew we were talking about Eddie and Art. I told you I won't go into that house. I won't, ese!"

"Órale, don't come, ese; but we won't forget this."

"Hey, what can I say? That's the way it goes."

Back in the house Eddie called out, "All right, Art, ready? There's 2 of us and around 13 of them."

"Yeah, Ed, it doesn't matter if there's 13 or a 100 of them. It's all the same. The important thing is I'm here backing you up." It didn't matter because there were so many of them. We were going to lose if there were 13 or 100. I knew that only in the movies could one win against such odds.

From where we were in the living room, we could hear all the guys marching toward the house, like soldiers marching into battle. "Here we go," I said, voiceless.

The first guy to enter was the oldest of the brothers, Juan. He came in swinging a bat. Around and around it was flying in the living room. Eddie and I took shelter under the door frame leading to the hallway. The guy kept swinging the bat over his head toward us. He hit the walls a few times, trying to hit us; but he couldn't because he'ed make contact with the door structure. I knew there was no reason to try to rush him because he wasn't doing any damage to us.

Just at that moment I heard another car come to a sudden stop. From where I was standing, I saw my little brother Victor with his best friend Chris. Victor had made a steel cane for fights like this; he had it in his hand. They rushed into the house ready to fight. Eddie and I saw Victor run right into the waiting arms of Juan's brothers and their friends, standing behind their brother swinging the bat. Right away Victor started struggling with four guys. Chris was swinging, right, left, another right. Then he was tackled by a few guys and was on the ground with them on top of him. Victor was trying to hang onto his steel cane, swinging it every which way as the four other guys were struggling to take it away from him. Once they took it away from him, Victor kept right on swinging with his fist before being forced onto the ground.

"Man," I thought, "I have to get to Victor to help him!" However, Juan didn't tire of swinging the bat. Now Eddie and I knew we couldn't stay where we were. We had to find a way to tackle Juan as he swung his bat and give Victor and Chris the help they needed.

I was going to rush Juan, thinking that then we could get to the guys who had Victor and Chris. Victor's steel cane was now in his opponent's hand, as he was banging it on Victor's head. I yelled out, "That's it, man! I'm going to kill one of you!" One of the guys who was by Victor looked at me as I dashed away.

I took off running down the hallway, around to the washroom, and into the kichen that was on the other side of the living room. Part of the wall that separated the kitchen and the living room was a place where my mother sometimes put flowers or plants; it was about five feet high. Juan's brothers, who were now in the back corner, could only see half of my body. I yelled out. I yelled standing still where I was, "Hey, man, you guys better split or that's it! Someone is going to die!"

I meant that I was going to where Victor was, even if the bat was swinging! I knew if Juan turned his attention to me Eddie would rush him. I was going to help Victor if they liked it or not. Someone might die!

Juan and his brothers were only able to see the top half of my body because of the planter. They couldn't see the bottom half or see my hands. One of Juan's brothers heard me yell that someone was going to die. He thought I went to the back washroom to get a gun or a rifle and returned to take care of business.

One of the brothers yelled, "Carnal (Brother)! He has cohete (firecraker, slang for gun)!"

I didn't move. Heck, if they wanted to think I had a gun or a rifle, the better off I was. I looked at the guy who yelled and said, "That's it, man!"

"Carnal! Come on. Let's get out of here! He has a cohete and is going to use it! Come on, Carnal! I don't want any us to die here!"

All the others, the brothers and friends of Juan, backed to the door while Juan was still swinging the bat. I ran to where Victor was and was going to start fighting, but they were already on their way outside. They all ran to their cars, jumped in, and left.

We laid Victor down. He was bleeding from his head where they struck him with the steel cane.

In a few minutes the cops arrived and came to the door. We locked both the screen door and the outside door. The cops banged on the doorway. Eddie answered. He showed just his head and kept the screen door closed and locked. "Yes?"

"What happened here?"

"What do you mean what happened here?"

"You know all too well what I'm talking about. Open this door!" the cop insisted.

"Officer, do you have a warrant?"

"No, I don't need one! Let me in now!"

"You can't come in, officer. Everything is all right here."

The cop appeared frustrated. He wanted to come in; however, he knew if Eddie didn't want to let him in and he really didn't know what was happening, there was nothing he could do. The cops all talked outside for a little while. In a few minutes they left.

Victor was bleeding badly from the head; but Chris was doing OK, just a little beaten. We took Victor to the hospital. Eli's brothers took him to the hospital. In the next few days Eli almost died from his wounds.

I was really glad I didn't have to go to jail for any of this. This wasn't what I wanted. No one told the cops what really happened. Eli knew it was part of the neighborhood's unwritten rule that you do not tell the cops who did it. He probably made up a story about what happened.

When my mother arrived home, she was really upset about the mess in her house. She was upset because the living room was full of blood. When she found out about Victor being hospitalized, she really blew up! Of course she only received our side of the story with a few facts changed, but she believed it. It was all Eli's fault, and he was to blame for everything. She called her friend Sarah, the Lopez's mother and told her our side of the story. Sarah knew how to reach Juan, Eli's oldest brother.

Sarah called him and told him my mother was very upset that he went into her house with his friends and destroyed her home. She told him my mother was going to call the cops and put him in jail. It wasn't long before Eli's older brother Juan called my mother and told her he was really sorry. He pleaded with my mother not to call the cops on him. He told her that if she called the cops he would be taken away to jail for a few years. He explained to my mother that if this were to happen, there would be nobody to take care of his children. Juan told my mother that he would pay for any damage done to the house.

That is where the mess ended. I went home and didn't have to worry about anything. Victor's stitches came out the following week.

We never had problems with that family again. Tita didn't see Eli anymore. We heard that he almost didn't make it in the hospital, but he was back on the streets in a few weeks.

21 DONUTS AND MILK

One day Eddie came to my house. Yolanda called me from my bedroom to the living room. When I entered and saw Eddie, I greeted, "Hey, Ed, what's going on?"

"I came to show you my new van. It's really cool. They say there are going to be a lot of vans like this one later. The dealership said this is the first one that has ever been made."

"Oh yeah, a van? I see a lot of vans around." There were a lot of Dodge vans in the area, but most of the time companies used them for deliveries and other business. Not too many people had them for pleasure; the few who did had seats in them with windows surrounding the van.

"Yeah, come outside and look at it," Eddie invited.

As we went out the door, I saw his new van. It was really cool, different. I said, "Man, look at that paint job! Looks psychedelic!" That was a word we used to mean cool, hip, nice.

"Yeah, wait till you see the inside."

He opened the doors. I had never seen anything like it. It had red carpet on the floor and on parts of the walls. It also had paneling on the inside. A cool, black chair, the kind you would find in a living room; a cooler that looked like a refrigerator; and a large sofa, also black, were part of the interior. It was fixed up with cup holders made of wood, really cool. This was something new, something different. People in general had never seen vehicles like Eddie's van. It was really something new.

"What is it called, just a van?"

"No, it's called a Busy Body."

"Cool, Ed."

"Yeah, let's go to the store to buy some beer, unless you have some."

"No, we can go and get some," I said as I stepped into his new Busy Body.

"No, not in here. Let's go in your car."

I thought it was cool he wanted to go in my old 1963 Chevy. It looked great but not as cool as his new van.

Once we were on our way, he looked around my car and asked, "Do you know why I wanted to come in your car?"

"No, why?"

"So I can appreciate my payments!" My car was older and his was cool and new.

Man, I felt bad. "You are cold blooded, Ed. Remind me never to go in my car again." We laughed.

As time passed, Yolanda was drinking more and more. I didn't like the friends she was associating with while I was at work. Every year we would go on vacation somewhere. On one trip I rented a trailer and had a really nice time. For that reason I rented one again for another vacation. I wanted to rent a trailer to have a lot of fun camping.

One time we went to Arizona camping. We went to Arizona only in the spring because we were not accustomed to the heat Arizona has in the summer. There was a nice river in the area we visited, allowing us to spend most of the day swimming. We camped for four nights and were planning on staying three more nights.

One evening Yolanda and I stayed up late, after we had put the boys to bed in the trailer. Yolanda was drinking wine. I had four beers and was feeling all right. She was already slurring her words a little. It was ten in the evening when I said something that made both of us start laughing. We were having a pleasant evening. When we stopped laughing, she looked at me with a serious expression, gazing at me for a second. She looked nice with her smile, but then her smile disappeared and an ugly expression overcame her face. She said, "There's something I have to tell you." Her expression changed again, and she appeared sad, as if what she was going say was something that would damage our marriage.

At that instant I knew what she was going say. It is an indescribable feeling a man has when he sees that expression in his wife's face and eyes. I knew what it was. I just knew! I stood up to change the subject. If it was what I thought, I didn't want to be told so far away from home. If it was what I imagined, what was I going to do about it in nowhere land?

"Hey, it's late. I want to get up early tomorrow. I don't want to sleep in late," I expressed.

"What's your hurry? I thought we were going to take it easy on this vacation," Yolanda expressed, wanting me to keep her company and keep her laughing.

I felt as if my heart was going to explode. I knew because of the way she had been acting at home, drinking too much. I just knew the tragedy that was going to take place.

"What should I do? Put more wood in the pit or let it burn down? I'm not going to stay up. I'm going to bed."

I couldn't bear to stay up with her if she had dreadful news she was going to give me, news that was going to change our lives.

"I don't know. I might stay up a little more, if that's OK with you," she said, as if she didn't know why I was acting strange. I wasn't acting strange as far as I was concerned; I just knew what was going to happen soon. I loved my family. Even though we had a rough marriage, I didn't want it to end in a bad way, a very bad way!

"All right, no problem. I'll throw some more wood in for you. I'll even stack more here next to the pit, so you can stay up as late as you want. And if your fire goes down, you can throw as much wood in as you want."

I went into the trailer, not wanting to stay up with the thoughts and feelings I was having. What if she was to tell me? What would I do? I didn't know, and I didn't want to take a chance to find out what it was.

It took me a long time to go to sleep. In an hour-and-a-half, Yolanda walked in and came to bed. I acted as if I were asleep, not wanting to talk, my mind racing. What was I going to do? How should I handle this right now? Am I going to lose my family, my boys? I loved them so much! What does all this mean? Later in the night I finally fell asleep.

The following morning I was up early. The sun had just come up, and I started putting everything away. The folding chairs and the bar-beque pit we brought were put away; I had to wash some of our things. I also put our fishing rods away. Everything was clean, just the way it was when we arrived. I sat on the picnic table waiting for everyone to awake, thinking about a lot of things. I wondered what she wanted to tell me. What was I going to do? I hoped I was wrong. If it were true, I didn't know how I was going to handle the news. I wanted to call someone and talk about it; however, I didn't have anyone to call with whom I could speak personally. There was my family, but I couldn't tell them such terrible news. It was too unthinkable.

In a little while I took a long walk, wondering where this change was going to take my life. "But it just couldn't be!" I thought. "It just can't be happening!"

I wondered why I was thinking this way, not even knowing if it was so. I was letting myself think too much. Yolanda and I had known each other for so long, ever since I was released from jail. I remembered back to when I first met her, at her house. I remembered what her father Juan told me about taking care of her and being good to her. I was really trying to do that. I just hoped what I was thinking wasn't so.

People were starting to get up and come out of their tents and motor-homes. I thought I should return to our campsite because my little boys were going to get up and want to do something. When I arrived, the trailer door opened and closed. I didn't see anyone. I went to the trailer and opened the door. "Jorjito, what are you doing?"

"Daddy, are we going now?"

"Why?"

"Because it looks like it."

"Maybe," I answered.

"My other son came to the door and said, "Daddy, I'm hungry."

"OK, Mijo, I'll get you something. Want a donut?"

"Mmm, yeah," Jorjito said. I stepped into the trailer and gave them both donuts and milk. Now they were happy.

"After you get done eating, do you want to go outside and play?"

"Yeah," David answered.

When they were done eating and drinking their milk, I changed their pajamas and put on their play clothes, taking them for a walk to give Yolanda time to get ready. When we returned, we sat on the picnic table and talked. I loved these little guys so much.

In an hour Yolanda opened the door to the trailer. "Hey, what's this? Everything is put away. What is this, are we leaving?"

"Yeah, we are."

"Why? I thought we were going to stay a few more nights, right?"

"Well, I remembered something I have to do back home. I forgot all about it," I answered. It was odd she didn't ask what it was. She just accepted it as fact.

In a little while when Yolanda was ready to leave, I hooked up the trailer to the van; and we drove away. I drove all the way home without stopping. When the kids needed to use the bathroom, I pulled off the road. They used a portable toilet that I had in the van. When Yolanda and I needed to use the restroom, we stopped at the next rest area or gas station. It took twelve hours to drive straight home. I didn't want to stop because I wanted an answer to what Yolanda brought up at our campsite.

We arrived home in the morning at nine o'clock. On the way back Yolanda didn't talk much; neither did I. It seemed as if she knew why I was in a hurry to get back home. Once we arrived, she stepped out of the van and went inside the house. I started to unload everything we had taken. I had rented an Aristocrat trailer from Baker Rentals.

Once everything was unloaded, I washed the trailer really well, scrubbing the floors and even the walls. I wanted to get back my deposit, which was a lot. When everything was done, I unhooked the trailer from my van and unloaded the van. By the time the van and trailer were cleaned, it was noon. I went into the house and dialed Phil's number.

"Hello?"

"Hello, Mary?" At this time Phil had married a girl named Mary.

"Yes, it's me."

"Hey, this is Art. Is Phil there?"

"Hi, Art. Yeah, let me get him for you."

In a few seconds Phil came to the phone. "Hello?"

"Hey, what's up?"

"Hey, Art, are you back already? I thought you were going to be gone for a week?"

"Yeah, I was, but I came back early. I want to know if you can do me a favor."

"Sure, anything, if I can, that is." Even though Phil was married, he still liked to drink heavily. He definitely had a problem with drinking.

"I rented this trailer that I told you about. And if I don't call you back, can you take it back to Baker's Trailer Rental on Bascom Avenue?"

"Yeah, I know where that is. Sure. I have a ball for it somewhere around here. I'll look for it. If I can't find it, I'll stop and buy one." Phil was referring to the round ball that is put on the back of a vehicle to hook it to the trailer in order to pull it.

"You know what, Phil? I'll just take mine off and leave it on the trailer. If you need it, you can use it. Once you're done, keep it until the next time I see you."

"Sure, that sounds good. What do you have to do? I mean because you can't take it back yourself?"

"Hey, partner, I can't tell you. But it's something important."

"OK, Art, I won't ask. If I don't hear from you, I'll take care of it."

"OK, thanks. I'll leave the paperwork in the trailer, and I have a deposit coming back. Hold onto it for me. Next time I see you, I'll get it."

"Sounds good, Art."

"All right. Thanks, man. Later."

"No problem, later Art." We hung up the phones.

I went outside and removed the ball because I didn't know what was going to happen in the next few minutes. I was about to get the shocking news I was expecting but didn't want to hear.

My sons were in the living room playing as I entered the house. "Hey, you guys, why don't you go to your room or out in the back yard because I have to talk to your mother."

"OK, come on," Jorjito told his brother David.

Once they were gone, I called, "Yolanda, come in here."

"What?" she said from the kitchen.

"Come in here. I want to talk to you."

She entered the living room, cleaning her hands on a towel. She looked pretty. When I met her she was gorgeous. Was that beauty going to change now? Would I see her as ugly in a few minutes?

Trying to be calm, I requested, "Sit down for a minute. I want to ask you something." I could feel my voice shaking.

She sat on the love seat. "Yes?"

"When we were camping, on the last night, you said you had to talk to me about something. What is it?"

"What are you talking about? I don't know what you are talking about."

"You know, Yolanda. You know what I'm talking about. You have to tell me now. I have to know. I want to know."

"No, I don't remember. It must have been nothing. Is that why we came back? Just for that? I thought you came back for something important?"

"No, Yolanda, you know what I'm talking about. You have to tell me. I have to know. You have to tell me right now. It's my right to know now."

She sat for the longest time thinking, silent. Then in three long minutes she started to cry. "I don't know what to say."

"Just tell me. That's all. Just tell me."

"Oh," she said, still crying as she spoke, "I don't want to hurt you. I have loved you for a lot of years. I want everything to be right. I can't tell you."

"Yolanda, you have to tell me. You have to tell me right now."

She started to sob more and was holding back the words she needed to express. "OK, OK, I'll tell you. You are going to hate me for it. You'll never forgive me," she said, covering her face with the towel.

"Just tell me. Get it out, and it'll be over. You don't have to say anymore," I expressed. I wasn't going to let it go.

"OK, I'll tell you. I have a boyfriend, and I have been seeing him while you have been at work. I met him at the store."

"You what? You did what?" I shouted, not knowing how to act. I started to become angrier as the seconds were passing, not believing my wife was unfaithful. With my voice quivering as I started to cry, I continued, "You what? How could you? Why? Why would you do that?"

Crying, she answered, "I don't know. I just don't know. But I do know I have to tell you."

"But the boys, what are we going to do about the boys?"

She looked at me and declared, "If you leave me, the boys are staying with me."

I asked, "But . . ." I didn't know what to ask. There were many things I wanted to know. How could this happen? What was I going to do? My wife messed up on me! How could that be? Maybe I wasn't a good man because this terrible thing happened!

"Yolanda, I . . ." I started to cry more. "My wife! My wife! Oh, man! I can't believe it."

I felt that my manhood was taken away from me. Something bad had happened, and I didn't know how to handle it. "But . . ."

I felt like slapping her. I had never hit my wife and knew I never wanted to do it. However, this time I felt that I had a right to punch her out! I wanted to but couldn't and knew I couldn't stay in the house right then, or I might become violent. I stood and walked out the door, going to my van and stepping into it, starting the engine. I couldn't hold my tears back. As I started driving away, I saw my children standing at the front door. They must have heard us crying as we were talking.

I drove away not knowing where I was going. It was a very bad feeling knowing my wife had been unfaithful. It was unthinkable and just couldn't have happened. "My wife!" I thought.

I stopped not far from home and bought a half gallon of whiskey. Stepping back into the van, I started to drive. I took a large drink of my bottle and thought, "What in the heck happened? My wife, how? How could this have happened? I can't believe it!" I slapped the steering wheel and took another large drink, entering the freeway, beginning to drive north. I didn't care where I was going, just had to get as far away as I could.

As I was driving, my mind drifted and then came back to what had happened. I pulled over on the freeway and broke down again. I could not believe what had happened. I did this several times.

The next thing I knew I was hundreds of miles north of San Jose. My plans were to pull over and to get a room when I passed Redding; but I was so stoned, I went to the back of the van, did a lot of thinking and feeling sorry for myself, and fell asleep.

The following morning I awoke not knowing where I was. When I realized what had happened, I again broke down. I thought of my little boys. "What will happen to them?" I knew Yolanda wasn't like other mothers, loving their children and giving them a lot of attention. I knew that if I left she wasn't going to do a good job with them. In a few years my sons would end up in the streets and be in jail, just the way I grew up during my childhood. I didn't want this type of life for them. Now I cried for my little boys. I loved them so much; I didn't want to lose them.

I grabbed my bottle and took a drink, doing something to relieve the tremendous pain in my heart. I went to the front of the van and sat in the driver's seat, not knowing if I was close to Redding or had passed it. There were fields all around me. In the distance I saw a ranch house. I started the van and turned around, wondering where the freeway was. As I drove down the country road, I saw the freeway in a distance and looked for a sign that would tell me where the entrance heading south was located. I found it, entered the freeway, and drove.

I was just a little over the state line into Oregon. Once I passed the state line leaving Oregon, I started thinking again about my situation. What was happening could not be true. Maybe I was dreaming and was about to awake. If this were not a dream, surely this would be the hardest thing I would ever face in my life.

I took a big drink from my whiskey bottle. Half the bottle was gone. My family always had a high tolerance for liquor. I could drink a lot before I became drunk. Now that all this was happening, I didn't care how drunk I became. At that time I was one of those people who could drink a lot, and I wouldn't lose it. I was still able to drive all right. When I now think back to this time, I am glad I didn't crash into anyone and hurt others because of my grief.

By noon I was feeling the effects of the whiskey again. I thought to myself, "I'm a man, and I have to be strong! That is the way it is, and it's too bad things are turning out as they are!" But then I thought, "How could my wife do this? How? I can't tell anyone! I have to keep this to myself! How can I tell anyone that I wasn't man enough to keep my own wife?" I felt sorry for myself. With all this thinking I was hurting myself even more.

That night I do not know where I pulled off the freeway and parked. I wasn't looking for signs and didn't care what happened to me. I felt like dying rather then facing the situation. "What am I going to do? What do I have to do, not for myself, but for my boys? If I love them this much, what am I willing to give up for them?" I answered myself, "My manhood and stay with Yolanda for them!"

I knew I was experienced in life and that sometimes we have to give everything up for those we really love. I sure loved my boys. Before them I have to say I loved my wife. But now as the days, hours, minutes, and seconds were passing, my love for her was fading. My heart was deeply damaged because she had been unfaithful. Because I loved my boys so much, I was willing to give up my life and well being for them. I also cried for myself, knowing I was hurt and that I would always have to live with this. I wanted to release it all, so I wouldn't have to look back and suffer later.

As I was driving, I noticed a sign that said, "Mexican Border—15 miles." "Man, I'm here already!" I thought. I pulled over, still drinking my whiskey. I was done with the bottle and stopped to buy a new one but had no intention of going across the border. I wasn't on a vacation, merely taking a ride to decide what I was going to do with myself. On the third night, again, I pulled over and went to the back of the van to sleep. When I awoke in the morning, my stomach wasn't feeling well. I didn't care; I just washed the feeling in my stomach down with gulps of whiskey. In a little while the pain went away. The pain in my heart and the pain in my body didn't disappear. I drove north again, following the signs.

After the three days I wondered what I was going to do. I had to decide before going back, to stay or to leave without my sons. I took another large drink as I had the two previous days, trying to kill these childish thoughts of feeling sorry for myself. "I'm a man, and I'm going to act like a man!" I said in a low, strong voice.

I was really putting away the bottle I was drinking. I just could not help it; I felt this was too great of a crisis. I could not get through this experience without my mind and heart healer, liquor. This was a wrong thing to do. I should have used my faith in God, but instead I used liquor. I gave way to my imperfection.

At that time liquor served its purpose. It helped me think in a calm way. I felt I could have blown up and caused many problems for everyone. Then again, I was drinking too much, so much in the last three days that I went back to my original thoughts, "My wife messed up on me? What the heck! How can this be fixed? Why?"

"Art, get a hold of yourself!" I thought. I had to! A sign passed overhead. It said, "Sacramento—15 miles." I pulled over and fell sleep.

When I awoke, I thought about where I was and looked at my bottle. "Enough. That's it! I'm OK now! Man, I need a shower!" I started my van and began driving home. I was only two-and-a-half-hours from home.

I pulled into my driveway. The trailer was gone, so I knew Phil had taken care of business for me. He was all right. I stepped out of the van and into the house, not knowing what I was going to say. I had decided that for my boys' sake I was going to sacrifice myself and stay with Yolanda, although I didn't feel I could love her anymore. In fact, I knew I couldn't. Yolanda heard me in the house and came out of the bedroom to see who was there.

"You're home," she said when she saw me.

"Yeah, I am. Where are the boys?"

"They're out back playing."

I wanted to see them before I took a shower. I felt very distant from Yolanda as I was standing there. Everything had changed between us. I didn't want to know any details about what happened. In my heart I was going to remain in our home, but I wasn't going to be with her. I had given thought to when we met, how I grew to know her, and how I cared. It was all over now, all over.

I asked, "If I leave, can I take the boys?"

She appeared sad and answered, "No, I want you to stay. So no, they can't go."

The boys were happy to see me. When they saw me, they yelled, "Dad!" Both ran to me and gave me big hugs and kisses. They missed my reading to them and doing things with them. "Dada, are you going to go again?" the little one asked.

"No, I'm not going again. I'll be here for you, OK?"

"OK, Dada," he answered and went back to play.

I went into the house, where Yolanda had been in the living room. I thought I would try one more time and asked, "Are you sure you won't let me have the boys? You do know that you can't handle them, don't you?"

She stared at me, knowing I was right; but she knew I wouldn't leave without the boys. Yolanda answered, "No, they have to stay." She appeared as if she wanted me to take her in my arms; however, I just couldn't. I would never be able to embrace her with meaning as I had done before her affair. She would never be my honey again, never my babe, never my partner, never, ever! It was a sad day.

22 FREEDOM

e moved from the place where we lived to the eastside. During the next year I still felt a lot of grief and pain. I was a guy of few words. With great sadness everyday I thought about what had happened. It was still unbelievable. This was the kind of thing you only read about or watch on T.V.

Everyone at work knew something tragic had happened in my life because I changed so much. They wanted to know what was going on with me. What was changing? However, I only had a few words in response.

The girl in the office, whom I had known for years, asked, "Art, what's wrong? You're not the same laughing and joking guy I knew. Is there anything I can help with?"

"No, Sue, there isn't. I'll work it out, but thank you."

Three months after the fact, I was stopped by a good friend leaving the yard at work. "Hey, Art, I want to talk to you for a minute."

"Sure, Dave," I answered and stopped. We were standing outside the yard in front of the large cyclone fence. Behind the fence were eight Roll-off trucks in a straight line. One of the trucks was the one I drove.

"Hey, Art, everyone knows something happened to you. But no one knows what. The way you've been acting and the sad way you look, I can only guess what it could be."

"Yeah, Dave, I'll work it out. It might take some time, but I'll work it out."

"Well, I was talking to my wife about you. I told her that I was going to say this to you: I know whatever happened is really bad. It hurt you terribly. You are the kind of guy that God will take care of because you are good with everyone. Don't worry, Art. You're going to be like Job in the Bible. God is going to give you back ten times more than you have lost. I just know He will. You watch, five years from now you are going to look back at this time and remember what I told you. Sure enough, it's going to happen, you'll see."

I wondered if Dave was guessing right about what happened in my life. I wasn't going to tell him, but how did he know? I suppose the way I had been acting, he and other people presumed the worst and thought they knew what really happened.

"Think so, Dave? I don't know. Life is rough right now. I've been through a lot of things in my days, but I think this is the toughest time I ever had. I hope I make it through without doing anything stupid."

"Aw, Art, I know you won't. I have known you for a lot of years. I know God is going to take care of you. Just hang in there. My wife and I will pray for you."

"Thanks a lot, Dave. I got to go."

"OK, Art. I'll see you tomorrow. Take one step at a time. Remember that!"

As I walked away, I felt really bad that my marriage was in crisis and people could tell something was wrong with me. "Later, Dave. Thanks man!"

Everyday was torture. The only thing that brought good feelings to me was seeing my little boys. I would always be there for them when they needed me. I knew that later in life I would be finished raising them, and they would become individuals with their own minds and do what they wanted to do. However, I was going to do everything in my power to help them obtain a stable life. I had been reading the Bible for a few years, and I was going to teach them to have morals in their lives.

Many times during this period, I went to my mother's house, wanting her to help me with this crisis; however, I couldn't bring myself to tell her. My mother had started with heart problems at an early age. Many times I would go to her bedroom. As she lay in her bed, I would lie next to her. Even as an adult I rested my head next to her and hugged her. As I would rest next to her, I remained sad and quiet, thinking about my life and what had happened to my wife. My mother knew I could not tell her what had broken my heart. She would comb my hair with her hand.

"Mijo, I wish you would tell me what's wrong. I know it's something bad, but I have no idea what is it. I know you don't have to tell me; whatever it is, you can talk to me about it. I'll listen and tell you what I think."

I didn't comment right away. In a minute or so I answered, "OK,

Mom, I know you are here." I was more convinced then ever that I could not tell anyone. It was too embarrassing.

This scene repeated itself many times during this period of my life.

A few weeks later my mother decided to change her bank account. She wanted me to open an account in my name in order to deposit her money into it. It wasn't a problem with me. She said she would come to my house to pick me up to take care of the change. I was ready and waiting for her that day.

Yolanda was in the living room. I was in the kitchen when my mother drove into the driveway. I said, "There she is. I'll be back."

I stepped out of the house. Yolanda came to the door to wave to Mom. As I entered my mother's small car, she said, "Shouldn't we tell her to come, so she can sign also?"

I gazed at the front door where Yolanda was standing and thought, "No, Mom, you don't know the real Yolanda. She isn't the person you knew. She will be leaving soon, and your money will be in jeopardy."

"Mom," I answered, "no, it's OK. You don't need her signature. It's not important." I really meant that she was out of my life and would soon be out of my house.

As time went by, I remained in the same house as Yolanda. We continued doing the things we always did. Moving to the other side of town was a good decision; I couldn't live in the same place anymore.

As the months passed, Yolanda continued to go out with her friends. I really didn't care what she did. It was almost a year since she had confessed her unfaithfulness to me. She became very irritable with the boys and even told me she didn't think she loved them. I didn't know if it was something she was going through, or if it was really true. The way she treated them, it appeared she really didn't care for them as a mother should.

As the weekends continued, she would arrive home late at night. I didn't have any romantic feelings for her anymore and felt that living with her was a thorn in my life that I had to bear for the sake of my sons. I wasn't going to let them go only to have a hard life, as I did. I loved them too much.

Yolanda told me the boys irritated her. Because of that she couldn't take them with her when she went out with her friend.

My older son was a rough kid. Sometimes he would fight excessively with his younger brother; he was hard to handle. I thought his behavior might be occurring because of the manner Yolanda treated them. It is unnatural for a mother to feel this way with her children.

One Saturday night I waited for her. I was getting tired of her coming home at all hours of the night. On this night I waited until 3 a.m. I was sitting on a chair next to the door with all the lights off when I heard her drive up in her small Nova. She stepped into the house, closed the door, and removed her coat.

"Where you been?" I asked, calmly.

She turned on the light, looked at me, and asked sarcastically, "What are you doing? Waiting up for me?"

"What does it look like? Where were you?"

"What do you mean where was I? What do you care?"

"Yolanda, I don't want you to stay out so late. You still live with me, you know." I tried to talk as calmly as I could, not wishing to blow it and really mess everything up for myself.

She stepped to the chair where I was sitting and stood right in front of me. She stuck her finger in my face and demanded, "You don't tell me what I can do and what I can't do!"

I really felt as if I should stand and take a good hard swing at her, knocking her out! I really did. However, I thought of the consequences and realized that I would end up being the bad guy in all of this. I remained seated and asked, "You keep saying that one of these days you're leaving. When is that going to happen?"

"You want me to leave? I'll leave tomorrow if that's what you want!" she sarcastically said.

"What about the boys?" I asked, hoping she was going to say she didn't want them and that she would leave our children with me. The way she had been treating them lately, I couldn't see her wanting to keep them. I hoped her answer would be in my favor. I felt that if she was a good mother I wouldn't mind their being with her. Children, I feel, are always better off with their mother if the mother is good and dedicates herself to her children.

"I don't want them. You can have them! They are better off with you anyway!"

"Good. Then you can leave tomorrow!" I answered, really feeling rewarded.

For the last year it seemed as if there was light at the end of the tunnel. Now the tunnel had come to an end. A new life at last! I wanted her out of my life.

I told her that the following day she could leave. I would call my sister to pick up the boys. Or, she could leave them at Tita's house. I would pick them up after work.

"All right! Then, do you want me to leave?"

"Yeah, I do, if you are going to leave the kids."

She turned around and walked away, and I went to bed on the couch where I had been sleeping for a while.

The following morning I went into the boys' room and found them both in a deep sleep. They looked so peaceful, not knowing what I had been enduring for them for so long. I kissed them both; one of them turned over with my kiss.

I went to work feeling much better about my life, feeling this change was going to provide happier days for me. If Yolanda was going to leave, I was going to be a happy man. Lately I had been staying after work with some of the guys, drinking two or three beers because I didn't want to go home. I sure wasn't going to stay after work on this day!

I had called my sister Tita, told her part of the story, and let her know that Yolanda might be calling to leave the boys. She told me she had not heard anything from her as of yet.

I clocked out of work and drove home, hoping I would not find Yolanda, as if nothing had happened. I hoped she realized it was over between us. From this point forward it wasn't even thinkable that we could continue together in any form or fashion.

Pulling up into the driveway to my house and seeing her car in the driveway, I thought, "Oh, man! What the heck? I thought she was going to be gone!"

She was in the kitchen when I walked into the living room. I sat in the same chair as the night before when she was pointing her finger in my face, wanting to know why I was waiting for her.

She knew I was now home and was slamming dishes around as if she was really angry. I sat quietly for a few minutes. She peeked into the living room to see if I was there.

After a few minutes of thinking, I asked, "I thought you were going to leave today. What happened?"

She stepped into the entrance way of the kitchen and the living room. "What? You really want me to go? I thought you were saying that last night because you were drunk!"

"I wasn't drunk! I haven't had anything to drink for a while. You said you were leaving. Now I come home, and you're still here!"

"All right then. You do want me to go? All right, I will!" She turned around, departed into the kitchen, dialed a phone number, and said, "OK, I'm ready! Come and get me."

When she was done speaking, she slammed the phone down and stepped into the living room, making her way to her bedroom. I was still sitting in the same place. She exited her bedroom carrying a large suitcase, stepping by me and taking her suitcase outside. She returned for another one and placed it beside the first one. Once that was done, she grabbed her make-up bag and stepped into the restroom. By that time someone pulled in the driveway and honked. I didn't look out to see who it was. I really didn't care.

She walked through the living room carrying a large suitcase and returned twice for two other large boxes. She didn't look or speak to me as she walked back and forth. I could hear her talking and putting her things in the trunk; she stepped into the car and drove away, not telling the boys good-bye or anything.

I sat in my chair feeling very relieved. "Now I'm free!" I said in a low voice. A ton of bricks had been lifted from my back and my heart. I went to the back door and called the boys into the house, sitting them on the sofa. "Boys, I have to tell you something."

"What?"

"Your mother is gone. She left."

Jorjito answered, "Oh, we know."

"How did you know?"

"Because Mommy always tells us one day she is going to leave because she doesn't like us."

"She told you she doesn't like you?"

"No, but if she leaves, that's why."

"Come here. Sit on my lap, both of you."

They came and sat on my lap. I wondered if they knew what really happened. At the moment it didn't seem as if it mattered. In a minute they wanted to know if they could go back outside and play. I let them go.

I took the rest of the week off from work.

23 LOVE AT FIRST SIGHT

hat next Saturday I went to a picnic. I had a friend named Jim who invited me. The picnic was held outside of town, going south to Anderson Dam where the drain-off was at the dam, a nice creek. When water was released from the dam, it was a raging river. I took the boys, and they had a lot of fun. I now had this feeling of freedom and felt happy. We all had a nice day. I also had the opportunity to meet a few new friends. Some of the girls whom I met asked where my wife was. They thought I had a wife because I had two little boys.

"Oh, I don't have one right now. She left."

"I see. So do you have your boys for the weekend?"

"No, I have custody of them."

I really liked my new life. Although it had just started, I enjoyed coming home from work and not having to contend with a woman who didn't love me.

"Oh, that's nice. They look like two nice little boys." Once the girls knew I was alone, they became nicer; however, I wasn't interested in anyone at the time. I didn't want to be seeing anyone.

One evening I arrived home to find the telephone ringing as I stepped into the house. It was the neighbor I had on Emory Street, where I previously lived. She also had two young children the ages of my sons. "Hello," I answered.

"Hi, this is Loretta from Emory Street. I heard you are not with Yolanda anymore."

I thought, "Man, news travels fast."

I answered, "That's right. She left."

"Where did she go? Does she have a boyfriend she went to stay with?"

"I really don't know where she went. I haven't heard from her. All I know is that she left," I answered, trying to be polite. Loretta was always a nice neighbor. She was the kind of person who, if she baked a cake, would bring half of it to us, saying it was too much for her small family.

"I don't know if you know; but Mike also left me, about a month ago."

"Really, where did he go?" I had a feeling I knew why she was calling.

"He's living with his girlfriend. He comes by on the weekends to see the kids. But only for a little while. How are your boys?"

"Oh, they're doing really well. I think they are handling it really well." That is what I told everyone because that's what I really thought. As I became older, I found this wasn't true. Children are affected very much when a crisis occurs in their lives, such as a separation or divorce.

"I'm glad. Well, all the time I have known you, I've known you were a good father. I wished Mike was like you. Mike always drank too much. I know you heard us always fighting. That was because he always hit me and then hit my kids. They're too small to be hit." Her children were very small for their ages.

I answered, "That's too bad. I know. I would hear you guys fighting all the time. Hey, was that you who would always go out to the car, start it up, and hold the gas pedal down to the floor?"

She laughed, "Oh, yeah, that was me. I used to lock the doors, so he couldn't get into the car to stop me. I knew how much he loved his car, so I would try to blow it up!"

Man, I thought, "That's too bad."

"Did you ever blow it up? I used to look out the window and see sparks flying out of the back pipes."

"No, I never did. But if I knew then what I found out later, I would have set his car on fire!"

She changed the subject and asked, "Art, I was wondering if I can come over tomorrow? We can let the children play. I know they will enjoy it, and you and I can get to know each other better."

I was afraid she was going to ask something like that. She was lonely and wanted a boyfriend; but I wasn't ready for a relationship at this time, especially with a woman who might want to burn up my car if she became upset with me. I tried to think fast because I wanted to let her down easily. "Well, Loretta, tomorrow I'm busy. You know, these last few days I've been really busy with the boys. Tomorrow I have to wash clothes and get them ready for their babysitter."

"Oh, who is going to take care of them?" she asked, sounding as if she had something in mind.

"Right now I have my sister taking care of them. But I have another lady who will be watching them in the future."

"Oh, I can do that for you; and I won't even charge you. I would love to do that for you."

I didn't want to get involved with Loretta and knew if she took care of my boys it would put me in a bad situation. In time she would be cooking my meals as if I were her boyfriend. I didn't want that. "Oh, that's OK; I think I'll try this lady first. Thanks a lot. Hey, listen, I have to go. But it was nice talking to you."

"Oh, OK. I'll call you back again, and maybe we can do something."

"Sure, that will be fine; you can call me if you like. But Loretta, I have to be honest with you. I'm not ready to have a girlfriend. I don't know if that's what you're thinking. I would rather not get involved with anyone at this time," I said, not beating around the bush. I had learned how to be truthful and frank when it was necessary. I had to be that way sometimes and wasn't afraid to speak openly.

"Oh, I see. OK, but I'll still call you as a friend. Is that all right?"

Loretta wasn't my type of girl, but I told her I didn't mind.

The next two weeks I had a difficult time adjusting to all the work with so little time. However, I didn't mind that I had to clean house, wash clothes, iron, cook, and wash dishes. I had to do everything.

I called Yolanda's mother Sandy and told her I was sorry about what happened. She felt bad and told me she wished our problems would work themselves out in time. I told her maybe they might. No one knew what happened the year before and how that led to the situation we were in now. I knew our relationship would never work.

One evening there was a knock at the door, two guys from work. The guys who worked with me had a lot of respect for me because of the way I conducted myself.

I answered the door. John and Robert were standing there with bags in their arms. They both had two six packs of beer, "Hey man, come in."

"Art," John greeted, "we wanted to come over and give you some encouragement. We heard you were having a rough time, so we came to comfort you." Both of these guys were older guys. They were in their forties or fifties.

"Yeah, man, I appreciate that. Sit down," I said as I wiped my hands with a towel. The boys and I had just finished having dinner, and I had started to clean.

Robert pulled a six pack out of one of the bags. He gave one to John, took one for himself, and pulled another one for me, walking across the room to hand it to me. "Here you go, Art."

"Hey, I just have to tell you. I can't drink a beer right now, but you both can have one. Then you have to leave."

They both appeared surprised. "Oh, all right, buddy."

"Haven't you heard?"

Robert answered, "No, heard what?"

"Heard that a woman's work is never done!"

Both Robert and John laughed. John asked, "Is it true?"

"Heck, yeah, man, it's true. I still have to clean the kitchen, give the boys a bath, wash a few loads of clothes, and get the boys ready for their babysitter tomorrow morning. Yeah, a woman's work is never done. I know if I have a beer with you guys, that's it. Man, I won't get anything done."

They both looked at me and appeared to feel sympathetic. I felt that it was all worth it. I didn't mind doing all this for my sons. I loved them. If I had to stay up all night, then that's what I had to do.

The guys drank one beer each and said their good-byes.

The following day there was a knock at the door. It was Yolanda's father Juan. "Hey, Juan, what's up? Come on in. Have a seat."

He entered my house and sat down. "Hey, Art, what can I say. I'm really sorry things are going this way for you. I don't know what to say about my daughter leaving her kids."

"Yeah, Juan, I know, but. . . Hold on, let me get the boys." I stood and went to the back bedroom across from my bedroom.

"Hey, boys, come and say hi to your grandfather."

They both came running out and said hi to Juan, embracing him. In a few seconds Jorjito told David, "Come on! Let's go back and play."

"I don't want to. I want to stay here."

"No! Come on!"

The way Jorjito behaved, I knew in a minute we were going to have a big scene. "Jorjito, why don't you sit in here for a few minutes and listen to us."

"I don't want to. I want to go play."

"OK, you can play; but David wants to stay here for a little while."

"OK," Jorjito answered.

"So, Juan, how is work? How are you? What's new in your life?"

"Well, Art, things are not going too hot. Ever since my divorce, I have had a bad time trying to make it. But you know this booze doesn't help any. Are you drinking now that my mija left?"

"No, Juan. I don't have a problem with that. I can maintain. Hey, I have a lot to keep me busy," I said as I looked at David sitting there becoming bored.

"Daddy, can I go back with Jorjito?"

"Yeah, you can go. I didn't tell you that you had to be here. You wanted to stay here, remember?"

"Oh, yeah," he answered as he jumped off the sofa.

"Yeah, I know you have been drinking." I continued with Juan, "I never had a problem like you."

"You know Juan, if Yolanda could handle the boys, I would have let her have them. But she isn't that kind of mother."

"Yeah, I understand. I know you are a good guy, and you really tried to be a good man for her." As Juan stood he continued, "Well, I have to go. I just wanted to stop and see how you're doing. Art, if you need anything, just let me know. I'll help anyway I can."

"Thanks, Juan."

I called the boys, so they could say good-bye to their grandfather. It was a short but nice visit. Juan was all right. He just let the liquor take over his life. Liquor was cool to me at that time. However, one had to keep it in check.

Four weeks went by, and Yolanda called. "Hello," she greeted.

I knew her voice right away. "Hello?"

"Hi, it's me. How are you?"

She sounded as if she were a changed person, speaking very nicely, as if she were going to ask for something. "Yes, what can I help you with?" I asked harshly.

"I'm calling to see how you are. Is everything all right?"

I knew, I didn't want anything to do with her. She was trying to talk to me without asking how the boys were doing or anything. "What do you want? Do you want something?"

"Are you mad?" she asked, now sounding irritated.

"If I'm mad? Are you asking if I'm mad? Listen, I don't want you to call me anymore. I don't want to talk to you anymore, only if it's about our boys!" I hung up the phone, feeling upset that she called for me and not her sons. Why would she call me after all that had happened?

In two weeks she called again. The conversation was the same as the previous call. It went the same way.

Weeks turned into months. My life was a routine—working, washing, cleaning, and shopping. I was happy with my lot in life and knew one day things were going to change. However, I wanted to make my life as enjoyable as I could.

During this period I was invited to a lot of social gatherings. I usually accepted when it involved children, events such as dining, bowling, pizza, the park, the theater, and parties.

If there were woman at these gatherings and they became aware I was single, their form of communicating with me changed dramatically. They went from normal, friendly faces to flirty, batty eyes, complete with scheming smiles. Their eyes moved around in a curious way. I believe it's a natural response when one single person meets another. They blink a lot, and their eyes roll. Sometimes if a woman had children, as she expressed this body language, her children would run to her and interrupt our conversation. The mother, the woman who was flirting with me, would start to look toward the child. Her face would then change. The smile would disappear, a frown would appear, and she began to express a wicked look as she stared at her kid with a look that seemed to say, "Why are you bothering me? Can't you see I'm flirting? Now go back and play, or you are in trouble!"

The woman's face would start to glance up and, as if she were going through a transformation, she was then smiling and had goo-goo eyes by the time her eyes were back on me.

I would think, "Nope, you are off my list. If I were to pick you, someday you will look at me that way!"

There was a person I knew who had a friend who cleaned houses. A few months after I separated, I asked if she could ask her friend to clean my house once a week for half a day. The friend gave me Francis' phone number. I had known Francis previously. She was related to friends of mine, and I had seen her around. She said she had just lost a client and would be happy to clean my house, putting me down for Thursday morning. She started to work at my home the following week.

I had it all planned. She would come on Thursday mornings when I would be out of the house at work. When I arrived back from work with my sons, the house would be nice and clean. My plans, however, didn't work out as I thought. I would keep it clean through the weekend. On Monday it started to get a little messy. By Wednesday it was worse, with clothes all over, washed, but not ironed and not put away. By Thursday when she arrived, the house looked as if it had been hit by a nuclear device. It was a disaster!

After the first week she came and worked for ten hours but charged me for four. She stayed the extra time because she felt sorry for me. Even though she didn't know me well, she liked me, not in a romantic way but in a friendship way.

During this time my father came from Mexico to visit every six months or so; he would stay for four to six weeks. We all, my brothers and sister, nephews and nieces, got together a lot. We always had a good time.

One day my little brother Victor called me to say Dad was coming to visit, but he was going to go to Victor's house first. Victor asked me to join them at his house. Eddie was then married to Martha, his next-door sweetheart. We all loved Martha very much. Eddie and Martha would be there too. I told Victor I needed only to take a shower and would then leave to his place. He agreed.

Mona, Victor's wife, was a fun person. My father really liked her; he enjoyed joking with her. Mona was a playful fighter; that's what my father liked about her. On one of his visits, while all the women were cleaning up after dinner, my father ordered everyone else to do the work except Mona. He wanted her to sit next to where he was resting, so he could fight with her!

By the time my father arrived, I was there. We had a great time that evening. It was always nice visiting when he came to see us.

Dad took out the tequila from his suitcases and started to open the bottles. He always brought the best tequila from Mexico, the unadulterated, 100 percent agave, as it said on the bottle.

Dad asked how I was doing, if I had heard from Yolanda as of yet. He asked if I was hurting because she was gone. He felt I would be much happier if she were back with me.

I explained to him how everything was, telling him I didn't want her back. If she did call me, I didn't want to speak to her about us, only about our children. He listened as I told him how I felt. I didn't tell him she had another boyfriend nor what happened the previous year.

However, from what I told Dad, he could easily guess.

"OK, Mijo, I understand," Dad acknowledged as he took a puff of his cigarette. He was drinking Ancient Age whiskey, his favorite. "Good, good. I'm glad you are being a man."

I sure was glad Dad hadn't seen me when I broke down the day I found out about Yolanda and her boyfriend or that I had decided to live with her for a year for the sake of my boys. Dad never heard my version of what really happened. I didn't know how he would take it.

During the following week I went to see Dad twice for an hour because I was very busy. On Thursday when Francis, my cleaning lady, was done, she left an invitation to go to a small dinner for singles. It was at one of her friend's home.

Victor called on the phone, "Hey, big brother! How are you?" I was able to see Victor everyday because we worked together driving roll-off trucks.

"Yeah, Vic, how you doing? What time did you get into the yard today?"

"I got in right after you, around three. Dad asked if you were coming over today. He wanted you to be here."

"Tell him not today. I have a lot of things to do. I have a little washing to do and need to get caught up with some other things."

"OK, hold on. Let me tell him." I heard Victor tell Dad, and then I heard my father tell Victor what to tell me.

"Hey, Dad said not to worry about the clothes. They're not going anywhere. He said they will be there when you get back," Victor repeated as he laughed.

"No, I can't go today, Vic."

"All right, I'll tell him. Hey, do you want to come with us Saturday? I'm going to take Dad and Eddie to a shooting range. I'll take my guns and play around."

"Sure, what time?"

"Around one."

I had just remembered the dinner I was invited to attend. The dinner was at 4 p.m. I really wanted to be there because I wanted to meet new people. "Do you think we'll be back at your house by 4 o'clock?"

"That's about how long we will be there. Most of the times that I go, I actually don't shoot more than an hour. Why, do you have a date?"

"Well, it's not a date. I'm invited to a dinner with some people. The woman who cleans my house invited me, and I would like to go to meet new people."

"You mean to meet a girl?" Victor was joking.

I laughed, "Not really. Vic, you know I'm not in any hurry to find a girlfriend."

By this time I had told Victor what had happened, the whole story about Yolanda and me. Victor replied, "No, I know you are not looking for a girlfriend. Heck, big brother, if I were in your shoes, I would have a line of girls standing outside my door. Then I could take a different one out everyday," he said as he laughed.

"Yeah, but I have to think of my sons."

"Come on, big brother, I'm just kidding. You are too serious! Laugh. It's a joke!" he said, laughing again.

I also laughed, realizing Victor was right about my being too serious. I needed to lighten up. "OK, Victor, I know. I know. You're right. Hey, I'll be at your place on Saturday around noon. Sound good?"

"Sure, cool. I'll let Dad know that you won't be with us all day, that you have a date after!" We both laughed because I was taking it as a joke now. I told Victor to tell Dad I would come back to his place after dinner. We hung up.

The following Saturday I awoke the kids. We dressed and ate breakfast before going to Victor's house. Now, as a man, I always enjoyed Dad's company. I had a very difficult time growing up with him; however, as adults we got along very well. I grew to love him very much.

Dad was lying on the couch when I arrived. "Dad, how are you? Are you enjoying your visit?"

Dad looked at me and answered, "Oh, yes, Mijo, I'm fine. I always have a good time when I come here."

My father had a girlfriend in Mexico, who worked in a warehouse for the government. She managed medical supplies for doctors; she also sold these same supplies to my father for pennies on the dollar.

Dad traveled every few weeks to doctors' offices, doctors who lived in small towns. He sold his inventory at very low prices because the doctors worked in poor communities. Government prices were much too high. On a few occasions Dad came to San Jose and bought surgical supplies or whatever his customers used the most. He would keep paperwork with receipts, just in case he was ever caught by the government.

"I'm glad, Dad. Were you going to stay at my house?"

He knew I had a hard time with the kids, so he really didn't want to make it more difficult on me.

"No, Mijo, I think I'll stay here with your brother a few days, then stay with Eddie, and then at Tita's house."

I wasn't offended; I would rather he not come to my house. It would only make more work for me. I didn't have a wife to help me.

We talked and had appetizers, enjoying our time together. Victor told my father to be ready at 1 p.m. Victor knew we were leaving at 2, but he knew my father too well. He told Dad 1 p.m. because Dad liked to wait for the last second to get ready. He always made us wait on him, so Victor played it smart and said 1 p.m.

Eddie and Tita were also there. I had asked Dad how his business was doing. "Mijo, it's doing really good. I have my doctors who always buy from me. A few weeks ago I went to a hospital that is owned by the church. The person who I leave my supplies with told me they did not know if they were going to keep buying from me. He told me I had to talk to Mother Superior. I went into her office, and Mother Superior told me to have a seat next to her desk. She said, 'Well, Pepe, I do not think we can buy from you anymore.' I asked 'And why is that, Mother? Because a man came in last week, and he sold the same merchandise as you do; however, his prices were much lower than yours.'"

My father laughed, as if this was going to be really funny. "So I told her, 'Why, Mother, you know if that man has lower prices than I do, you know his merchandise is stolen! And I do not think the church wants you to buy stolen inventory that belonged to the government. I think I am going to talk to the priest about this!'"

"The nun sat there for only a second and replied, 'Yes, you are right, Pepe. We will only buy from you!'" We all laughed because we knew Dad's stuff was also stolen!

It was getting close to one o'clock, and we told Dad it was nearly time to leave. Dad remained lying on the sofa, looked at his watch, and said, "OK."

Victor had a Semi automatic rifle, and a 22 hand gun. Eddie had a .38 handgun. I didn't own a gun.

At 1:20 we left and arrived at the shooting range a little before 2 p.m. I had a great time with my brothers and father. It was fun seeing my father, who was all knowing, give everyone lessons on how to use a gun.

When we arrived back at Victor's house, I asked my sister if she could watch my boys for a while because I was going to a party. "What kind of party?"

Tita was glad to see me go out and do something besides stay home and take care of my sons. She agreed to watch the boys and told me not to worry about coming home early. She said if I was having a good time to stay as long as I wanted. I told her I really didn't want to stay very long. I didn't know if I knew the people who were going to be there. I didn't know the lady who cleaned my house very well. All I knew about her was from the notes she left telling me where she put things when she cleaned.

I left Victor's house and arrived at the party a half hour late. The house was on Arden Farms Place, off Senter Road. I parked and stepped out of my van, feeling a little nervous; I was going to a party where I didn't know anyone. I approached the front door. As I waited, I wondered who was going to answer, the person who lived in this nice home or one of the guests.

The door swung open. There was a beautiful, slender girl with long, black hair standing on the other side of the entrance. She was wearing a red sweater, black pants, and red high heels. She had a very nice smile and large, black eyes. I felt as if I had met her somewhere. Her smile grew larger, and her eyes shined. She greeted me, "Hi! You must be Art."

I was stunned. I didn't know what to say. Now, at this moment, I felt as if there was such a thing as "love at first sight." Her mannerism, as she was waiting for a reply, was stunning; she carried herself as the girl of my dreams would have. "Yes, Art Rodriguez. What's your name?"

"Flora Muñoz. Come in! Come on in!" she exclaimed. She sounded like a princess.

I stepped into the house. "Have we met before?" I asked.

"I don't know. I work as an x-ray tech. Sit down. Everyone is in the kitchen, but we can talk for a minute."

"Oh, and do you do that now, still?" I felt as if I was stumbling over my words.

"Yes," she answered as she giggled, knowing I was having a difficult time speaking. "But, I have been working for a private doctor for a few years now. I like it much better than working at a hospital or a clinic."

Gazing at her, I knew I could sit there all night, not saying a word and enjoying the feelings I was having being close to her. It was her beauty.

Someone stepped into the living room where we were. "Flora, I think the turkey should be done now."

Dan looked at me and greeted, "Hey, Art, how are you? Remember me?"

"Yeah, I do, Dan. Good to see you. How have you been? Good to see you here."

"Yeah, it's great to be here." I had seen Dan around a few times in the past. He knew people I knew. Dan was a good guy and wasn't a rough kind of person. He had been married, but I heard he was now divorced.

"Art, why don't we step into the kitchen. I'll introduce you to the others who are here," Flora invited me as she stood in the living room.

"Hey, that sounds like a good thing to do." I thought it was nice for her to stay in the living room alone with me to talk for a few minutes. She must have also liked me to do this. Maybe she felt the same way I did when she opened the front door, love at first sight.

I stepped into the kitchen and saw Francis, my house cleaner, "Hi, Art. Nice to see you!" she greeted, smiling as if she was happy to see me there.

"Yeah, same here. Hey, I want to thank you for all the work you do at my house. I know you're doing a lot more than I pay you for, and I really appreciate it. Thanks." Francis was a very pretty lady.

"Oh, you are welcome, Art. I do so much work because I feel sorry for you, and I know it's hard for you because you are taking care of your two little boys."

"Yeah, thanks." If she charged me what she should have for all the work, I would probably have had to pay her what I received in a week's salary!

Flora said, "Art, let me introduce you to Lydia, Virgie, Dan, and Jim. You know Francis and Danny."

I went down the line and shook everyone's hand. "Hello," I told them. They all greeted me in return.

Flora checked the turkey and asked Dan to take it from the oven; it was done. "Art, can you do something special for me?"

"Sure, if I can."

"I don't just ask anyone to do it. But you are so nice, I want you to do it."

"OK, what is it?"

"Cut the turkey for us."

I told her it wasn't a problem. She asked me if I knew how to cut the turkey. I told her it was easy. All you do is get the knife and move it back and forth. Everyone laughed and thought that was funny. I laughed, too, even though I was serious.

Once the turkey was carved, I as well as everyone else served ourselves. There were trays where the plates were placed. When I was ready to eat, I went into the living room and sat on a large love seat. Flora served herself and followed me into the living room. She sat next to me. We had a pleasant talk. I asked her who the children were whose pictures were on the wall. The living room had a television set, three lamps, a sofa, a love seat, and three bean bags.

"Oh, they are mine. That's Tito," she answered as she walked to the pictures and pointed to them. "He is my oldest. He's nine years old. That's Gina," she said as she pointed to each of the pictures. "She is seven years old. And my baby Lisi. She is my sweetie. She is three years old."

"They look like cute kids. Are they?"

Flora didn't understand what I asked. As she stepped back to where she had been sitting next to me, she asked, "Are they what?"

"Are they really cute?"

She laughed and answered, "Of course they are."

"Good," I answered. I have two boys, also."

"Yes. That's what Francis was telling me. How old are they?"

"Jorjito is seven and David is five years old."

Flora nodded her head and smiled. She looked so beautiful when she smiled. As I looked at her, I had the urge to grab her, to kiss her, and to give her a tight hug.

I wanted to get up to go to the kitchen to find more bread. However, I was so attracted to Flora that I didn't want to leave her side. As I sat next to her, I felt as if I were glowing. She gave me a very pleasant feeling, as if I were high on something.

"Maybe someday I can meet your children," I stated.

It seemed as if Flora was my date, and we planned being here together. I could feel a buzz between us, as if there were electricity connecting us together. In these few minutes I felt as if I had known her all my life, but I had just met her.

"Yeah, I would like to meet your little boys, also."

"Art, you're almost done with your food. Would you like to get more?"

"Well, I'll get it myself in a minute."

"No, let me get it for you! I'll be happy to get it." She stood and took my plate. "Would you like everything?"

"No, I'll just take a little meat and bread, dark meat."

"OK, I'll get it," she said as she stepped away.

Danny was sitting across from me. He asked, "Art, are you still working for the same company?"

"I haven't seen you for a long time, Danny; so I don't know what company you're talking about. Right now I work for a business driving a truck, picking up large dumpsters, American Waste Systems."

"Oh, yeah. You used to work for a company making fiberglass, but that's been a while."

"Yeah, I've been working at this place for a while now," I said as Flora came back with my plate. I looked up, smiled and said, "Thank you, Flora."

She returned the smiled and answered, "You're welcome, Art."

I liked the way she said my name. She said it in a caring kind of way.

"Oh, I think I remember something about a garbage company. Someone was murdered or something."

"Yeah, it's true. Would you like to hear the story?"

Danny sat up, "Yeah, I would."

I looked at Flora and then the others, "I mean, I don't want to bore anyone with a story. But if you want me to tell you, I can. It'll only take a few minutes to tell it."

Flora smiled as if she was going to enjoy the story. "Yes, I'd like to hear it." Everyone else also agreed to listen. I told them it wasn't a love story, but it was one that really happened. They were all eager to hear my story, so I told it.

24 BANG

Montana was a thin Portuguese man with a long face. Even though he inherited his garbage business from his family, he built it to accommodate the growing businesses in the surrounding areas. He worked in the same business with his great grandfather when he was a boy. In those days they used horses and wagons. The old man looked as if he lived in the streets. He wore oil-stained clothes and heavy work boots; his shirts were never tucked. Even though he appeared this way, he always carried a wad of cash of $100 bills and didn't care who saw it. He liked wearing baseball caps, most of the time with no logos. He shaved only once a week. Although he was a very scroungy looking man, he was very generous and kind to people who didn't have much.

He and his friend Sam, who was better dressed than Montana, went on a fishing trip to Baja California in Mexico. Sam was bald and had a round face and round body. His cheeks were always blushed pink. Sam was Italian.

The weather was warm. They had been on the gulf beach for two days. Both days had been hot and clear. One could see the mountain scape clear across to the other side of the Gulf of Cortés. There was no wind as the two friends sat on buckets with their large surf fishing poles cast far into the water. They were bringing in a large fish every few hours. To them, sitting and doing nothing but waiting patiently for the fish to drift past their hooks was enjoyable. They sipped on their cheap wine. It was the wine Montana grew up drinking.

They arrived at a location only thirty miles from Guaymas, Mexico, in Montana's new Ford truck. The truck pulled his old, small trailer. The trailer appeared as if it had been lived in and had never been washed. The inside didn't appear any better than the outside.

The sand was as white as snow. In both directions from where they sat, there wasn't a person on the beach as far as they could see. The trailer and truck were parked a hundred yards from where they sat.

Along the back of the sandy beach, there were a few rows, six to eight feet high, of sand dunes. There were one-foot high plants around them. Where they parked the truck and trailer, there were no dunes for a hundred feet. Fifty feet behind the sand dunes was the two-lane highway. The desert appeared dry with an occasional cactus and other desert plants. Traveling this road, one could see the ocean as the sand dunes cleared every few hundred yards.

"Isn't this beautiful, Sam? I love this, just us and our vino!"

"Yeah, it is. I'm glad you asked me to come with you, Monty." Through the years Sam called Montana "Monty" for short. "I think this is the farthest south we have ever come."

"No, we were a few hundred miles south about fifteen years ago. Remember the señorita who wanted to take you to her room?" Montana replied as he laughed.

"Yeah, I do." Sam wanted to change the subject. He didn't want to remember that event. Montana teased him about it for a year. "I think this is the last bottle of vino we have. I know we have beer, but I don't think it's cold anymore."

"I'll make you a deal, Sammy. You go to the store this time, and I'll go next time," Montana suggested as he took a long gulp of his wine, hoping Sam would agree. He wasn't in the mood to go for a 20-mile drive. And he wasn't in the mood to find he would have no more wine in a few hours.

"Sure, that sounds like a deal, old man. I'll go this time. Do we need anything else?"

"I don't think so, just vino and ice. If you think of something on the way, go ahead and get it."

"All right, Monty," Sam said as he stretched his legs to stand from his homemade chair, the five-gallon bucket. "I'll be back, in about an hour. Catch one for me if you get yours next."

"No, that's not part of the deal. When you get back, you have to catch your own." Both laughed as Sam walked away.

Upon leaving, Sam went into the trailer to see if he needed any other supplies. He could not think of anything. He really could not think straight. The cheap wine was having it's effect. He stepped out of the trailer and into the truck, turning the key. The engine started. As he looked toward the road, he saw a taxi drive by and disappear behind the sand dunes. A thought crossed his mind. He wondered what a taxi was doing so far out in no man's land.

He drove out to the road and made a left down the two-lane highway. A quarter mile down from where their trailer was, parked on the opposite side of the highway was the taxi that had passed them. "He must have turned around and parked," Sam thought.

As Sam drove past the taxi, he slowed and saw both the driver and the passenger with their heads facing down, as if they were reading a map. The passenger was sitting in the back seat directly behind the driver. Sam didn't know what to think of it. He knew they should have looked up because there were not very many people in this area. "What are they doing, sleeping? No, they couldn't be asleep because they just drove by. This is the first sign of life they have seen for a few hours, and they didn't even look up at me. I wonder if I should go back and see if they need help."

As Sam was thinking about this, he put his foot on the brake but then released the pedal, thinking they were probably going to stop with Montana and ask for directions. He realized Montana would help them anyway he could. Sam released the brake and kept driving down the road.

Montana sat on his bucket as the small waves splashed on the shore. Just a few feet from where Montana sat, there were dead sea plants that were washed in by the waves with hundreds of little flies swarming over them. He could smell the saltwater and seaweed, loving it even though it stunk.

Montana looked back toward the trailer when he heard a car approach. The driver stopped, and a man stepped out of the cab. The passenger seemed motionless. Putting his wine bottle down next to him on the sand, Montana stood, wondering what they wanted. He started walking toward the taxi. In a few minutes Montana approached the driver.

The driver was a big man, well dressed. He wore a black suit without a tie. He was balding and appeared to be about fifty-five years old. He had a big round face, was clean shaven, and had a large nose. He wore wingtip shoes, very shiny, that looked odd for the desert. He had drops of sweat on his forehead but still wore his suit coat.

Montana asked, "What is it? Are you lost?"

The big man pulled a gun from the inside of his coat. Montana froze. "Hey, I don't want any trouble. What do you want?"

The man smiled. He said, "I didn't think I was going to find you alone. But I did. I have been waiting a few hours to make my move. Now that your friend left, it makes things a lot easier. Inside!" he demanded, moving his gun as if he was pointing to the trailer.

"What? What do you want, money?"

"I said, inside! Or I'll blow your head off!"

Montana's eyes scanned the road, hoping Sam forgot something and would return. He then looked at the man inside the taxi. It appeared as if he were the real taxi man.

"He's dead. He's not going to help you. Now inside! Or you're going to be just like him! Now, go!"

Montana stepped to the door of the trailer and opened it. He stepped inside the small trailer. The big man followed him. Montana took two steps inside to give the man room to enter.

"What is it? You want money?" Montana asked, willing to give him all he had.

Montana heard the big man squeeze into the small door of the trailer. The big man didn't answer.

BANG! Montana saw a bright light. Then everything went black.

"Wow, did that really happen, Art?" Danny asked.

Flora was wide-eyed as if she were in a trance.

"Yeah, it really happened. They killed the old man."

"Who do you think it was, Art?" Flora asked.

"Me? I know it was the mafia. There was a guy who hung around there all the time after the old man was murdered. His name was Joey. I think he had something to do with it. Don't get me wrong, he was a really cool guy."

Jim asked, "Does this guy Joey still work there?"

I laughed, "Does he work there? No, he never worked there, just hung around with the new owner. I heard he is there to look after things. When they opened the old man's will, they found that Montana's children didn't inherit anything; but Rick, the old foreman, the owner now, received everything. Yeah, the cops still come around asking questions to try to find out if there is any new information about the murder. When they ask me, I tell them that I had just started working there when all this happened."

Dan asked, "So you weren't there when he was murdered. You started around that time?"

"Well, what happened was I had a friend who worked there. His name is Leo, good guy. He told me to go to the office and ask for Rick, that Rick was the new owner and that he would talk to him before I went in. He wanted me to work there, so he would have one of his friends working there with him."

Flora asked, "So you went to the office right after they killed the real owner?"

"Yeah, one day I asked my boss at Owens Corning Fiberglass if it was all right if I left work early. My boss said it wasn't a problem. That's where I worked before working for the company where I now work.

Arriving at American Waste Systems at 2 p.m., I walked into the yard where all the trucks were parked. It appeared as if all the trucks were in their parking spots and as if the trucks were done for the day. "Man, these guys get off early," I thought.

I saw a mechanic working on a truck in the garage. "Excuse me, but I'm looking for Rick. Can you point me in the right direction?"

The mechanic was Latino. He had a dark complexion. He was standing next to the big garbage truck wearing dirty overalls and had a wrench in his hand. He was tall and had thick, black, shoulder-length hair. As he took a puff of his cigarette, he answered, exhaling smoke, "Over there," he pointed, "in the office trailer."

"Thanks, man," I replied as I started walking across the yard. The double wide office trailer had a six-foot wide redwood deck completely around it. On the side there was a window that opened with a counter on the outside as well as on the inside. A lady was sitting at her desk on the inside next to the window. It appeared as if the drivers deposited their day's paperwork through that window.

There was a new, black Cadillac and a new, blue Buick, along with a green Chevy pickup parked in front of the office.

I entered the trailer. It had nice, plush green carpet. The desks and furniture were made of oak. The lady who was sitting behind the window appeared older. She had red, short, curly hair and was very thin and frail looking.

She sat behind a desk next to the window with the counter that opened facing the door. She was talking on the telephone. I stood patiently as the lady was taking an order on the telephone for the delivery of a dumpster. She sounded harsh as she spoke to the customer. There were three other desks, that were not occupied. I looked around at the office. I could hear men talking in one of the back offices. I looked up at a picture of the company and the surrounding area that was shot from an airplane.

The older lady hung up the telephone. As I turned back around to face her, she asked, "May I help you?"

The conversation in the back office became a little louder. "Yes, I'm here to see Rick."

The woman seemed annoyed as she turned her head in the direction of the loud voices. She paused for a second then looked back at me.

The lady spoke rudely. "What is this about? Do you have an appointment?"

"Well, my friend Leo, who works here, said you needed a driver. He said Rick wanted me to come in today and talk to him."

The woman looked toward the back office again as the voices turned into yelling. "I think you'll have to wait a little. Would you like to have a seat?"

I looked around. I didn't see any chairs to sit on when I came into the trailer, only the ones behind the other desks. "Sure."

"There is a folding chair behind that file cabinet. You can take it out and sit on it; or you can come back later, whichever you prefer."

I really didn't want to come back another time. I felt if Rick didn't have time for me right then, I was going to forget about the job. The cranky old lady and the yelling in the back gave me the creeps. I reasoned that maybe I should wait for a little while. It might turn out to be a good job. "OK, I'll get the chair and wait."

I pulled the chair out and unfolded it. I sat next to the file cabinet, behind the grouchy woman. I asked, trying to be friendly, "How long have you worked here?"

"A long time!" she snapped. "Too long!"

"So you're not happy here?" I asked, reacting that way because of the tone in her answer.

She stopped writing, glared back at me over the rims of her glasses, and snapped again, "I did not say that!"

I thought I had better shut up. I knew the older lady wasn't going to be very friendly if I tried to continue the conversation.

The back office door flew open, and a man came out followed by another man. The first man was tall and thin, maybe forty years old. He looked as if he was Latino or Italian. He was wearing black slacks and a white shirt with no tie. His face was loaded with acne scars. As he walked through the office, he blew smoke upward from his cigarette. The second man was speaking as they were walking toward the front office where I was seated.

"He must be Rick," I thought. He appeared to be in his late fifties. He had one of those faces that looked as if it had been pushed in like a bulldog. He had short, curly hair, was thin, and was clean shaven. He appeared stressed.

Raising his arm, trying to be persuasive, and attempting to catch up, the man I thought was Rick said, "Look, I'm doing the best that I can. Tell him he is welcome to come and look at my books. I can't do any thing more than what I'm doing."

Both men were in the front now and heading toward the front door of the office. Neither man noticed me sitting by the file cabinet. The older lady stopped writing and looked up at her boss.

The man in his forties said, without turning around, "OK, I'll give him your message. I'll let you know what he says, but I can't promise you anything."

When the first man approached the front door, he opened it and stepped outside. Rick followed him out and closed the door behind him. As the door shut, the old lady shook her head disapprovingly, as if she was really disgusted.

I wanted to strike up another conversation with the old lady; however, I thought from her last response that it might be better not to say anything. I heard the two men conversing out by the cars. I stood to see what I could see from where I was standing. Rick was doing all the talking. He was trying to convince the other guy of something. Then the car's engine started, and he drove away.

I waited for Rick to re-enter the office. I stepped to one of the windows to see if Rick was still around the building. If Rick had also left, I was going to leave and not return. I didn't need to get a job where it seemed as if the people didn't get along with one another. I could see that Rick was still standing where the car had been parked. He lit a cigarette and stood on the same spot for a few seconds.

"Does that man work here?" I asked the older woman. I asked even though I knew she didn't like conversing, but I didn't care.

"No, he doesn't work here. But he might as well! He comes here almost every day as if he owns the place! Maybe Rick will be working for him someday!" she answered sarcastically.

I didn't reply, not knowing what in the heck she was referring. Whatever she meant, I knew she didn't like her boss Rick very much.

Outside Rick took another puff of his cigarette as he turned to return to the office. I moved away from the window. Rick stepped into the office and saw me. He had not realized someone was there when he exited the trailer. "Hello, do you need something?" Rick asked, surprised.

"Yes, my name is Art; and Leo told me you needed a driver. I told him I would come in and talk to you."

"Oh, yeah, Leo did speak to me about you. Come in."

We stepped into Rick's office at the back of the big mobile home. Rick's office had one large oak desk with a very nice huge oak table against the wall. There were two large, freestanding fancy lamps that made the office appear very attractive.

"Sit down," Rick invited, pointing to one of the two large comfortable, cushioned chairs in front of his desk.

"Thank you."

"Well, what makes you want to work for my firm?"

Before I answered, I recalled the story about Rick, and Montana. I remembered being told that Rick was a foreman for Montana, and Rick even drove the trucks himself in the past. But once Montana was killed in Mexico, and his will was opened, they found that Rick had inherited the company and the land. Montana had a son who was in his thirties and a daughter who was in her late twenties. Neither of them received anything in the will. Everyone thought it was strange the way things were finalized. I had heard someone say Rick contracted Montana's murder; however, no one really ever found out what really happened up to this point.

"Well, my friend works here; and he told me what a great job it is. I think he really likes it here. He called me and asked if I wanted a job, so I came down."

"Good. Leo is a good worker. He has been here for about five years. Have you ever driven a roll-off truck before?"

"No, but I'm sure it's not different than any other truck. I have driven bigger trucks than what you have here."

"Yes, but you know, roll-off trucks are not the same because you do not only have to know how to drive a truck but you also have to know how to pick up the dumpsters without dropping or tipping them over on someone's house or car."

"I'm sure I can handle it. I see Leo out on the road all the time. It looks like a piece of cake."

"Where do you work now?"

"I work at Owens Corning Fiberglass."

"OK, I'll try you out. You can try out tomorrow and go with Leo."

I didn't like that. I had a job already, and it paid my bills. Plus I could not just walk away from my old job without giving them a notice. "Well, you know, I'm working at Owens Corning Fiberglass like I said; and I have to give them a notice."

"How long of a notice?" Rick asked. Rick didn't care about my other job. He wanted me to start as soon as possible.

"I think two weeks will be fine."

"Give them one week and come here next Wednesday. I really can't wait for two weeks. I need a driver right away."

I thought it over and felt this would work. I wanted to get out of Owens Corning Fiberglass really badly. "OK, Rick, that'll be all right."

"Good!" Rick said as he stood. "I'll look forward to seeing you next Wednesday."

I also stood and shook Rick's hand thanking him for the job. "I'm sure I will like it."

25 HER LARGE, BLACK EYES

"So that's when I started to work there, right after the old man was killed in Mexico."

Flora commented, "Poor kids of his. You mean they didn't get anything from their father?"

Dan replied, "But then again, maybe they got paid off. You know, that's what they do sometimes."

"Oh yeah, or put a dead horse's head in their bed!" one of the other guys who was there said as he and Danny laughed. Their thoughts came from the movie, "The Godfather."

"Art, do you think Joey scared them?" Flora asked, worried and concerned about the old man's children.

"Joey? I don't know. I don't think it was Joey himself because Joey is really a cool guy. I got to know him pretty well, and he's just not that kind of person."

Just then I looked at my watch and said, "You know what? I have to get going now. My father is down from Mexico, and I told him I would return this evening to visit him some more.

"Oh man," Jim said, "just when we were really into the story!"

I stood and Flora did too. She looked at me and gave me that pleasant smile. I loved the way she looked at me with her large, black eyes.

"I'll walk you out, Art."

"That will be very nice. Thank you."

I said my good-byes to everyone and shook hands with the guys, telling them I would see them later and tell them more stories. They enjoyed having me there, and I was glad they did. Flora put on a sweater and opened the door, so we both could step outside. We stepped slowly down the walkway. The winter air had become chillier with the evening.

"Flora, I really enjoyed being at your house. You are a very beautiful girl, and you are so nice. I don't think I would have ever met anyone like you."

"Thank you, Art. What a sweet thing to say. I'm so happy you were able to come to the dinner. I think we were meant to meet each other this evening. I hope we can talk again."

"Sure we can. I'll call you."

When we arrived at my van in front of her house, I opened the door and reached for a pen and paper. "Let me have your phone number."

I wrote it down and put it in my shirt pocket. "Thank you, Flora. I will call you for sure in the next few days."

"Well, it will be very nice if you do. I'll be waiting for your call."

I felt like kissing her, but I knew that I didn't have to rush. I sensed she was going to be the woman with whom I was going to spend a lot of time. I felt a great happiness inside of me, a really special feeling that no one was going to change. It seemed as if I had known Flora all my life, although I'd just met her.

I reached for both of her hands and looked into her eyes, telling her she had the most stunning eyes I had ever seen. She liked the compliment and thanked me. I used to tell all the girls the same thing. However, as I said this to Flora, I knew I really meant it. She was the lady, the one for me, my soul mate.

"OK, Flora, I know I will call you and see more of you. I hope you don't get tired of my pestering you so much as time goes by."

She looked up at me and said, "I will never think you are pestering me. I will always enjoy your company."

"Don't forget you said that!" We both laughed.

I let go of her hands and stepped into my van, as she stayed on the sidewalk. I started the engine and pulled out of the parking space. Driving to the end of the court where I had to turn around and head out the other way. Flora was still standing in front of her house waving good-bye.

She was a very nice and attractive girl. As I turned the corner, she continued to wave to me. "Man," I thought, "she is still sanding outside smiling at me. How did she fall into my hands?" I really felt like going back and spending the rest of the evening with her. My father was going to be visiting in San Jose for a few more weeks, and I realized I'd be seeing a lot of him anyway. However, I had already said good-bye, and I knew this wasn't the last time. I was going to be seeing a lot of Flora and her children.

When I arrived back at Victor's house, Dad was there still drinking from his bottle. We spent the evening talking and telling stories, having a nice time. Dad was drinking his Ancient Age whiskey as we spoke.

By the time I was back, Dad seemed as if he knew more about what had happened between Yolanda and me. He commented, "Arturo, Yolanda is no good for you, Mijo. Let her go. She is no good!"

With that comment I was sure my brothers and Dad talked about me while I was gone. "I know, Dad. Don't worry. I don't even want to talk about her."

"And your sons?" he asked as he raised his chin, as if he was asking how they were handling it.

"Dad, my sons are great. They are getting what young kids get. I'm going to take good care of them. Later, I'll find a wife who will treat them as her own." When I said this, I wanted to announce that I had already found that girl, the girl of my dreams. I wanted them to know her and to see her the way I saw her. However, I didn't say anything about Flora. I was quiet, thinking of her.

That day turned out to be very nice. I enjoyed it. It was a day I will never forget. I loved every second of being next to Flora, my true love and my soul mate.

On Monday I saw Victor, and we stopped to have lunch. We both drove roll-off trucks and enjoyed our work. People noticed at work that everything was now going well for me. No one looked at me oddly any longer, as if they were trying to guess my situation.

That evening I was going to call Flora, but I lost her telephone number. I knew it was in my shirt pocket; however, somehow I had misplaced it. During the week I tried to call Francis to obtain it again but was unable to contact her. That Thursday, when Francis came to clean my house, I left her a note asking for Flora's phone number. Later in the evening the phone rang. "Hello?"

"Hi, Art?"

"Yes?"

"This is Francis. I received your message today at your house. I'm calling to give you Flora's phone number. I didn't have it when I was at your home." She gave me the number, and I thanked her for doing all the work in my house as she did every week. She said it was no problem. On this day she did a lot more than she usually did. She brought the first lady I knew, the one who referred Francis to me. With the two of them working, they finished a lot more cleaning. I thought, "Oh man! Someone else is looking at my ugly mess here!"

I thanked Francis and hung up the telephone. I dialed Flora's phone number. It was busy. I thought maybe it was Francis calling Flora to tell her I was given her phone number. I dialed again. It rang. "Hello?"

"Hi, Flora. This is Art."

"Hi there. I was wondering if you were ever going to call. How have you been?"

"I've been good. How about you? Have you been busy taking a lot of x-rays and taking care of your kids?"

"Oh, yeah, but that's life. My mother helps me a lot. I take my kids to school, and my mother picks them up for me. After work I pick them up. Mom cooks for us about every other day, so that makes it nice. My parents are good to me."

Our conversation went on for forty-five minutes. During that phone call I learned a lot about Flora and her children. I wanted to keep talking to her, knowing that I could easily spend another two or three hours on the phone. However, I didn't want to overdo it on our first call. We hung up; and I remained seated on the love seat in the living room, thinking about our conversation.

In two days I called her again, asking who was there. She said her children were home from school. I asked if I could come over to meet them, wanting to know them. I knew I was going to become someone important in their lives. I had my boys get ready, and we left to meet Flora's children.

I knocked at the front door. A young boy answered. "Come in," he said as he unlocked the screen door. He didn't say anything more and stepped back a few feet to watch T.V. Just at that moment as we were entering the house, Flora stepped in from the kitchen. "Hey!" she said as she bent down on one knee to greet David. "What's your name? I bet it's David?" She gave him a hug. "And you must be Jorjito. How are you, Jorjito?"

"Fine," Jorjito answered. Both of the boys were shy. They didn't know what the big deal was. They expected just to meet someone, and this lady was making them into something special.

"So this is Tito. Hi Tito," I greeted as I took a step toward him.

Tito acted as if he wasn't paying attention. Flora said softly, "Tito, say hi back, Mijo. Don't be rude."

"Hi," Tito acknowledged, not seeming very enthused.

Just then a young girl stepped in to the room. I greeted, "Hi, you must be Gina."

She looked at me wondering who I was, since I knew her name. "Yes, I am. Hi."

"And my baby Lisi is taking a nap. It was a long day for her."

We sat on the sofa, and we talked for a while. Flora asked how long I had been alone. I told her, and she told me she had just received her final papers from her divorce. She said that her ex-husband still bothered her, but she didn't want any part of him, he was really a pest.

It was a relaxing evening. As we left, I told Flora I would call her the next day. I told her children good-bye, and she parted with my boys in a warm and friendly manner.

"Art, I'm sorry; but I can't walk you out to your car. I don't want to leave my children alone."

"That's all right. I wasn't expecting you to. I understand. I think I know where I parked my van." We both laughed.

As the weeks followed, Flora and I talked a lot on the phone. I saw her every few days. We had only known each other for a short time, but we were really getting to know each other's feelings, our likes, and our dislikes. We had so much more to learn about each other.

One day I called Flora and asked if she and her kids wanted to go with us to have pizza the following Saturday. She answered, "Sure, that'll be very nice. It'll be nice seeing you again."

"How was work today, Art?"

"Work was work. It was fun. I really enjoy my job. I work with my little brother."

"Oh, how many brothers and sisters do you have?"

"I have Eddie, my oldest brother; he is two years older than I am. Then I have Tita; her real name is Mildred. She is two years younger than I am. Then last but not least is my little brother Victor. He is four years younger than I."

"Do they all live in San Jose?"

"Yes, they do. I'm glad because if any of them were to move away, I would really miss them."

"Yeah, I bet. What does your older brother do? Drive a truck, too?"

"No, he works for a company that sells plumbing supplies to other businesses, mostly plumbers.

"What about your sister?"

"She takes care of her kids. Right now she has a boyfriend named Charlie. He's a good guy, and they are probably going to get married soon."

"That's nice."

"What about your family?" I asked, wanting to get to know her well.

"Well, my father works at a foundry, hard work. He's been doing that for a long time. My mother works for the cannery. She's been doing that ever since I was a little girl."

"I understand when ladies have been at the cannery that long, they work hard; I mean, they work as hard as a man."

"Yes, my poor mother. It is hard work. I worked at the cannery with her only one time. I couldn't take it and was there only two weeks," Flora said as she laughed.

"Well, some people have to do hard work. Their bodies can handle it, and some can't."

"What about brothers and sisters?"

"I am the oldest of my brothers and sisters. After me there is my sister Elise; we call her Lisi. She is six years younger than I am."

"Does she live in San Jose?"

"Yes. She's very nice and loves to go dancing. She has a son and takes good care of him, like a good mom should."

"That's nice. A lot of that comes from the way you were raised. Your mother must have done a good job with all of you."

"Yes, my mother did. I think it's easier with girls. My brothers get into more trouble. My father has a hard time with them. My mother was really good with all of us. She still is."

"After my sister Lisi, I have my brother Rick, who is three years younger than she, followed by Anthony, and then my youngest sister Suzie."

"Oh, so then there are five of you kids?"

"Yes, five of us. My brothers and sisters are still young, so they like doing young people things."

"Yeah, and we're stuck raising our kids!" We both laughed. I enjoyed hearing Flora's laugh.

"What about your other sister. How is she?"

"Which sister?"

"Your youngest,"

"Oh, that's Suzie. She is really a nice sister, smart. She's a young girl. We're so far apart in age, plus I am so busy with my kids that we don't get to do a lot together. I love her. One day I'll get to know her really well. And my brothers, well, they're my brothers, teenagers! My mom and dad have a lot on their hands. They like to do a lot of things. But I love them. They are my little brothers."

Flora changed the subject, "So you work for that garbage company, right?"

"Yeah, I do, American Waste Systems."

"How do you like it? What kind of job is it?"

"It's one of those jobs that's a lot of fun. I really look forward to going to work. Everyday is an adventure."

"That sounds like a great job. What about what you were telling us the other day, about that man getting murdered? Did they ever find out who did it?"

"I think they know who did it or had it done, but they can't prove it. The cops still come around to ask questions."

"Really, have they ever asked you?"

"Let me tell you a story about what happens all the time. This story happened a few months ago; however, it still occurs maybe once or twice a month."

"I was done with my route for the day. I parked my large roll-off truck and was turning in my paperwork at the office window when I saw Rick, the new owner of the company, and Ruben, one of his supervisors, trying to peek out the window at two men on the sidewalk. Joey, the guy I was telling you about, wasn't there."

Ruben was a supervisor at the company. He moved up from being a garbage man. When Rick took over the company, he wanted someone who could take his place, someone who would work with the employees and also be loyal to him.

Ruben and I had always gotten along well. As far as I was concerned, Ruben was one of the best supervisors for whom I had ever worked. He was the kind of man who always defended the workers, one time going so far as to quit his job and not return to work unless Rick hired back the man he had fired.

Ruben was Latino. He had old acne scars and was dark complected, appearing rough but really having a mild manner. He was a good guy. He had short, wavy, black hair; was 5'10; and was well built from all the years he carried a large garbage can on his back.

"Hey, Rick," I greeted. "Are those guys friends of yours?"

Rick turned and looked at me, not liking my comment. He answered, "No, not mine. Have you ever seen them around or talked to them before?"

"No, I never saw these guys around. Are they cops? They look like cops to me." When I was a kid, I had my problems with cops and didn't like them very well. Although I hadn't had problems with them for a long time, I still didn't care for them. I felt most of them considered themselves better than others. "Are you worried about their being out there?" I asked, jokingly.

Rick and Ruben both turned and looked at me. They didn't like my smart remarks.

The old lady, Judy, sitting at her desk, receiving my paperwork, moved her eyes up to mine with an expression as if she were saying, "What's wrong with you? Shut up!" Judy was a strange person, but I was always able to get on her good side. Judy became fond of me as the years passed. I picked up a dumpster that was from a flower shop. When I found fresh flowers, I would wrap them up and take them to Judy. She loved it. She thought I bought them for her.

Rick and Ruben were motionless as they looked out the window. I also turned to see what was getting all of their attention. Rick saw that the two detectives had stopped one of the garbage men. It seemed as if the conversation was intense. I saw their hands moving around wildly as if they were arguing.

Judy looked at me and asked, "Art, did this man on Walsh Street say he was going to come in and pay for his dumpsters? He was supposed to have a check for you."

"I don't know, Judy. He didn't tell me anything. I just had the worker sign my tag. If I would have known he was supposed to pay, I would have asked him for a check."

"Oh, that's all right. I'll take care of it. Thank you, Art."

"You're welcome, Judy. I'll see you tomorrow," I said as I turned to step away from the office; however, I stopped when I saw the two bosses still motionless, staring out the window.

"Hey, Rick, want me to tell them anything for you if they stop me?" I asked teasingly.

Rick turned and glared at me. He had an expression that could have killed. Ruben was standing behind Rick. He stared at me as if he were saying, "Don't say anything, man! This isn't funny! This isn't the time!"

"Later! See you tomorrow."

Only Ruben answered, "OK, Art, see you tomorrow."

As I started my walk toward the front gate, the two men let the other worker go and appeared as if they were waiting for me. As I passed the mechanic shop, one of the mechanics was standing behind one of the trucks in front of the shop, smoking a cigarette. He said as I walked by, "Be careful. They're waiting for you."

I stopped my walk and asked Raul, the mechanic, "Hey, what do you think those guys want to know now?"

The mechanic took a puff of his cigarette and answered jokingly, "They're cops, and they want to know if you robbed a bank."

"Yeah, right. I always rob banks. That's why I work here!"

"You'll see. But be careful," the mechanic said as he looked toward the office. He continued, "He's watching you. Don't say anything too loud, he might hear. He has good ears!" Of course Raul was kidding because the office was all the way at the back of the truck yard.

"All right, I'll let you know what they say," I replied as I continued my walk toward the front gate.

As I approached the men, I felt their eyes analyzing me. I have always had a bad feeling when I was around cops. Maybe it was because of my young days when I was frequently getting into trouble with the law.

"Hello, sir. You have a minute? We would like to ask you some questions."

"Yeah, I have time. What can I do for you?"

The taller one had a long, thin face and appeared to be in a pleasant mood. He took out a badge and showed it to me. I looked at it and replied, "OK, cops." I acknowledged as if I didn't already know.

"How are you today?"

I had my back toward the yard and the office. I knew Rick and Ruben were watching. I could feel their eyes on me.

The shorter cop asked, "We would like to know if you heard anything new about Montana's murder?"

"No, I didn't know Montana. That guy died before my time at this company. I'm just like you guys. I only heard about it."

"When did you start working here?" the taller cop asked.

"Right after he died. Why?"

"We wanted to know what you know about his death. What's the talk here about who killed him?"

"What do you mean?"

The shorter cop seemed a little annoyed and asked, "When you started working here, did you hear about how he was killed? And have you heard anything about who did it? From the men who work here, I mean?"

"No, not me. I only read about it in the newspapers, just like most people. No one here really talks about it. I thought this thing was over a long time ago."

"No it's not. We're still investigating. Do you know a man who comes here quite often by the name of Joey?"

"Joey, yeah, I know Joey. What has he done?"

"We didn't say he has done anything. We're just asking if you know him."

"Sure, I know Joey. Everybody here knows him. He's a really nice guy."

"Do you know if he had anything to do with the previous owner's murder?"

I smiled as if they were putting me on by asking me this question. "No, not me. I don't know anything!"

The taller cop appeared relieved because he was making progress. "What can you tell us about Joey? What does he do here? Is he on the payroll?"

I knew cops and knew how they were. I needed to be very careful with them. From experience I knew that a cop will very easily twist what is said into something you didn't say or you didn't mean. They will tell you it is confidential and then tell everyone you said it.

"I'm sorry, but I can't tell you anything about him."

"You know, you are responsible if you do not tell us and later we find out something. It might not go well for you," the shorter cop implied, sarcastically.

"What do you mean it might not go well for me? What are you saying? Who do you think you're talking to?" I asked, now feeling upset because the cop was trying to intimidate me.

The taller cop looked at his partner, as if he himself were annoyed with him. He said, "Sir, I'm sorry. He didn't mean anything. What's your name?"

"Art. Why? Am I under suspicion for something like he said?" I asked, raising my chin in the direction of the shorter officer.

"No, you are not under anything. That's OK. Thank you very much for stopping and speaking with us. We really appreciate it. I'm sorry if we upset you. We understand you just work here and have nothing to do with any of what happened," the taller cop expressed. The shorter cop looked upset and didn't say anything.

"No problem. I'll see you later," I answered as I started to walk away.

The nicer cop called out, "Hey, here is my card. If you hear of anything about the murder of Mr. Montana, please call us."

I took the card and didn't say anything. When I arrived at my car, I looked at the card. I didn't want the card and felt I wouldn't tell them anything even if I knew something about the old man's murder, which I didn't know.

As the months went by, I heard many rumors about the death of Montana and how Rick took over the company. I also heard how Joey and his friends helped Rick get things going after Montana's death.

Joey didn't stop by the company very much anymore. I later heard the company wasn't doing well and might even lose many of its contracts.

26 HONEYMOON

"That's what's still going on at my company, Flora."

"My gosh, it sounds like they are really trying to find out who did it. Do you think that man Joey did it?"

"No, Joey is a good guy. Everyone likes him. I know he wouldn't have anything to do with it. Joey is a cool guy."

I continued, "All the guys we work with are all good people. Everyone gets along. Every morning we stop at a coffee shop and spend an hour there for break."

"An hour? That's a long break."

"Well, what we do is combine all of our breaks and lunch together. We don't stop for the rest of the day. Everyone knows we stop there, even Rick, the owner. Sometimes when he's driving a truck, he will also stop."

"Really, he still drives a truck?"

"Yeah, but not very often. I think he goes out on a truck because it makes him feel good. When he does stop with us, we kind of cut our breaks short, to a half hour, and leave. You know how that is. We don't want to take any chances when he's there. But hey, it's all right because we don't stop the rest of the day. Besides, it's a lot of fun. I know if Rick was to find out we stop for an hour, he wouldn't mind as long as he knew the rest of the story."

"Like all business owners, all they see is the dollar. They say that the old man Montana used to go up to each truck every morning as they were leaving the yard and tell the driver, "Don't use the brakes! Every time you step on the brakes, it's a cup of coffee you are burning up!"

Flora laughed. She added, "He must have been crazy!"

I laughed and replied, "Yeah, I think he was. I think they all are!"

"You make the job sound like fun. I think I'll try to get a job there and drive next to you," Flora said as we both laughed.

We were on the phone for a long time. It was getting late. "Flora, I wish I had met you a long time ago."

"Really? Why?"

"So I would have someone to talk to every night. It's nice talking to you. You know you are my kind of girl, don't you?"

"Oh, that's sweet of you to say that, Art."

"It's true. I hope we can keep talking every evening till we fall asleep."

"Yeah, me too."

"Flora, what school did you go to?"

"I went to Andrew Hill. What about you?"

"Overfelt. Do you remember the busy signal?"

"No, what is that?"

"It was a busy signal on KLIV radio. I thought maybe you used to talk on there, on the phone."

"Oh, no. When I was young I was a school girl and a book worm. My father didn't let me talk on the phone very much. In fact, he didn't let me do very many things at all, like going out with guys and things like that. Only to school dances, games and to the movies."

"Yeah, sometimes that's really good. Your father was smart. Sometimes girls go out too much, and they start to change. They're not the same anymore."

Flora yawned and agreed with me.

"Flora, are you tired? We can hang up and talk again tomorrow. I don't mind."

"OK, if you don't mind. I can talk to you all night, but I am getting sleepy and have to go to work in the morning."

"Yeah, me too. It was really nice talking to you, Flora. I think I really care for you."

"Do you? I'm glad. I think I care for you, too."

"Oh, I wanted to ask, would you like to go for pizza on Friday night? We can take the kids and have fun."

"I'd love it, Art. Let's do that."

We said our good-byes and hung up the telephone. I lay in my bed before knocking out, thinking about Flora and how nice she was. I wondered how we would get along if we were to get married. With that last thought I fell asleep.

The following day I did what I had always done, took care of my boys and went to work. That Thursday I went to work and had another adventurous day. This is why I enjoyed my work so much.

My route on this day was in a business park where every building housed a different company. I drove my truck behind a sheet metal company to pick up a dumpster that was on my schedule.

When I drove behind the building, I saw a large machine out in the weather. I knew that if it stayed outside for a long period of time it would get ruined. Rust and other damage would start to take its toll. I didn't know the name of this piece of machinery, but it appeared as if it had been taken out of the shop a few weeks earlier. I took out my Polaroid camera that I carried in my truck for times like this and took a picture of it. I picked up the dumpster I was to haul away and took it to the landfill. In one hour I returned with the large, empty trash box and returned it to the location.

I left that company and went to another business two blocks away where my next pickup was scheduled. Next door to this building was another sheet metal shop, however, much smaller. I parked the truck in the street and walked to the large open bay door where people were working with the sheet metal inside the building. There was a guy who looked at me as if he was in charge. He stopped what he was doing and stepped out to meet me as I approached. He looked at my large roll-off truck and asked, "What can I do for you?"

"Hey, how are you?" I asked.

"I'm fine."

I took the picture out of my pocket, handed it to him, and asked, "Do you use this kind of machine in your business?"

"Yeah, we would if we had one. They are hard to find used. We can't afford a new one at this time; they cost thousands of dollars. We need a small one like this one," he said as he handed back the picture. He continued, "Are you selling this shear?"

I thought, "OK, now I know what it's called."

"Yeah, I wanted to sell this shear. Would you have a need for it if the price is right?"

"Oh yeah. What do you want for it?"

"What will you give me for it?"

"You better tell me that. You're the one selling it. Is it OK? I mean, does it work?"

"Let me find out. I'll be back in about one or two hours. I'll be back."

"OK, sounds good to me. I'll be waiting. We were looking to pick one up; but if you have a good price, you might have a sale for it."

I started to walk away, saying, "OK, I'll be back in a little while."

I walked away, jumped in my truck, and drove to the back of the building next door, to the building behind the one where I had been. I picked up the dumpster with my truck and drove to the landfill. When I returned to the track of businesses, I drove to the building where I took the picture, parked, and went into the office.

"May I help you," a girl asked who was sitting behind a counter.

"Yes. I would like to talk to someone in regards to the shear in the back of the building."

"Hold on," she said as she reached for the phone, dialed a number, and asked someone to come to the front.

In a minute someone opened the door and asked, "Can I help you?"

"Yeah, I was looking at the old shear you have in the back. Were you looking to get rid of it?"

"Yeah, we were. I hated to throw it away because it's still good. We just bought a nicer, new one. Do you want to buy it?"

"How much do you want for it? And does it work OK?"

"Sure it works OK. That's why it's not in the dumpster. If you want it, give me $500, haul it away, and it's a deal." I knew they were worth a lot of money, but I just wanted to make a little for the time being.

"Cool. Let me get back with you in about an hour."

The guy started to open the door to exit the office. "Just let me know, and it will be a deal."

I put the dumpster down in back of the building where I originally loaded it onto my truck. When I was done, I drove the truck out to the street and parked. I again stepped to the large bay door where I had earlier spoken to the guy. "Hey, how are you doing?"

"Good. What did you find out?"

"Well, here is what I got. This one," I stated as I took the picture out and showed it to him. "It has a price of $1,500, and it works. Nothing is wrong with it. You have to pick it up."

"Where is it?" he asked.

"Right here down the street, a few blocks away."

"I'll take it. What's the address?"

I didn't want to give him the address. He would then know where it was and go to the place to buy it himself, leaving me out of the picture. "You can give me a check. I'll go and pay for it, and then you can go and pick it up. If you need help picking it up, I can do it for you; but I'll charge you."

"No, we can do it. We have a fork lift and a truck. Let me get you a check." I told him to give me two checks. One made out to me with my name for $1,000 and the other for $500. I asked him to leave the section blank on the check that states, "Pay to the order of."

In a minute the guy had the two checks for me.

I told the guy I would get back with him and drove my truck to the other business. I paid for the shear and told him that someone was coming to pick up the machine. Then I returned to the other business and told that guy where to pick up the shear. He said he could kick himself in the behind because he knew the people and could have bought the shear a lot cheaper than my price.

Everything turned out fine for me. I was happy with the $1,000 profit I made without having to do very much work.

On the following night we were going to have pizza. I invited two other families, telling them I would pay. We met at the pizza parlor that next evening, Friday.

It was really nice seeing Flora again. As I drove into the parking lot, I spotted her as she and her children were stepping out of her car. I felt excited when I saw Flora. She had a cool black Duster. She had bought it new 7 years before this time. She thought it was a jewel behind the large glass window at the dealership. She still kept her Duster clean and shiny after all these years.

When she saw me as I drove up, our eyes met, she smiled very sweetly. I returned her smile. "Hi, Flora," I greeted as I parked next to her.

"Hi, Art. It's good seeing you," she answered as I turned off the engine and opened the door. I helped the boys out and turned to face her. As I looked into her eyes, I found myself wanting to get closer and wishing to kiss her; however, all the kids were standing around watching us. I didn't know if they noticed how dazed I was looking into her eyes. In a second I realized where I was and what we were doing.

I looked down at her children. "Hey, Tito," I greeted as I reached for his hand to shake it.

"Gina! Hi, little girl. How are you?"

She smiled as she stood there holding onto her coat. I reached to shake her hand also.

And Lisi, was the little one. "Hi Lisi," I expressed as I felt her little cheek. I wanted to get close to these children because I knew I was falling in love with their mother. This meant these children were going to be very special to me as my life progressed.

Flora smiled at Jorjito and David; she hugged both of them. They were a little shy at first, but in a few seconds all the kids were talking with one another. We entered the Straw Hat Pizza Parlor and walked to the tables by the large movie screen and the games.

"Hey, Art!"

I turned toward the voice calling me. I saw Roy and his wife Linda.

"Hey, Roy and Linda!"

Roy laughed and said, "You made it! I thought I was going to have to pay for our own food!"

"Roy and Linda, this is my girlfriend Flora."

Roy rose and extended his hand, "Hi, I'm Roy; and this is my wife Linda."

Flora smiled, "Nice to meet you. Art told me you were good friends of his."

"Yeah, we're old buddies. Sit down. Sit right here across from us. Those Cokes are for my kids, but it's OK. We'll move them to the next table."

"Are you sure, Roy? I mean, I don't want to kick your kids from their tables."

"No, no, don't worry about it. They don't care. Hey, what else can we ask for? You are already buying our pizza!" he exclaimed as he laughed. When I invited Roy, I told him I would pay.

I looked at Flora and asked where she wanted to sit. "Anywhere is OK," she replied, "Would you mind if we sat with Roy and Linda?"

"That's fine."

Roy and Linda were a step family. Linda had three children when she met Roy. Now with one son of their own, it tied the knot for Roy and Linda's step family.

Roy was a good father to his stepchildren. I admired him because good stepparents are hard to find. There are usually a lot of problems in step families. If one works at it, then it can be done. I knew if I married

Flora, this was the way I wanted my family to be, a good one. One of Roy and Linda's sons, Johnny, was a few years older than Flora's daughter Gina. Little did I know then that one day Johnny would be my son-in-law.

We ordered pizza for everyone, took our seats, and enjoyed our meal. It was nice talking to Flora. We spoke about our families and other things, really getting to know each other. I talked to her every night on the phone. Through all these times, we were able to get to know each other well.

On this pizza night when we were leaving, Flora and I were the last to go. I walked Flora and her children to her car. "Would you like to go out with me tomorrow?"

"Yes, that will be fun. Where do you want to go?"

"I think we could go out for dinner and then maybe dancing. What do you think?"

"Sure, I think that will be a lot of fun. I'll ask my mother if she can watch my children. I'm sure she will say she will. My mother has always been good with me in watching my kids."

When I arrived home, the phone was ringing. It was Flora. Again, we talked until late. The following evening I picked her up, and we went out for dinner and then dancing. It was very nice. She was really a lot of fun and great company. I loved every second I was with her and knew where we were heading. We dated like this for the next two months.

One night we were all at my home for dinner. Flora and I were sitting in the living room, talking. All the children were in the family room watching a movie. In my house one of the back bedrooms was turned into a very small family room. The window to that bedroom was taken out, and a sliding door was installed. On the other side of the sliding door was a patio where I had tables and chairs and a barbeque pit. The kids were watching a good movie while Flora and I were sitting on the sofa in the living room. The lights were dimmed, and we were getting a little light from the kitchen.

I gazed into Flora's eyes and said, "I want to tell you that I love you."

She was sitting close to me as I held both of her hands. I had already told her that I loved her a few times in the last few weeks, and she repeated that she felt the same. "What are we going to do about it, Art?" she asked.

"I want to marry you. Will you marry me?" I asked softy, not taking my eyes from of her. I brought her hands up to my lips and kissed them a few times.

She looked deep into my eyes and answered, "Yes, I will marry you. I will be happy to spend the rest of my life with you, Art."

I kissed her very gently on her lips and held her close, telling her I knew she was the one for me and that I knew this the first time I met her. She said she also knew. "How did you know?" she asked.

"I knew. I knew I felt the same way. I loved the way you smiled at me, the way you looked at me, and the way you talked. That day I knew you were the one for me."

"Really, why are we going through all of this when we could have been married the first day?" We both giggled. I held her tight and whispered in her ear, "I love you and will always treat you like a queen. To me that's what you will always be, a queen."

"Oh, Art, thank you. I love you, too. I know you'll be a good husband, and I know I will always be a good wife to you. I love you."

Still holding Flora closely, I said softy, "Flora, not only will I be a good husband to you, but I want you to know that your children will be my children. I will marry them when I marry you."

I could feel Flora squeeze me tighter. She felt delighted when I told her I cared about her children. I knew every woman wants the best for her children; and because I loved Flora so much, I would love hers as well.

Flora pulled away and looked at me. She stroked my hair back and said, "Thank you. Thank you for being so sweet. I love you."

We embraced for a while as we remained silent, meditating on what we had just told each other.

A few seconds went by, and I continued, "Flora, I'll do my very best to make you happy. I want us to be together until we leave this world. I know that if you're faithful to me I will always be here for you."

"Art, I will always be faithful to you. You never have to worry about that. Remember, I'm not her. I'm me."

Just hearing her say this made me feel good. For a few years I had feared the same thing would repeat itself as had happened with my first wife.

In a few minutes her baby Lisi stepped into the living room looking for her mommy. "Mommy?" she called.

Flora answered, "I'm right here, honey. Come here, baby. What's wrong?"

"I'm tired. I want to go mimi, Mommy."

"OK, lie here with me." Lisi climbed on the sofa and rested her head on Flora's lap.

I hadn't bought any rings for Flora at this point in time because I didn't know our relationship was going to become serious so quickly. That evening was a very nice and special evening. We all enjoyed it.

The next day Flora and I talked about marriage. We both went shopping for rings at Eastridge Mall in San Jose.

In the next few weeks, we planned our wedding. At first we wanted a big wedding; however, with such short notice in the San Jose area, we could not find a hall to rent. We decided to have the wedding in my back yard.

During the weeks before the wedding, we had a lot of fun. I took Flora and the children for rides in my van. When the children grew up, they said I would take them for rides and wait until they all fell asleep so that Flora and I could make out. Really, I waited to be alone so we could talk.

A month after my proposal, we married in my back yard. It was a small wedding, a few friends and family, but a very beautiful one. A minister officiated a very inspiring ceremony. As the minister was speaking, I turned and looked at Flora, I thought, "I know I will have a happy life being married to her." She looked very beautiful. I couldn't believe that I was actually marrying this woman. I was being blessed. I thought back to when David talked to me outside the gate at American. I remembered his words as if it was the day before. He was right. His words came true. I smiled.

After the ceremony we had a reception that lasted until the evening. Most there dressed nice for the event. We served Champaign and beer. No one drank too much. The important thing to us in our marriage was that we were truly happy. All five children were also happy for us. In fact, three weeks before we married, the children asked if it was all right if they started calling me "Dad." I told them it was fine, and I was happy with it. They could call me "Dad" anytime they wished.

We left the party and headed to our first stop, a reserved a room at the La Baron Hotel in San Jose. At the time it was a first-class place, almost new. We were given keys, and Flora had a bell boy carry our few items to our room. Once he was gone, we felt so happy that we were finally going to spend our first night together. It didn't bother us that inside the bathroom were cans of opened paint and brushes. We laughed because this room was being painted at the time we arrived.

I then opened the curtains to have a nice view of San Jose from the sixth floor. All we were able to see was a brick wall in front of us. If this had been any other time, it would have been very upsetting; however, we were so happy to be together that we didn't care. We had each other, and that was it. We had an extraordinarily graceful and romantic night.

The following morning we left San Jose for our honeymoon to Mendocino on the coast of California. The drive was magnificent. Everything was green, and the weather was mild. I know it was even more beautiful because I was with Flora.

We reserved a room at an inn, and we had the most incredible four days one could ever expect. We had no television in our room; however, we didn't complain. We didn't need one. We had a view of the Pacific Ocean from our room. Every meal we enjoyed with a view; but best of all, we had each other and knew it was going to last a lifetime.

On our return home the children were very happy that we were now going to be one family.

The Monday after our honeymoon, I returned to work. That afternoon when I returned home, I was really looking forward to seeing my new family.

"Flora!" I greeted my new bride as I took her into my arms and gave her the longest kiss. I really missed her that day. Flora appeared to be sad. I asked what was wrong. She told me the boys, Jorjito and Tito, had a big fight and that Jorjito told Tito I would never be his real father. Jorjito maintained that I was his father, and that was it. Jorjito told Tito I would always love my real sons and could never love them. Tito took this very seriously.

The children were all playing in the back yard. Tito was in his bedroom with the door closed. I called everyone into the house. When the kids heard my voice, they were really happy and ran inside. I also called Tito into the living room.

"Hi, Dad," each one of them greeted me, followed by a hug. I asked them all to have a seat because I wanted to talk to them. They obeyed my request.

"I want to tell all of you this. I want all of you to know that when I married Mom I married all of you. In my heart I married you Tito, Gina, and baby Lisi. David and Jorjito, I love you boys, as you know; but now I have more kids to love. You are all my children; I am adopting Tito, Gina, and Lisi into my heart. So you will be as if you really are my family. I'll treat all of you as my children. If you are well-behaved, you will be praised and treated the way you should be; and I will really appreciate it. If you act disobedient, then I will discipline you, just as if you were my children. Does everyone understand?"

They all agreed. They were all happy. "Jorjito and Tito, do the two of you understand?"

Tito responded, "I understand, Dad."

"Jorjito, do you understand?"

"Yeah, I understand."

From that day forward our family relationships were really nice and went well. We treated one another as if we had been together all along.

As time went by, we grew even happier. We did things together as a family, and I took care of my part of the marriage and did my best. Flora did the same. I shared my time with all of them and wanted them all to grow up to be good people to have a good life. I didn't want them to experience what I went through when I was a youngster. I told Flora I had to treat all the children right because they were going to grow up to become adults. They would remember everything I did, good as well as bad.

27 MAFIA STORIES

our years passed, and our marriage grew even stronger. Flora and I never fought. We got along all the time and were very happy. The kids grew fast. People who knew us never knew we were an step family. Being married to Flora was like day and night compared to being married to Yolanda. When I was married to Yolanda, I thought that was the way marriages were supposed to be, always fighting. That's the way I remembered my father and mother, always fighting.

I still worked at American Waste Systems. One day, after being employed at this company for six years, my friend Danny called me to ask if I was interested in buying a roll-off truck, the kind of truck I drove.

"Who's selling it?"

"These two brothers in Santa Rosa have a wrecking yard business and bought it to haul junk cars, but they found it's cheaper to have them hauled by a local hauler." Santa Rosa is about an hour-and-a-half drive from San Jose.

"What were they asking for the truck?" I asked. I didn't have plans to buy one. But if the deal was right, I could sell it and make a profit, as I had been doing for years.

"I think the guy I spoke to said he wanted around $10,000."

"How is the truck? Do you know?"

"Well, the guy told me it has a rebuilt engine, new tires, and new brakes. So it must be good. He also said the truck looked good. But you know how that can be. I think you'll have to look at it to see if you want it."

"Do you know if he has any dumpsters he wants to sell?"

"I don't know. I'll give you his phone number. You can ask him. If you want, I'll go with you to look at the truck. I don't mind going for a ride."

When I hung up with this friend, I called the number I was given in Santa Rosa. After a conversation with the owner of the truck, I knew that even if the truck didn't look as good as I was told, I still could sell it for at least $18,000. That would give me a $8,000 profit.

The owner of the truck also told me there were two dumpsters that were included with the truck.

I made arrangements to see the truck the next day. I bought it and drove it along with the dumpsters to San Jose, putting the smaller dumpsters inside the larger one.

I wasn't sure what I was going to do with the truck and dumpsters. I even considered starting my own business; but I knew if I did, it was going to be difficult. I was taking everything into consideration. My present job was secure, and I enjoyed it. Even though it paid well, it was still difficult to make ends meet. The cost of living in San Jose was and still is very expensive.

A few days after purchasing the truck, Rick, the owner of American Waste Systems, confronted me to ask if I was going to start a new business in the same area in which I worked. I was surprised Rick knew I had bought the truck. He didn't like competition.

During this time Rick was having a lot of problems with the drivers and the union. He had fired two men in the last week.

The following day after confronting me about the truck, Rick left the yard and instructed his secretary to give me my walking papers. I could not believe that I was fired for being in competition with American Waste Systems. I had not even started a business as of yet.

Since I was fired from American Waste Systems, I had no choice but to go ahead with a new business. I bought ten old dumpsters, as well as ten new ones that were very expensive. I placed an advertisement in the local newspaper for people who were cleaning their homes or remodeling. It wasn't long before business started to increase.

Things fell into place and Number "1" Disposal progressed well. My wife Flora and I enjoyed being in business, and most of the time we did well. As time went by, there were good months and bad months; however, overall, business went fairly well.

During the first two years of having my own business, we were not able to afford vacations. In time, we enjoyed our vacations and doing enjoyable things during the slow months of the year.

One year when our business was struggling, I received a phone call. "Hello, this is me."

"Hello, how are you, me?" I answered, playing around. For a second I didn't know who "me" was, but then I remembered that voice.

"Hey, Art! How are you, buddy?"

"Joey, is this you?" I recognized Joey's voice. It had a bit of a southern tone to it.

"Yeah, I was wondering how you were doing?"

I wished I had been doing much better during this time; however, in the last few months, things were not going well at all. The bills were not getting paid as they should. A new company had moved into the area. They were renting dumpsters for a lower rate, trying to put the smaller companies out of business. Because of this everyone else had to drop their prices, making it difficult for smaller companies such as ours. I had no idea business would be such a roller coaster and would take so much time for Flora and me. In a few months everything would be all right, but it was going to be a while before that time arrived. Flora and I had now accumulated a lot of debt.

"I'm OK, Joey. Things are coming together now," I answered, falsely.

"That's good, Art. Hey, can we meet to have lunch or something? I sure would like to talk to you."

I knew I had to be careful with Joey. I remembered the first time I saw him; it was the day I went to apply for the job at American Waste Systems. I remembered Rick following him and pleading with him about money. I never wanted to do that. I could not see myself begging anyone. However, I felt having lunch with Joey would not hurt. I just needed to be careful not to accept any money from him. If I did, then, "Who knows where that will go," I thought.

"Sure, Joey. What time and where?" I asked.

"Let's do it tomorrow. Are you really busy tomorrow?"

"Yeah, but that's OK. A guy has to eat, you know," I said laughing.

"OK, Art. That sounds like a winner."

"Hey, Joey, is there anything specific you want to talk about? You know, so I can be ready and think about it?"

"No, Art. I just wanted you to know that I'm with you and want to help you and your business in any way I can. I don't know if you know, but I really let Rick have it when he fired you. I told him I wanted to see you back at work. I don't know why he had it in for you. Well, I think it was the fighting he was doing with the union. There was no reason for it. The union told him the same thing. I just want to have lunch with you to let you know that if there is anything you ever need, you can just ask. I know a lot of people. Well, we can talk about it tomorrow. Where do you want to meet?"

"How about Denny's on Tully Road, right next to Highway 101?"

"It sounds like Denny's is where we're going to have lunch. OK, I'll see you tomorrow. About 12 noon?"

"Well, why don't we make it 11:00; so we can beat the crowd. You know how it gets at lunch."

"Yeah, tell me about it. All right, I'll see you there, buddy."

"OK, Joey, later," I answered. Both of us hung up the telephone.

I sat on my living room sofa and thought about the conversation I just had with Joey, thinking back to when I went to the office with the union rep after I had been fired. Once the meeting was over and I left with the union rep, Joey stepped out to talk to me by my car. Joey didn't care if we were being watched by Rick; Joey didn't care if Rick didn't like it. No one told Joey what to do.

I remembered Joey telling me that he wished me luck, as well as urging me to call if I ever needed anything. He handed me a business card and told me to call him if there were any favors I wanted to ask of him. After all those years I still carried his card in my wallet. I always thought I might call Joey if I was in a jam, and I really needed help. Then I would be able to see what Joey was really able to do. It was my ticket to get out of jail free!

"Art, who was that on the phone?" Flora asked as she stepped into the living room, wondering why I seemed as if I was in a trance.

"It was Joey. Remember Joey, the guy I told you about at American Waste?"

Flora sat on the sofa facing me. "What did he want?" Flora remembered my always telling her that I thought Joey was a gangster, that he was a wise guy in the mafia.

"He wants to meet with me. He said he wants to talk."

"Talk about what?" Flora asked, concerned.

"I don't know. He just said that he knows I'm having a hard time in business, and he wants to talk."

"How does he know that? We haven't told anyone."

"I don't know. Maybe he knows everyone who starts a business has a hard time."

"Just be careful, Art. You don't want to make any deals you'll regret later."

"I know. I sure don't want to have any of those troubles. We're having a difficult time keeping this business going as it is. If I only had more dumpsters, then we would have enough money coming in to make it. But with what we have, man, we're barely making it!" I said worriedly.

The business was growing; and, in turn, more dumpsters were required in order to pay business expenses. I wondered if I had more dumpsters if I would be able to place them. I wasn't placing all the dumpsters I had as it was, especially at this time of the year.

"Yeah honey, I know. But things will get better. They always do." Flora moved toward me and gave me a kiss. She held both of my hands. She didn't like to see me worry over business. If it were up to her, she would have liked to see me find a new job back when I was fired from American Waste. She felt if I went to work and received a payroll check every week, there would be no worries. However, I didn't want to do that. Even though I had a difficult time in business, I enjoyed it much better than if I had to work for someone else.

"Art, look at the good side of life. I love you, we're happy, and our kids are doing well. That's the important thing. As you know, we have seen our business do well and seen it do not so good. But we're still here and still in it. I know it'll be all right."

"Yeah, honey, I know you are right. But you know me, always worried about money. There are so many things we need to get for our home and for our company. If we only. . ." I said as I stopped and wondered where I could come up with money to get my business moving again.

Flora and I had already tried to get a business loan to purchase more dumpsters, but we were turned down.

The next day at 11:00 a.m., I parked my large truck in the back parking lot at Denny's Restaurant. I stepped off the truck and walked into the large glass doors hoping to see Joey at a table. Standing at the entrance of the place and looking both ways, I didn't see Joey anywhere. Five girls sat at a booth next to where I stood. They were noisy, laughing, and having a good time. A few tables down sat a young couple with their little girl sitting on a high chair. The child was crying as the mother tried to place food in her mouth. Farther down was an older, slender African-American man who had his coffee up to his lips, smelling the aroma.

I went out the glass doors and waited, standing there for a minute. Joey drove into the parking lot in a cool, black, new Buick.

Joey parked, stepped out of his car, and walked hurriedly toward me.

As he approached, he asked, "Hey, Art, were you waiting long?"

"No, I just got here. How are you?" I said as I opened the big glass door for Joey.

"I'm OK. Just running as always, trying to make deals here and there." I wondered what kind of deal Joey was going to offer me.

The waitress put two fingers up as she picked up two menus. I nodded my head and said, "Yes, two please." Joey and I followed her to our table.

We sat at a window booth next to the thin, black man. The waitress took our order while Joey and I spoke about how things were going for each of us. Then we spoke a little about American Waste. Shortly, our lunch arrived; we ate and talked about our families.

During this time people were filing in and filling the restaurant. Four men were seated across from us; two ladies were seated at the booth next to us. At the window booth behind Joey sat an older woman with a lady who seemed to be her aged mother. The restaurant was in full swing with the sounds of clinging and clapping dishware as well as the aromas of a coffee shop at lunch. The yells of the cooks letting the waitresses know their orders were up was also part of the background noises. I wondered when Joey was going to speak to me about his reason for meeting.

Joey reached for his napkin and wiped his mouth, pushing his empty plate to the side. "Well, Art, I wanted to talk to you about a deal we would like to make with you. Really, it's a deal you can't refuse. That's how good it is."

"OK, Joey, I'm all ears. But first, who is 'we'?"

A smile came across Joey's face. "You are the first one to ever ask me that. I think everyone else with whom I do business knows that answer even before I deal with them."

I thought about all the things I had heard about Joey. I had heard mafia stories but was never really sure if they were true. I felt it was none of my business to verify the stories.

I sat waiting for Joey's answer and knew I was now going to hear it firsthand. "Well, let me see, who are we? How can I say this? Art, you really don't know who 'we' are? I thought all you boys knew that."

I smiled and said, "I have heard things, Joey, but never knew if they were true and never really tried to find out because it was none of my business."

Joey was just preparing to answer, when the waitress came to the table and asked if we needed anything else. "No, we're fine, thank you." I answered. I looked at Joey and asked, "Is everything OK with you, Joey? Did you want anything else?"

"No, I'm fine, thank you."

The waitress placed the check on the table and stepped away.

"What kind of things did you hear, Art?" Joey wanted to know, paying close attention, wanting to know if negative rumors were going around about him and his organization.

"Well, first of all, this was a long time ago and to tell you the truth, you might not want to know what I heard. It's not too cool. Some things are OK, but not everything."

"Is that right? Like what?"

"Well, I heard about all the times you went into the office defending the guys at American. Everyone had only good things to say about you and how you helped them," I answered, wanting Joey to feel good.

"That's good, Art. I'm glad the guys appreciated it. I worked really hard at times for them. Sometimes your union shop steward Ochoa didn't do anything for the guys, and I didn't like that. I called him a few times to let him know how I felt."

"Yeah, I heard you did that. That was really cool of you to step in for the guys, Joey."

"Well, you know, I really like all the guys at American Waste. You said you heard some other things about us? Like what?"

I felt comfortable with Joey, so I didn't mind telling him. I also felt I was going to be able to hear if the stories others shared were true or not. "Well, I heard that you and your people had the old man in Mexico killed. I don't know if it's true, but that's just what I heard a long time ago."

Joey didn't like this comment very much. "Who said that? I don't know how those kinds of rumors get started. I would like to know who said that, Art. I really would."

"Well, Joey, I'll tell you this. Every time the cops came around to the yard, the guys liked you so much that no one ever told the cops anything about what they heard and what they knew."

A surprised expression came over Joey. "What do they know?"

"Do you really want me to tell you? I mean, I don't want you to feel bad or anything, Joey."

"Of course I want to hear, Art. I'm a big guy. I can handle it."

"Well, they know you are there all the time and tell Rick what to do and get on his case a lot. And they know that when you really get upset you make Rick do what you want. He doesn't like it, but he does it. Hey, Joey, did you have anything to do with the old man's murder?"

"No way, guy! Not me! My people and I don't do things like that. We're good people and always try to help with others' problems. I have helped Rick out a lot. My people are business people. We care about companies and try to do what we can to help them. We never hurt anyone we're trying to help. The only time we get upset is, and you know, any organization would get upset, if someone tries to burn us. You know, just like you. If you were to take a dumpster to someone and they give you a bad check, what are you going to do? Let it go or try to get your money? And if they just don't want to give you any money, what are you going to do? Go to the next step, right? Whatever that next step is going to be for you. You will have to decide, right?"

"Yeah, that's right. I'd probably drop the guy, man!" I answered, thinking how hard business was.

"Yeah, but you won't try to drop him if you know you can get your money through other ways, like going to court or dumping the box right there at his place, right?"

"Yeah, I guess that's true."

"Sure it is."

The waitress stepped up to the table, asking if Joey wanted more coffee and I another Coke. "No, we will be leaving in a minute," Joey answered.

Joey continued, "It's something like this. We do you favors, and you do us favors. And if someone tries to move in on you, we're there for you. That's the way we do business, Art."

As Joey was speaking, I was wondering what Joey had in his bag of deals for me.

"I understand, Joey. You're a businessman."

"That's right. And those cops who came around the yard at American Waste? They don't know jack, Art! They think they are onto something, but they don't know anything. If they did, they would have talked to my people or me; but they haven't. I don't know if you know how cops are, but they want to make something out of nothing. Hey, why would someone want to do a dumb thing like kill the old man in Mexico when it could be done right here? I know if I wanted to do someone in, I would just follow him and let him have it when no one was around. Wouldn't you?"

I thought about it and knew Joey had a good point. Why would they want to kill the old man in another country where you'll get more time in prison than you would here? "Yeah, you are right. I never thought of that."

"Hey, let me tell you why I wanted to meet with you, Art."

"Yeah, I've been wondering about that. What's up?"

Joey sat back in his chair as if he was relaxing and said, "Well, my people and I want to do a little business with you. We want to make you an offer you can't refuse."

I thought to myself, "I can't refuse? Oh yeah I can!"

"Yeah," I asked, waiting for the offer.

"How much do you charge right now for, let's say, for a 20-yard dumpster?"

"$330."

"OK. We want you to go and bid on some companies' trash needs. But we want you to bid $430. That's $100 more than you charge right now. We guarantee you will get the contracts, some for five years and some for one year."

"How do you know I will get them?"

"Because the people on the list we're going to give you owe us favors, and the contracts are already set up. All you have to do is go and bid on them. I don't care who else and how much other companies bid, you'll get the contract. Trust me."

If this were true, I wondered what I had to do and if I would be married to the mob for the rest of my life. "And what's in it for you, Joey?"

"OK, here is the way it works," Joey said as he sat up on his seat. "We have to make money, too. As I told you, we're businessmen and have to make money for you and for us. Some of the companies you bid on will have one dump a week. Others will want a dump everyday. When you charge $100 more for each dump, you keep $75 and kick back $25 cash to us. It's that simple. You make money, and we make money. Art, it's a deal you just can't turn down. To start off with, we will give you five accounts to work with. And if you can handle five, then we will give you five more."

"What if things change for me, and I have to raise the price?"

"You put that in your contract with the company. That's your part of the business deal. You have to take care of them. If you don't put that in the contract and your expenses go up, you aren't going to make any money. So you have to write some new contracts and state that if your dump fees, taxes, or anything goes up, dumpster prices go up. But you have to remember, Art, we're giving you a good deal. No matter what, we want our money. If the company goes out of business, then it's not your fault. You don't have a contract with them, and we won't have one with you. Or if the company starts to go under and they only have one dumpster a month, then that's OK. You don't have to pay us. The only time you have to pay us anything is when you make money. Then we make money. Doesn't that sound like a good deal?"

"Yeah, it does. Who are your bosses, Joey?"

"My bosses are in Chicago. They call me everyday, and I go see them every so often. Once in a while they come down here. They will be coming down in about a month. If we make a deal, I want you to meet them. I want you to know they are good people and will take care of you."

I was unsure what I should do. "What's the name of your company, or what does your company go by?" I was hoping he wasn't going to say the mafia.

"The name of our business is Financial Enterprise. But if you try to look us up, you won't find anything. We don't want people to be calling us, if you know what I mean." Joey studied my eyes to see my reaction.

I played the part as if everything was all right. I liked the deal and wanted to tell Flora to see what she thought about it.

"Hey, Art, you can't go wrong, buddy. I know. I work with other companies. They are all happy with our deals. The only thing we ask out of the ordinary is that when you pay us we want you to hide the payment. You know, like pay in cash. If you were in Chicago, then it would be all right to make the check out to our company. But not here. We had some problems in California, and they don't like us much. But you know how that is when you have problems with the law; they have you over a barrel!"

I wondered what Flora would say about this offer. I knew she might not like it, but I knew it sure would help us out with our financial crisis. Some months it seemed that our money just didn't stretch out enough.

"Well, what do you think, Art? Does it sound like a good deal, buddy."

"Yeah, it sounds like a good deal. I'm just thinking, that's all. I have to think about it for a while. I want to make sure I do the right thing. One problem I have is that I don't have enough dumpsters. If I place a dumpster with a company and they only get dumped once in a while, then I really lose out."

"Well, we can help there, too. We can get you dumpsters for a really low price. We will even ship them in from somewhere else for you. You can give us an IOU and pay us later when money is coming in. Like I said, Art, we're here to help."

"How much do you think the dumpsters will cost me?"

"It depends where we get them from. It could be $300 to $500 each. They might not look really good; but, hey, they are cheap dumpsters. You know, cheap as in price."

I knew those were really good prices. A new dumpster costs around $3,000. "Yeah, Joey, those are good prices."

"Art, we trust you; and we want you to trust us. You don't have to pay us right away. To us it's like having money in the bank. When things are going well for you with our deal, you can pay us then. Nothing in writing. Like I said, we trust you, Art," Joey's tone seemed sincere. He continued, "Hey, if you go with us, you are doing the right thing. How can you lose? You can't! It's a sure thing to make money. Like I said, you just have to make sure you put everything in your contract so that there are no misunderstandings with the other people."

I had to ask Flora what her thoughts were but didn't want to tell Joey. I didn't want Joey to think I was going to run home and ask for Flora's permission. Also, if things didn't work out right, I didn't want to put Flora in harm's way if it came to that.

We needed some kind of break in our business. The way things were going, we would have to shut the doors and call it quits soon. That meant I would have to go to work for someone else, and I sure didn't want to do that.

"Well, Joey, I need a little time to think about it. But it does sound good. And besides, I know I'll have some more questions before I say yes. I need a little time to think about those questions."

Joey took the check the waitress left on the table and started to stand. "That's fine, Art. Take your time and think about it. I'll meet you here again tomorrow, and we'll talk about it some more," Joey said as he looked at the check, took out $20, and placed it on the table along with the ticket.

As I stood, I thought the next day was a little too soon; however, I felt it best not to say anything. "What time?"

"Same time is cool with me, Art. If there's a problem, I'll call you."

During the rest of the day, I thought about what Joey and I had discussed. I felt it was a good deal and reasoned that this was the break I needed.

When I was done with my work for the day, I went home and was anticipating talking to Flora, seeing what she was going to say. I hoped she felt as I did.

When I stepped in the door of the house, Flora was there to greet me. She walked up to me and kissed me, putting her arms around my shoulders. "Art, I'm so glad you are home. I missed you, honey."

"I missed you too, Flora."

Just then Gina stepped into the kitchen from the family room. "Hi, Dad. How was your day?" Gina stepped over to give me a hug.

"Good, honey. How was your day? Are you doing well in school?" I asked. Gina was Flora's second child. She was a just 14 months younger than her brother Tito. She was a very bright girl and full of love.

"Yeah, it was good. And I'm trying to get good grades, but sometimes the work is really hard."

"Do you have homework?"

"Yeah," Gina answered as she walked into the kitchen and opened the refrigerator. "Yes, of course. I'm doing it in the family room right now."

"Art, I'm glad you are home," Flora said. "I wanted to go over some of the bills with you. I don't know what to pay with the money we have right now. Lately we just never seem to have enough money to pay everything we owe."

"First, how was your day?"

"I'm sorry, honey. I should wait till later to talk to you about this," Flora said as she took a step away from me, still holding my hand.

"No, that's OK. I don't mind. But first I want to know how your day was." Even though we spoke all day on the two-way radios, I still enjoyed asking her this question because I cared about her. She stepped up to me, put her arms around my neck, kissed me, and hugged me again. I squeezed her when I embraced her. She didn't release me for a few seconds. When she pulled away, she looked up at me and apologized again, "I'm sorry, honey, OK?"

I chuckled and answered, "That's OK. Don't worry about it. I don't mind. No big deal."

We both sat down on the living room sofa. "OK, my day. Let me think. OK, here it is. First I talked to you on the radio. Then I ate something and took care of Marina, changed her diaper. Then I talked to you again on the radio. Then I gave Marina a bath. Then I talked to you again.

Do you want me to keep going?" Marina was our first baby together.

I laughed and answered, "Sure. Why not? I like hearing about your day."

Flora raised her hand. With her index finger she tapped my nose. She asked, "What about your day? How did your meeting with Joey go?"

"Well, here is what he said and the deal he made me," I explained. I shared the entire meeting, almost word-for-word. Flora cut in periodically to ask a question. At times I knew the answer, and other times I guessed. Flora listened intently, not taking her pretty, large, black eyes from me. "Well, that's it. That's what he offered me."

We both sat quietly, not saying anything for a minute. Then I asked her what she thought. Flora didn't answer right away. She was in deep thought. "That doesn't sound like a bad deal. As long as it is like he said," Flora answered, thinking of the money we would eventually make on the deal. She continued, "If we go along with this offer, then we will need more dumpsters."

"We talked about that, too. He said he could get us dumpsters, and we can pay him later. Nice, huh?"

"Are you sure this is all on the up and up? I mean, it isn't illegal, is it?"

"The only part of it that might be illegal is the cash part. But I think we should claim it so we can't get into any trouble. We will just pay Joey the $25 out of our income. Then it won't be illegal because we will be paying taxes on it."

"Good."

"I think it's OK. I mean, we're not doing anything wrong by bidding, right? What they do on their end, well, that's up to them. They have to take the responsibility. Oh yeah, I forgot. It must be all right because he said his company has a name, and they are based in Chicago."

"Really? What's the name?"

"I can't remember. But I'll find out when we meet tomorrow."

"Tomorrow? Why are you meeting him tomorrow?"

"He told me to think about it, and we were going to meet tomorrow to see if I am going to go for it. He wanted to give me time to think about his proposal. He said so we can get things started right away. What do you think, Flora? Do you think we should go for it?"

"Well, I think it sounds kind of spooky. What if Joey is in the mafia? Then what will we do? Can we stop working with them if we want? Or will we be stuck with them?" Flora went into deep thought again for a few seconds. Then she continued, "Maybe we shouldn't do it. I don't want to get into a big dilemma that we can't get out of."

"But why? It sounds good to me. I think if we want to, we can get out of it as soon as the contracts end."

"But what if they kill us? Or throw us in the river?" Flora asked jokingly.

"We don't have a river here, remember?"

"Oh, yeah. But we have a creek!"

"So, what do you think? What should I tell Joey tomorrow? Should we go for it? I think it'll be a good deal."

"Yeah, I don't see anything wrong with it. I don't know why those companies would give us contracts. But if they are willing to do it and if Joey's people are giving them some kind of kickback, then that's their business, not ours."

"Good. So that means you think it's a good deal, and I should tell Joey we will do it?" I asked, hoping this was what Flora was saying. I was the kind of person who didn't let my wife tell me what to do; however, I always felt better when I received her approval. I usually did what she wanted anyway.

"I really think we need to give it some time to think about it, Art. If we do go for it, I hope everything works out fine for us and that later we don't find ourselves in so deep that we can't get out of it."

"I don't think so, Flora. Anyway, if I want to get out of it, I don't think they can make me do anything I don't want to do. I mean, what can they do? Break my legs or put a dead horse's head in my bed?" I said as I started to laugh. "Yeah, but I think you are right. I'll tell them we're going to wait on it. Maybe in a few weeks we'll see. If we're still in business by then!"

Gina stepped into the living room again. "Mom, what are we having for dinner? I'm hungry!"

Flora stood from the sofa and said, "I'm starting dinner right now. Come and help me make tacos."

"Tacos!" Gina repeated. "I love tacos!"

28 WHEN PEOPLE START TO DIE

The next day, at 11:10 a.m., I drove into the parking lot at Denny's Restaurant. Scanning the lot, I saw Joey's car parked in one of the spaces. As I drove my large truck through the parking lot, I found it was full and had to drive a half block away to find parking. I wondered why there were more cars than the previous day.

As I entered the restaurant, I saw Joey sitting at one of the booths with another man, a guy who looked familiar but, at the same time, I didn't think I had ever met. It was a weird feeling.

"Hey, Joey, how you doing? Were you waiting long?"

"Art! Good to see you, guy! No, we were not waiting long. We arrived a little early to discuss some things. Art, this is my business associate Eddie. Eddie, this is Art."

Eddie was balding and appeared fifty-five years or so. He had a big round face, was clean-shaven, and had a wide nose. He wore wingtip shoes, very shiny ones. He put his hand out to shake mine and moved slowly, displaying a wicked expression. "Hey, Art," he greeted with his strong and raspy voice. "I have heard only good things about you, buddy. Sit down. Sit down!"

It sounded and looked as if Eddie was a heavy smoker. His face was saggy, and he appeared as if he lived a hard life. I didn't know why; but when I saw Eddie, it made me think of the old man Montana and his murder.

"Hey, Eddie, nice to meet you," I greeted as I shook his hand.

Joey spoke up, "Sit down, Art. What do you want? Coke, coffee? A beer?"

"I'll have a Coke."

"Excuse me," Joey called to a waitress. "Can you get my friend a Coke?"

The waitress nodded and went for it.

"Art, I invited Eddie here because he is going to handle the loan for the dumpsters you asked for. Eddie is a really good guy to work with, and he'll take good care of you."

"Yeah, Art, I will. How much do you need? A mil? Half a mil? You name it, my friend; and you'll get it. Anything for you and Joey."

I couldn't help it. I had to laugh. I felt as if this was a script for a movie, and these guys were not for real. "No, I don't think so. I just want to get dumpsters. That's all. I wouldn't know what to do with that kind of money."

"Hey, spend it, kid. That's what you do with that kind of money," Eddie answered. "We don't give dumpsters away, you know. We lend you the cash, and you go find them and buy them," Eddie replied.

"Yeah, that's right, Art. All we do with our connections is help you out with money, and you do whatever you want to with it. Hey, you are going to make a lot of money on our deal. You will be able to pay that money back in no time. Then what Eddie will do is lend it out to someone else who needs it."

"I thought you said yesterday that you would get me dumpsters really cheap? Or did I hear wrong?" I asked, hoping I didn't misunderstand Joey.

"Yeah, that's right. What I will do is offer you our dumpsters. If you want them, you can buy them with the money Eddie is going to lend you. But, if you find dumpsters for a better price and in better condition, then you can do whatever you want. Some of our dumpsters are in really good shape, and others need a lot of work. But, hey, it's your money; and you can do whatever you want with it. The only thing we ask is that as soon as you receive the dumpsters, before you put them out, you paint them your colors right away. You know, we don't want you to have any problems with anyone who might try to claim them."

The waitress stepped up to the table and put a napkin down with my Coke. "Thank you," Joey told her. When she left, I took a drink of my Coke.

"These dumpsters aren't stolen, are they, Joey?"

Joey perked up as if he didn't like my question. "Heck no, Art! What do you think I am, a thief?" Eddie looked over at Joey as if he wanted to laugh. I could almost tell he was lying. Joey felt Eddie's eyes on him and felt as if he had better fix the story to make it look good.

Joey continued, "Well, it might be something like that, but not really.

You see, Art, we get the dumpsters from people who owe us and went bad on our business agreement. Like I said, we get our money one way or another. Just like our deal with you. You do your part, and we will do our part. We're getting the dumpsters from someone who didn't want to pay us our share; so if someone doesn't want to pay, we take it."

"What if he goes to the cops?" I asked, becoming a little worried.

Joey and Eddie looked at each other as if they were saying, "What's wrong with this guy?"

"Oh, no, Art. No one wants to go to the cops. That's when people start to die," Joey replied.

I didn't like his answer at all. I knew right there that this deal wasn't for me. "I see," I acknowledged in a very low voice.

"But don't worry, Art. That won't happen to our relationship. I know you well, and you know me. If for any reason you can't make your payment to Eddie, you make sure you let me know. We will work something out with you. We understand that everyone has problems, and we want to help anyway we can. We believe that if someone is having a hard time we have to help each other. You are going to like dealing with us. You are going to get rich, and so are we. Others in this valley have been working with us for years," Joey said as Eddie sat next to him, nodding his head in agreement.

"I don't know, Joey," I answered, not really wishing to go ahead with the deal; especially after hearing how they get their money if someone didn't pay.

Joey laughed as if it were funny. "All right, Art, here are five companies you are going to give bids on; and like I said, don't worry. You are guaranteed to get them." Joey took a paper out of his shirt pocket and slid it toward me. "When you get these all set up, we'll give you five more. We'll see how many you can handle. The more you can handle, the more we will give you. You don't even have to go and have contracts printed. Just do them on a typewriter or a computer; it doesn't matter. You can even write it out by hand. And if these companies don't like it, they can type it out or have it printed. When they have it ready, they'll call you; and you and they can sign the contracts. If you decide to go that way, make sure it's what you wrote on the contract you submitted. Don't let them change anything you wrote. If there are any problems you can't handle, just call me. I'll straighten it out."

"Well, Joey, I really have to think about this some more. I don't know if I want to do this."

Joey had a wicked smile come across his face, one that I had never seen. Eddie didn't say anything. He stared straight ahead, as if he didn't want to hear the bad news Joey was going to tell me. "What do you mean, Art? It's a done deal already. If you didn't want to do it, you should have told me yesterday when we met here."

I didn't like this at all. I didn't like being told what to do by anyone. "What do you mean, Joey? I didn't agree to anything. I told you yesterday that I was going to think about it. You said it was all right and that we were going to meet here again today to talk."

A half smile came across Joey's face again as he said, "No, I, we must have misunderstood each other. We were coming back here if you agreed you were going to go for it. And when you said you would meet again, I took that to mean you wanted to make a deal with my company."

"I'm sorry, Joey. There was a misunderstanding because I'm not going to go forward with your deal."

Now a small, wicked laugh accompanied Joey's half smile. "No, Art, it's too late to change your mind now. I already told my people in Chicago. Remember I told you that we don't do anything in writing? Well, the deal is done. We're business partners. Here are the contracts you are going to get. As I said earlier, you are not going to regret it. You are going to get rich with us, Art. Trust me, buddy."

"No, Joey, I'm sorry; but I'm not in business with you. Now, if you would have handled this right, you would have had me because that's what I came here to tell you. But now after this, I am not going along with it," I said as I stood. I wasn't going to let anyone tell me what I had to do or could not do. No one told me how to run my business.

People in the surrounding tables stopped eating and looked, knowing we were having a problem. We had their full attention. The noise level in this section of the restaurant dropped. Everyone was wondering what the argument involved.

"Wait, Art, don't go yet!" Joey exclaimed, rubbing his face. He didn't want the deal to fall apart.

"Hey, kid! Sit down!" Eddie demanded as he extended his arm, motioning with his hand for me to sit. Up to this point Eddie didn't say much. He stood. Now with a softer voice, Eddie repeated, "I said sit down, man! Be cool! All we want to do is talk!" I stopped moving away and looked at Eddie, as if I were saying, "Hey, if you want to fight with me, I'm here and I'm ready."

"Come on," Joey repeated. "Sit down. This isn't the way to go. Let's talk. We don't want this to end in a bad way. We haven't even started our business relationship yet, and look at the way it's turning out. We don't want this and neither do you, buddy. Come on. Sit down for a few more minutes."

I thought for a second, "I can sit and just be very careful with what I say." I know these guys have nothing over me. So I'll listen to what they have to say.

"All right, let's see if you have anything to change my mind," I stated as I sat down again.

Joey took a deep breath and continued, "Look, Art, let's try this and see how it works. If you don't like it later, we can sit down and talk about it again. It's not going to hurt. Look, you already said you would do it."

"I didn't say I would do it!"

"Yeah, you did! You said that's why you came here, to tell me you were going to go for the deal."

"Yeah, but I didn't commit to anything!" I said, feeling myself becoming upset again.

Eddie put his hand on the center of the table and said, almost in a whisper, knowing the people at the surrounding tables were now trying to listen, "Hey, hey! Let's talk like men. We don't want to be fighting with people who we're trying to make our business associates. We want to have good relationships with our people. That's what makes our business work. OK?" Eddie looked at both Joey and me. I wanted to tell Eddie I wasn't fighting with anyone, even though I was ready to fight. Eddie asked again, "All right? At least can we make that deal?"

Joey went first, "OK, I'm game."

"Well, we can talk; but that's all I'm doing today. Like I said, I really have to think this through," I said, trying to keep the peace.

"Good, Art, good! I'm glad you are seeing things a little better. You know why Joey is so pushed?"

"No, why?" I asked, lowering my voice. The people who were sitting around us went back to their eating and their own conversations.

"Because he will be in hot water with the boys back home if this deal doesn't go through. That's why."

Joey didn't say anything. He had a sad expression. I wondered if this was all an act.

"Back home, as in Chicago?"

"Yeah, back home. Joey made them think you were in. So as far as they are concerned, you are in. If you back out after you are in, then it's not going to go well for anyone. Not for Joey because they won't like that he came out with a bad deal again. Joey's last deal wasn't a good one. They'll be upset with me because I'm not doing my job, and I'm not keeping everyone happy. And they won't be happy with you, Art, because they will think you backed out of a signed contract."

"Hey, wait a minute. I didn't sign any contract."

"We know you didn't sign one; however, giving your word is as good as signing a document. That's the way they see it. Even though you didn't actually sign a paper, they feel you did because Joey told them. Let me tell you, Art, you don't want those people to be on your bad side."

"I'm not worried about them. "Them," heck, I don't even know who 'them' are. But 'them' don't scare me. I can handle anything 'them' throw at me," I said sarcastically, knowing that 'them' was probably Joey and Eddie.

"I don't know if you realize what they can do, Art. Just think if you found dumpsters all over town missing. They'll put them on trucks and haul them across the country, paint them right away, and no one will ever find them. It happens all the time. Really, these guys are bad people!"

"Hey, nobody better touch my dumpsters. I paid a lot of money for them. They cost me an arm and a leg."

"Tell me about it. That's why I say, you need to work with them so they don't knock you out of business. Hey, Art, no one can afford missing dumpsters!"

Dumpsters were easy prey. They had no license number or no markings to show ownership. Some companies put engravings on them, but they could easily be removed. I was fortunate that up to this point no one ever messed with my dumpsters.

"Like I said, I'm going to think about it some more. I don't want any trouble with anyone. If you guys want to offer me a good deal without trying to make me do something I don't want to do, then maybe I will go for it."

Eddie spoke, "All right, Art. We will be waiting to hear from you.

Take this list of companies and call them, or turn in one contract as we said. Then see how good it'll work for you. I'm telling you, guy, you will really like it. That's what makes businesses go, when businessmen have good connections; and their connections are the ones who take care of you and make your business work."

I looked down at the paper. I really didn't know if I should take it because it might make them think I was going for the deal. Eddie reached into his coat pocket and took out a black leather envelope. "Here, Art, look inside this."

I reached for it. Eddie and Joey were still sitting down. I opened the envelope and looked inside. I saw a lot of $100 bills and some $1,000 bills. Without moving my lips, I said to myself, "Wow."

"Art, I brought this so you can tell me how much you want to borrow. I was going to give you a few grand to start you off." Eddie paused and then continued, "You can take a few of those bills right now if you want. Maybe you have some bills you need to pay. Go ahead. Go for it."

I had to really think about this. I thought to myself, "These guys are not messing around; they really mean business. Man, I can't believe that after the way I talked to them they are still willing to do business with me and give me some of this cash."

Joey and Eddie both knew I was taking a long time to respond. They knew I was dreaming about what I could do with that much money. I really wanted to say OK right there, on the spot, but thought about what they said about people dying. I didn't want anything to happen to the love of my life, Flora and our children. I then said, "Look, if I go for your deal, I want you to understand that my wife and kids are left out of this. I don't want them to know anything about this. All right? I mean, I'm still going to think about it. But if I decide to go for it, I want to make sure my family is safe."

"Art," Eddie answered, "we don't ever do anything to hurt women and children. We will only do business with you. If for some reason things were not to go well, which I know they will, we will only come to you. Your family will always be respected and safe. And let me tell you this, the way our people in Chicago feel about things like this, if anything were to happen to you, they will find out how your family is doing and do what they can to help them. When you are with us, we will take care of you; and that's a promise!"

"OK, I'll call you and let you know. All right?" I asked, now feeling better about the deal. I was still holding the envelope and hated to give it back.

Eddie reached for the money. When I handed it to him, Eddie held it and asked, "Are you sure you don't want any right now? I mean, hey, you can have some now to go on vacation with your wife and kids."

I was really tempted but answered, "No, I don't think it'll be a good idea. I'll call you."

"Look, Art," Joey said. "Eddie, why don't you give Art $500 to show our good faith? Art, you don't have to pay us back the $500. Why don't you take your wife away for the weekend? We want to do this so you know we do care. I know the both of you will think of us when you are spending the money." Joey took the envelope from Eddie's hand and removed five $100 bills. I sat back down because I didn't want the people nearby to see me taking the money.

"Well, I better not. If I take money, I will feel I have to go with the deal. If I do go with it, then it won't be for the money you want to give me." I stood and was ready to go back to work.

Eddie and Joey rose from their seats. Eddie asked, "All right. When can we expect to hear from you? Tomorrow?"

"I don't know. Let me think about it. I'll let you know within a week."

"That long?" Joey asked. He appeared worried for himself. I thought he had possibly gotten himself into trouble with his friends, wherever they were.

"What can I say? I already said I will let you know in a week." I felt if they didn't like my decision, they would have to whack me (kill me). A week was the amount of the time I wanted to think about it.

Eddie extended his hand and said, "OK, Art, nice meeting you. And remember, we will be good partners for you. If you come with us, we will take care of you. I will be looking forward to meeting with you again."

"All right, Eddie, it was nice meeting you. I'll call Joey and let him know my answer. If I decide to decline the offer, I hope you and Joey don't take it personally; but that's life, man."

Eddie didn't say anything. He just shook his head and looked down at the table, as if he didn't want to tell me what would happen if I decided not to go for their deal.

"Art," Joey inserted, "hey, what about the list with those company names, so you can call them and see how easy it'll be?"

"No, Joey. I think I better not take it. If I were to try it, you might think I want to go ahead with the deal. I better not."

Joey looked as if someone took away his candy. He answered, "But you might like it. Take it."

I didn't want to answer him again; I had already told him I didn't want to accept the list. All I said was, "OK, later, man. I'll call you." I walked away and stepped out of the restaurant to my truck.

When I arrived home that evening, Flora came up to me and kissed me. "Well, what happened at your meeting with Joey?"

"It went well. I didn't give him my answer yet. But they know I'll call them next week and let them know what I decided." I didn't want to scare Flora with all the details.

"You said 'they'; who are 'they'?"

"Joey brought his friend; his name is Eddie. He's the guy who handles the money, the one who is going to give us money to buy more dumpsters and build up our business if we take the deal."

I went on to tell Flora most of the conversation I had with Joey and Eddie. I didn't tell her about stealing dumpsters or about people dying.

"What do you think, Art? Do you think it'll be all right? I mean, I don't want anything to happen to us."

"Well, for now, I don't think we'll go with the deal. I just don't think the time is right."

"Next time you meet them, I want to go to see what they're like," Flora requested.

"Well, I don't think that will be a good idea."

"Why not?"

"Well, I don't want you to get involved. I told them that this was between them and me. I told them to leave you and the kids completely out of anything we do. I don't want you to get hurt," I said, taking hold of her hand and squeezing it.

"Oh, I, I want to be involved with everything you do. Besides, it's my business, too."

"I know, Flora, honey; but I want you to trust me on this, just in case things don't go well for one reason or another. I want you and the kids to be safe."

Flora felt as if she was being left out of the business deal. She had a sad expression as she said, "I don't think we should get into it if there is a chance that things could go bad. I don't want anything to happen to you, Art."

"Nothing will. Trust me. All right?"

After a little more persuasion, Flora agreed.

"Flora, why don't we go away for the weekend? You and I only. I think we need it."

"That's nice. Where do you want to go?"

I think it'll be nice if we take off to Mendocino. It'll help us think about what we're going to do."

"That is so nice. All right. Let me call to see if they have a room available at the inn where we always stay."

Flora called and was told that the room we stayed in on our honeymoon was available. We were going to be upstairs in a room with two large windows with a view of the ocean. It was going to be the two of us and nothing else to distract us from each other.

Mendocino is a very nice town that sits on a bluff on the Pacific coast. Everything built in the city of Mendocino has an old look to it. There are many small shops, restaurants, and a lot of tourists. It has beautiful sights of the coast with the ocean's large, blue waves banging on the cliffs. The inn Flora and I reserved was one mile from the town of Mendocino.

Through the weekend I thought of Joey and Eddie. My mind was on the move. I was considering a decision that could change mine and Flora's life for the better or maybe for the worse.

It was tough to resist the offer. I knew I should not get involved; however, the deal sounded so good. If it worked out, it would make business so much easier. We wouldn't have to worry anymore. I needed the contracts and the business.

On Saturday evening Flora and I were having dinner at a small restaurant. It took 45 minutes to be seated, but it was worth the wait because of the food and the nice view. Once we were seated, Flora asked, "You're really quiet, Art. Are you thinking of the deal with Joey?"

"Yeah, I am. I want to go for it, but at the same time I don't. Then I wonder what we will have to do if we don't get enough business without them. You know, if we're still going to stay in business. I wonder if we go with the deal, if we will really do well, if things will work out for us, or if it's all a big mistake and we're going to regret it later. I don't know, Flora."

Flora looked at me with her dreamy eyes. She loved me and didn't like to see me worry. "Art," she whispered, with her hand extended over the small table to hold my hand. I reached over and held her hand. "Don't worry about it. We already said we were going to wait and think about it. Now that I have given it more thought, I think it will be better if we don't do it. It's safer for us and our business. We'll tell Joey on Monday that we don't want to do it."

"Yeah, you're right. We think the same. I just hope everything turns out OK."

I thought of the conversation I had with Joey and Eddie, the way I became angry at them. I hoped things would work out, so I wouldn't have to become angry again.

"I'll try not to worry about it. I know it'll be all right. Let's enjoy our meal together and talk about nice things."

Flora smiled, and we spent the rest of the evening being romantic with one another.

29 SHE SMILED

On our return home on Sunday evening, I went upstairs to our bedroom. Flora and I added a family room and a large bedroom to the house right after we were married. There were no other rooms upstairs. It had two large five-foot windows on two of the four walls. On the other side there was a sliding door that leads to a wood deck, half as big as our large bedroom. The bedroom was neat, as always, except for the few clothes that were lying around from Flora's last few minutes of rushing to leave for the weekend. As I sat on our bed, I pulled out my wallet from my back pocket. I opened it and took out Joey's business card. Before dialing his number, I thought, "Should I? What if I'm making a big mistake? What if it's a really good deal, and I lose out? But then again, what if I'm doing the right thing and am going to save a lot of headaches? What the heck!" I picked up the phone and dialed the number on the business card.

The phone on the other end rang. "Hello. Answering service. May I help you."

"Yeah, I'm calling for Joey."

"Yes. Let me have your phone number, and I'll have him return your call right away."

"All right. This is Art Rodriguez and. . ."

"Oh yes, Mr. Rodriguez, He told me he was expecting a call from you. He will return your call in a minute."

I gave her my phone number.

"Thank you. I'll have him call you right back."

I put the phone down, experiencing an uneasy feeling. I lay back on my bed, looking at the ceiling, hoping I was doing the right thing.

The phone rang. I reached for it as I sat up. "Hello?"

"Art! This is Joey. I can't talk right now. Let me say this. Be careful. All right, buddy. Just be careful. I won't be seeing you anymore. I'm on the run, buddy."

"Wait, you are on the run? From who?"

"I can't say right now. I'll get back with you soon. Hang in there, Art."

I wanted to know what in the heck was happening. "Joey, what are you talking about, man?"

Joey hung up the phone and that was all the information I received. I sat up wondering what was happening.

I heard Flora coming upstairs. She entered the room and saw me sitting up, not doing anything. I lay back on the bed as I had been before placing the call.

"Hi," she greeted as she smiled.

"Flora, I don't know what's going on. Something's isn't right."

Flora rested on top of me, placing her hands next to my shoulders. She kissed me. Flora was a small woman. It wasn't uncomfortable having her small body on top of mine. She didn't want me to be overly worried because of this deal. Whenever I became worried about something, I was silent and reserved. Flora hated that because it was difficult for her to hold a conversation with me. "It'll be all right, honey. I know it will. We're going to do all right."

I returned her kiss and embraced her tightly. I really felt close to Flora. She was a good wife and had always supported me. "I know. Well, I hope anyway. As long as I have you, I know things will be all right." Still holding her, I continued, "I just spoke to Joey."

Flora lifted her body up and asked, "Oh yeah. What did you tell him?"

"Nothing. He told me he was on the run and to be careful."

"What? What did he mean by that?"

"I don't know. He hung up the phone. I don't know what he meant."

"Did you tell him you weren't going for the deal?"

"No. He didn't give me a chance to say anything."

The phone rang again. I reached for it. "Hello?"

"Hey, Art. How are you, buddy?"

"Eddie, hey, man, how are you? What's going on?"

"Hey, Art, I wanted to ask you. Did you just talk to Joey?"

"Yeah, I did. Why?"

"What did he say? Did he tell you where he is or where he is going?"

"No, he didn't tell me anything. All he said was for me to be careful."

"To be careful about what, Art?"

At this point the picture was becoming clear to me. After that meeting perhaps Joey and Eddie had it out; now Eddie wanted to get Joey.

Joey was running from Eddie. "He didn't say, Eddie. Just said to be careful. That's it."

"OK, Art, if he calls you again, tell him to come and see me. So we can talk. Tell him he has to come in to see me one way or another."

"All right, Eddie. I'll do that."

"Oh yeah, Art. I wanted to know if you are in the organization?"

"No, Eddie. I decided I don't want anything to do with it. I have no ties with you or your people."

"OK, Art, I'll get back to you and let you know what we're going to do about it." Eddie hung up.

"That was Eddie?" Flora asked.

"Yeah, he wanted to know what Joey had to say. I wonder what's going on with them."

"Yeah, that's strange. I wonder, too. He asked you if you were going for the deal?"

"Yeah. I told him I wasn't going with it. He said he would get back to me to tell me what they are going to do about it."

"About what, about not wanting the deal?"

"Yeah, if they are going to let it pass or take care of me."

"Take care of you? What do you mean by that?"

I laughed, "I don't know. Don't worry about it. I'm not worried about it. What can they do? Kill me? Heck, I'm not going to roll over and die. If they want to hurt me, they have a fight on their hands. Man, Flora, one of these days I am going to write a book about all the things I have gone through in life."

In the following weeks detectives came to our home, wanting to talk to me about Eddie and Joey. They said they found my phone number in Eddie's notebook and wanted to know what kind of relationship I had with him. I asked them how they came across Eddie's notebook. They would not answer me. Two visits by the police asking questions and that was it; no more visits from anyone. That was the last I ever heard from anybody.

View my photo album:
www.EastSideDreams.com

East Side Dreams

Travel with Art Rodriguez as he dreams of his past. He experiences an unpleasant childhood full of difficult obstacles that could have profoundly impaired his chance for a normal life. Life appears hopeless during those young years as he struggles to discover who he really is and at the same time contends with his dictatorial father. Travel with him as he takes you through the California Youth Authority, the prison system for young offenders. Although he grows up under such trying circumstances, he still finds enjoyment and excitement growing up in San Jose, California, hanging out with his teenage friends on Virginia Place in San Jose's east side. Experience with him his childhood as he reflects back on both pleasant and unhappy times. In this story that brings laughter and tears, both young and old can find comfort knowing that when life appears bleak and there seems to be no hope, events in life can change. There are ways out of a desperate situation. See how a bad relationship between a father and a son can change from resentful to an affectionate one.

This story is an encouragement to both young and old as Art leaves his delinquent life behind and moves into a promising future.

In 1985 Art Rodriguez started a successful business in San Jose, the city in which he was born. How did he start a business with such a delinquent past? Grow with him in his life and experience with him the hardships and successes of a new business.

Order
www.eastsidedreams.com

Sueños Del Lado Este

Viaje usted con Art Rodríguez, conforme sueña su pasado. Art experimenta una desagradable niñez, llena de obstáculos difíciles que pudieron haber disminuido sus oportunidades para desarrollar una vida normal. La vida aparece para él como una vida sin esperanza durante esos años de la juventud cuando se esfuerza para descubrir quien es realmente, al mismo tiempo que vive una continua batalla con un padre dictatorial. Viaje con él y acompáñelo a través del sistema carcelario de California, la cárcel para jóvenes delincuentes.

No obstante que creció bajo semejante estado general de tensión, él encuentra todavía disfrute y alegría al crecer en San Jose California, acompañando a sus amigos adolescentes en Virgnia Place, en el lado Este de San Jose. Experimente con él su niñez, conforme recuerda los tiempos pasados de infelicidad y los momentos agradables. En esta historia capaz de hacerlo llorar y de reir; tanto los jóvenes como los adultos pueden encontrar ánimo sabiendo que cuando la vida parece desolada y aparenta no haber esperanza, las circunstancias pueden cambiar. Existe escape de una situación desesperada. Vea como una mala relación entre un padre y un hijo puede cambiar, desde el resentimiento a una relación afectiva.

Esta historia es un estímulo para los jóvenes y para los adultos porque en ella pueden descubrir como Art deja su vida de delincuente y se impulsa hacia un futuro con promesas.

En 1985, Art Rodríguez comenzó un exitoso negocio en San Jose, la ciudad en la que nació. ¿Cómo pudo este hombre, un ex delincuente, comenzar un negocio con semejante pasado? Descubra junto a él y acompáñelo en el relato de su vida y experimente el sufrimiento, la privación y luego el éxito de su nueva empresa.

Order
www.eastsidedreams.com

Forgotten Memories
Turbulent Teenage Years!
But Life Goes On!

A re you having difficult teenage years? Does life go on? Travel with Art Rodriguez as he takes you through his teen years. You will see that life does get better, even though it appears confusing and harsh at times. You will enjoy his stories of growing up in San Jose, California. He will take you for a stroll; as he does, you will experience with him fun times and hard times. You will enjoy this sequel to *East Side Dreams*.

- This story will help you get through life's difficult times!

- You will take comfort in knowing that, if Art Rodriguez can make it, you can too!

- This story will help you to have a greater appreciation for your parent(s).

Order
www.eastsidedreams.com

The Monkey Box

Take a journey back in time with Art Rodriguez as he traces his family's past. In the 1800s Art's great, great grandfather was not only a duke in Spain, but he was also a priest. He had an affair with a young woman, and it became public knowledge when the young lady died at childbirth. The church was taking steps to excommunicate the priest, and the family was very humiliated because of the situation. His family offered an inheritance as well as family lineage documents for him to leave the country with his daughter Lydia.

As time went by in Mexico, the documents were stored in an airtight box that was carved with beautiful monkeys. What happened to the documents and the love story that followed 16-year-old Lydia? How did the family end up in the United States? This journey will reveal Art Rodriguez's family story.

- This story is exiting and will keep your attention throughout!
- It is a story that will inspire you or someone in your family to write your own family story.

Order
www.eastsidedreams.com